REALISM AND SOCIAL SCIENCE

REALISM AND SOCIAL SCIENCE

Andrew Sayer

SAGE Publications
London • Thousand Oaks • New Delhi

First published 2000

SAGE Publications Ltd
6 Bonhill Street
London EC2A 4PU

SAGE Publications Inc
2455 Teller Road
Thousand Oaks, California 91320

SAGE Publications India Pvt Ltd
32, M-Block Market
Greater Kailash - I
New Delhi 110 048

British Library Cataloguing in Publication data

A catalogue record for this book is
available from the British Library

ISBN 0-7619-6123-2
ISBN 0-7619-6124-0 (pbk)

Library of Congress catalog card number 99-75811

Typeset by SIVA Math Setters, Chennai, India.
Printed in Great Britain by Redwood Books, Trowbridge, Wiltshire

Contents

PART I

INTRODUCING CRITICAL REALISM

Introduction

Realism – or at least the 'critical realism' that I want to defend – is not what many people think it is. Many suppose that realism claims a privileged access to the Truth and thus involves a kind of 'foundationalism'. But such claims are inconsistent with realism, for if the defining feature of realism is the belief that there is a world existing independently of our knowledge of it, then that independence of objects from knowledge immediately undermines any complacent assumptions about the relation between them and renders it problematic. What reason have we for accepting this basic realist proposition of the mind-independence of the world? I would argue that it is the evident *fallibility* of our knowledge – the experience of getting things wrong, of having our expectations confounded, and of crashing into things – that justifies us in believing that the world exists regardless of what we happen to think about it. If, by contrast, the world itself was a product or construction of our knowledge, then our knowledge would surely be infallible, for how could we ever be mistaken about anything? How could it be said that things were not as we supposed? Realism is therefore necessarily a fallibilist philosophy and one which must be wary of simple correspondence concepts of truth. It must acknowledge that the world can only be known under particular descriptions, in terms of available discourses, though it does not follow from this that no description or explanation is better than any other.

In starting this book in this way, turning the tables on anti-realists, I am of course getting my retaliation in first, because I am aware that in certain quarters, 'realism' is synonymous with a form of naive objectivism, claiming unmediated access to the Truth. This misconception prevents realism getting a hearing. At the same time, I am also wary of naive supporters of realism who assume that it will indeed guarantee the production of true knowledge, when the independence of the world from our knowledge and the entrapment of knowledge within discourse imply the impossibility of any such guarantees.

Yet once such misconceptions are removed, I believe it can be shown that realism (particularly the critical realism pioneered by Roy Bhaskar) offers great promise for social science and theory. Critical realism provides an alternative to several philosophical and methodological positions which have been found wanting. Firstly, in the philosophy of natural science, realism offered a third way between empiricism and positivism on the one hand and the relativism that followed in the wake of Kuhn and Feyerabend's assault on conceptions of science as a cumulative foundationalist enterprise on the other. Secondly, in the philosophy and methodology of social science, critical realism provides an alternative to both hopes of a law-finding science of society modelled on natural science methodology and the anti-naturalist or interpretivist reductions of social science to the interpretation of meaning. By simultaneously challenging common conceptions of both natural and social science, particularly as regards causation, critical realism proposes a way of combining a modified naturalism with a recognition of the necessity of interpretive understanding of meaning in social life. For realists, social science is neither nomothetic (that is, law-seeking) nor idiographic (concerned with documenting the unique). Thirdly, with respect to debates around modernism and postmodernism, it opposes the reductionism and closure of some overly confident 'modernist' kinds of social science, evident in the determinism and flattening of difference common in some versions of grand narratives, and in the a priorism of neoclassical economics. Such approaches radically underestimate the openness, contingency and contextually variable character of social change. On the other hand, it rejects a defeatist strain of postmodernism which assumes that the absence of certainty, regularity and closure, means that hopes of reliable knowledge claims and scientific progress must be rejected (Stones, 1996). Accordingly, critical realism seeks to avoid both scientism and 'science-envy' on the one hand and radical rejections of science on the other.[1]

The chapters of this book are offered as realist contributions to debates on social theory and the philosophy and methodology of social science that have been prominent in the last two decades. While they are largely an attempt to apply and develop critical realist angles, at certain points I shall make criticisms of critical realism itself, particularly with regard to its account of critical social science. Although I have attempted to adopt a critical realist approach to my substantive work in social science – mainly in industrial and urban and regional studies and political economy (Sayer, 1995; Morgan and Sayer, 1988; Sayer and Walker, 1992) – I have not included any of this material in this collection, apart from drawing some examples from it in Chapter 1.

Insofar as this is a book of critiques, I should perhaps point out that I am more interested in ideas than who might have authored them and more interested in their evaluation than in their history. By and large I therefore avoid questions of how particular authors are to be interpreted. In many cases the ideas are not drawn directly from major theorists but are ones I have frequently encountered in discussions. In addition, as is common in philosophy, what follows may even include some lines of argument over which no-one claims authorship, but which nevertheless are interesting possibilities in themselves. One of the main sources has been discussions with research students in social science, especially those I have taught on courses in the philosophy of social science and social theory. I realize that engaging directly with the most prestigious authors would bring me more cultural capital, but they have had plenty of attention already, and utility is more important than prestige, even where its exchange value is lower.

A recent minor theme of debate in philosophy and social theory has concerned the role of logic and metaphor and rhetoric in science and philosophy (for example, Nelson et al., 1987; Norris, 1997; Mäki, 1993). Although these elements are often presented as opposed, critical realism takes a both/and rather than an either/or position regarding them. Both lay and scientific thought requires not only logic but metaphors and associational thinking. Scientific and philosophical discourses are rhetorical in the broad sense of involving persuasion, but that does not necessarily cancel out their dependence on logic and reduce them to a form of linguistic arm-twisting. Philosophy proceeds by making connections and distinctions. In the essays that follow, I, of course, deploy metaphors, rhetoric and associational thinking but I also try to work out what entails what, what is a non-sequitur, which conditions are necessary, which sufficient; more simply I attempt to distinguish rigorously between *can* and *must*, *all* and *some*, *often* and *always*. Following a philosophical argument is like negotiating a complex, twisting route through dense networks of streets. There are many opportunities for wrong turnings – unjustified inferences. One can take a wrong turning just by misreading 'can' as 'must', or 'some' as 'all'. Distinctions, especially in the form of dualisms or binaries, are regular targets of scepticism today, but whether they are good or bad is an *a posteriori* matter, and we can hardly avoid interrogating them logically – in terms of what they entail and don't entail – as well as in terms of their associations and metaphorical qualities. Simply to note the presence of binaries or dualisms does not constitute an argument until one explains what is problematic about the instances in question. Similarly, that a distinction can be deconstructed does not necessarily totally undermine it; it may just elaborate and qualify it. That a distinction is fuzzy is not necessarily fatal. Some of our most useful distinctions – like that between night and day – cannot be drawn sharply, but most of the time we have little difficulty with them. In other words my main aim in these essays has been to argue, to get beyond a sound-bite approach; if they are reciprocated with counter arguments I shall be happy.

It may help to situate the essays which follow if I offer a brief personal interpretation of the context in which critical realism has developed. Inevitably it will reflect my own situation within Britain. It is not intended as an overview; others are likely to have had different experiences.

The institutional context in which I began my first research was the University of Sussex, whose commitment to interdisciplinary studies forced me out of my early disciplinary parochialism in human geography and allowed me also to teach the philosophy of social science. This gave me free rein to explore the aftermath of the major debates in the philosophy of science of the 1960s and 70s – the conventionalist assaults of authors, such as Kuhn and Feyerabend, on empiricist philosophy of science, and the anti-naturalist approaches of interpretivism or hermeneutics in the philosophy of social science. This was also the context in which critical realism first developed in Britain in the mid-1970s, where the work of Rom Harré and particularly Roy Bhaskar, and others such as Russell Keat and Ted Benton, offered an alternative to empiricism and conventionalism in the philosophy of natural science, and to positivism and interpretivism in the philosophy of social science.

I started out with critiques of positivism, especially its expectation that the social world could be shown to be a composite of a number of behavioural regularities which would eventually be described by social laws akin to those of natural science. The empirical context was the prosaic one of studies of the development of urban and regional systems (Sayer, 1976). In attempting to develop an understanding of these that was both dynamic and spatial, it slowly dawned on me that social systems were necessarily open, and that they evolved rather than equilibrated, not least because people have the capacity to learn and change their behaviour. Consequently I realized the goal of finding rough regularities, let alone laws, to describe social systems, was a pipe dream. At the same time, realist philosophy was beginning to challenge the regularity or successionist theory of causation, and to analyse the explanation of change in open systems, so that it became clear that abandoning hopes of finding regularities in no way meant abandoning explanation.

From the late 1960s through to the early 1980s, the rise of the new Left revived some distinctly grand and modernist theories of capitalist societies. The world was to be seen in terms of grand structures while pluralism was associated with the much-despised liberalism, unable to see the structural wood for the interest-group trees, a tendency now – amazingly – inverted, with pluralism being associated with the intellectual avant garde and structuralism being seen as passé (McLennan, 1996). Particularly in its Althusserian form, structuralism exuded an extraordinary scientistic arrogance, later deservedly punctured by E.P. Thompson's withering attack in his unfortunately-titled *The Poverty of Theory* (Thompson, 1979). Much was excluded by those ostensibly all-embracing, all-explaining discourses – notably gender, race, sexuality and much of lived experience; here the rise of feminism, anti-racism and post-colonialism have challenged the old new Left with devastating effect.

There were also *within* the Marxist Left further reactions against homogenizing and reductionist tendencies, notably from Raymond Williams, of whose work nuance, complexity and sensitivity to local, lived experience were hallmarks. Many of those – myself included – who tried to apply Marxist theory empirically found that in confronting the social world in its concrete, that is, many-sided, forms, they had to develop more open, context-dependent and plural accounts, within which Marxism might have been an important ingredient but no longer a totalizing theory.[2] In urban and regional studies and industrial studies, this was associated with an increasing concern with *differentiation*, most strikingly evident in Doreen Massey's influential *Spatial Divisions of Labour* (Massey, 1984). This insisted on the enormously differentiated ways in which capitalist uneven development works out in practice and was critical of the reductionism of what later became branded as 'grand narratives', although 'grand analyses' would have been a better term since they generally neglected to tell stories and instead just absorbed empirical material into their pre-existing categories and frameworks (Sayer, 1981a). The focus on differentiation and pluralism might now sound familiar in relation to postmodernism and poststructuralism, but for many of those involved in this research, all this happened largely independently of their emergence. In some ways, critical realism, with its focus on necessity and contingency rather than regularity, on open rather than closed systems, on the ways in which causal processes could produce quite different results in different contexts, fitted comfortably with these developments. Realists *expect* concrete open systems and discourses to be much more messy and ambiguous than our theories of them and do not consider that differentiation poses a threat to social science.

Many reacted to reductionist accounts by shifting to middle range theory and empirical studies, for example from Marxist theories of accumulation to analyses of the institutional forms present in particular capitalist societies (Sayer, 1985).[3] This meant a greater openness to diverse empirical and theoretical influences, but what was and remains ambiguous about these middle range theories is whether they were intended to leave behind more abstract social theories or whether they were meant to build on them even if they don't acknowledge them (Sayer, 1995).

Another significant current within social studies which was critical of modernist social science prior to the rise of postmodernism and the turn to discourse was hermeneutics or interpretivism. These had developed a sophisticated philosophical critique of naturalism – the doctrine that the social world could be understood in the same way as natural science – and had theorized about the interpretation of texts and 'constitutive meanings' (for example, Schutz, Taylor, Winch, Ricouer). These represented a different source of criticism of positivism from that associated with Kuhn and Feyerabend.[4] At the same time there was a largely sympathetic critique of interpretivism's tendency to reduce social life wholly to the level of meaning, ignoring material change and what happens to people, regardless of their understandings (for example, Fay, 1975; Giddens, 1976). Critical realists argued that while interpretative understanding was an important and necessary feature of any social science, it did not mean that there was no scope for causal explanation.

In my neck of the academic woods, and probably many others too, all this happened before 'postmodernism' began to be discussed. This arrived mainly from across the Atlantic, out of architecture and the new dialogue between literary studies and social theory. This exchange, along with the more general turn to language and discourse, was useful in exploring the similarities and relations between literature and social science. Language could not continue to be taken as transparent and unproblematic by the philosophy of science; discourse and textuality needed to be taken seriously.

Postmodernism has also encouraged a more critical view of key categories of social thought, especially the ways in which binary distinctions or dualisms typically obscure connections, hierarchy and differences, and apparently comprehensive syntheses suppress the experience of certain groups, while concealing the identity of those whose particularistic stories they actually do express. Fundamental philosophical issues have been raised regarding the character of discourse, the limits of reason, and the question of truth. What the implications are of such developments for critical realism and social science is controversial:[5] for the 'defeatist postmodernists' they imply relativism, idealism and a rejection of the ambitions of social science; for others they point to a renewed social science which is conceptually cautious and more reflexive about both its implicit philosophy and methodology and its social and political coordinates. My sympathies lie with the latter view.

Differentiation is not the same as difference, interpretivism is not the same as discourse analysis, liberal pluralism is not the same as postmodern pluralism. These apparently similar concepts have different provenances and associations, but the parallels between them are intriguing. What is important to note, especially given the preoccupation in social science with novelty, is that some important critiques of modernism in social science predated postmodernism and did not share its predominantly idealist character.

If I have mixed feelings about postmodernism, there is one 'post' I feel committed to unreservedly – 'post-disciplinary studies'; indeed, since the late 1970s I have identified with social science rather than with a particular discipline. Disciplinary parochialism, and its close relative disciplinary imperialism, are a recipe for reductionism, blinkered interpretations, and misattributions of causality. The essays which follow reflect this post-disciplinary outlook. Several of the chapters have appeared before in journals. For the most part I have left these largely unaltered and, with the exception of changes needed to make them accessible to a broader and more contemporary audience, I have kept points made in hindsight to the section introductions. There are a few points of overlap but I have left some of these in order to retain the separateness of the essays.

I offer two kinds of introduction to critical realism. The first straightforwardly sets out some of the key features which bear most directly on the character of social research, leaving more fundamental epistemological issues to be addressed later. Given the growing number of books on critical realism and social science I do not attempt a comprehensive overview of its positions and philosophical defences here. Part II involves critical realist responses to many of the concerns which have characterized postmodernist tendencies in social science. In particular, Chapter 2 – 'Realism for Sceptics' – addresses a wide range of fundamental doubts which are typically raised about the whole enterprise and may serve as a more appropriate introduction for those coming from a postmodernist position. The other chapters in Part II deal with issues such as grand narratives, cultural relativism, essentialism and social constructionism. Part III addresses some issues which first arose in the 1980s concerning the role of space in social theory. Part IV addresses arguments that social science must necessarily be critical of the societies it studies and presents a case for integrating normative theories into social science.

Further Reading on Critical Realism

Both the term 'critical realism' and the philosophy it names were introduced by Roy Bhaskar, building on earlier work in realist philosophy of science, particularly that of Rom Harré. I would especially recommend Bhaskar's first two books, *A Realist Philosophy of Science* (1975, 1979) developing 'transcendental realism' for natural science, and *The Possibility of Naturalism* (1979, 1989) on the philosophy of social science. Neither of these is easy to read, but they are accessible compared to his later work and they provide an indispensable grounding for approaching subsequent books, such as his 1989 critique of Rorty. Andrew Collier's *Critical Realism* (1994a) provides a more accessible and not uncritical introduction to Bhaskar's work. Harré's realism is less elaborate and leans more towards social constructionism in social science. I would recommend his excellent introduction – *Philosophies of Science* (1972).

As regards the implications of critical realism for social science, in addition to my own *Method in Social Science* (1992), I would recommend Rob Stones'

Sociological Realism (1996); Tony Lawson's *Economics and Reality* (1997); Margaret Archer's *Realist Social Theory: The Morphogenetic Approach* (1995); Caroline New's *Agency, Health and Social Survival* (1996); Harré's *Social Being* (1979), *Personal Being*, (1983) and *Physical Being* (1994); and Alison Assiter's *Enlightened Women* (1997). With the exception of Stones' book most of these have little to say directly about postmodernism. However a prolific realist critic of idealist and relativist variants of postmodernism is Christopher Norris (1990; 1993; 1997). At a more substantive level concerning social theory I would also recommend the work of Norman Fairclough (1992), John O'Neill (1994, 1998), Kate Soper (1995a), and concerning methodology in empirical and evaluation research, the work of Ray Pawson (1989) and Pawson and Tilley (1997).

Acknowledgements

Parts of the book, especially the drafts of the chapters on space and social theory have benefitted from discussions with fellow members of the former Brighton Pier Space and Social Theory Group – John Allen and Doreen Massey. I am especially grateful to Michael Storper as co-author of an earlier version of Chapter 8. I have benefitted from the comments and suggestions of Bob Jessop, Norman Fairclough, Sarah Franklin, John O'Neill, Caroline New, Beverley Skeggs, Nigel Thrift, Dick Walker, and many anonymous referees. The usual disclaimers emphatically apply. Finally I would like to thank Eric Clark, Bridget and Roger Graham, and Frank Hansen for their support and also Chris Rojek for his encouragement at Sage, and my daughter Lizzie for being herself.

I would like to thank the editors and publishers of the following journals for permission to produce revised versions of material that appeared in their pages. To Blackwell for 'Postmodernist thought in geography: a realist view' (1993) *Antipode*, 25:4, pp. 320–344, 1993; for 'Essentialism, social constructionism, and beyond' (1997) *Sociological Review*, 45, pp. 453–487; and 'Critical realism and the limits to critical social science' (1997) *Journal for the Theory of Social Behaviour*, 27, pp. 473–488. To Pion Limited, London for 'The 'new' regional geography and problems of narrative', *Environment and Planning D: Society and Space*, 7: pp. 253–276 (1989) and for 'Ethics unbound: for a normative turn in social theory' (with Michael Storper), *Environment and Planning D: Society and Space*, 15: pp. 1–18 (1997).

Notes

1 In relation to the much-publicized hoaxing of the avant-garde journal *Social Text* by Alan Sokal, I find myself wanting to reject not only the charlatanism that he intended to expose but the naivety and overconfidence of Sokal's own position (Sokal and Bricmont, 1998; Osborne, 1997; Robbins, 1998).

2 Although there are many affinities between critical realism and Marxism, the former does not entail the latter. Thus the work of quite anti-Marxist writers, such as Hayek, have been argued to contain realist elements (Peacock, 1993).

3 This shift was no doubt related to the declining political influence of Marxism.

4 One of the peculiarities of these developments, was the blindness of the critics of orthodoxy working in the philosophy of natural science, such as Kuhn and Feyerabend, to the hermeneutic character of scientific knowledge, even though it would have helped their case.

5 For example, while many consider Derrida to be unmistakeably postmodernist and anti-realist, the realist Christopher Norris defends him from both his postmodernist disciples and modernist critics (Norris, 1991).

1

Key Features of Critical Realism in Practice: A Brief Outline

In this chapter I want to introduce critical realism by sketching some of the features which distinguish its approach to social science. There is of course a growing philosophical literature presenting and debating critical realism and rival philosophies and discussing its implications for social science. Rather than attempt to summarize such literature I will restrict myself to realism's key features, merely indicating some of the philosophical arguments in its favour. Those who are curious about epistemological issues associated with realism and want to know how it responds to sceptical positions, such as those of postmodernism, are recommended to start with Chapter 2.

We begin with some implications of the basic realist thesis of the independence of the world from our knowledge, introduce some features of critical realism's ontology (or theory of what exists) including its distinctions between the real, the actual and the empirical, its account of the stratification of the world and of the nature of emergent properties. We then move on to its distinctive view of causation, its inclusion of an interpretive dimension to social science, and its endorsement of the project of critical social science, that is, a social science which is critical of the social practices it studies. In the second part of the chapter we turn to realist approaches to empirical research and a brief discussion of examples from practice.

The Transitive and Intransitive Dimensions of Knowledge

We have already noted the basic realist tenet concerning the independence of the world from our thoughts about it. This relates to a fundamental distinction made by Bhaskar (1975) between the 'intransitive' and 'transitive' dimensions of knowledge. The objects of science (or other kinds of propositional knowledge) in the sense of the things we study – physical processes or social phenomena — form the intransitive dimension of science. The theories and discourse as media and resources of science are part of its transitive dimension, though as part of the social world they can also be treated as objects of study. Rival theories and sciences have different transitive objects (theories about the world) but the world they are about – the intransitive dimension – is the same; otherwise, they would not be rivals (Collier, 1994a, p. 51). When theories change (transitive dimension) it does not mean that what they are about (intransitive dimension) necessarily changes too: there is no reason to believe that the shift from a flat earth theory to a round earth theory was accompanied by a change in the shape of the earth itself. Things are a little more complicated regarding the social world for it is socially constructed and includes knowledge itself and it therefore cannot be said to exist independently of at least some knowledge, though it is more likely to be past knowledge than that of contemporary researchers.[1] When researchers change their minds it is unlikely to produce a significant change in the phenomena they study. For the most part, social scientists are cast in the modest role of construing rather than 'constructing' the social world.

This distinction between intransitive and transitive dimensions of science implies that the world should not be conflated with our experience of it, and hence that, strictly speaking, it is misleading to speak of the 'empirical world' (Bhaskar, 1975). Critical realism should therefore not be confused with empirical realism – equivalent to empiricism – which identifies the real with the empirical, that is, with what we can experience, as if the world just happened to correspond to the range of our senses and to be identical to what we experience. Nor should critical realism be confused with literary realism, as the former acknowledges and highlights the conceptually-mediated or theory-laden character of experience whereas the latter ignores it.

The Real, the Actual and the Empirical

Empirical realism treats the world as consisting of observable atomistic objects, events and regularities among them, as if objects had no structure or powers, and in particular, no unobservable qualities. Critical realism distinguishes not only between the world and our experience of it, but between the real, the actual and the empirical, defining these in a special way (Bhaskar, 1975).[2] When critical realists refer to 'the real' this is not in order to claim privileged knowledge of it but to note two things. First, the real is whatever exists, be it natural or social, regardless of whether it is an empirical object for us, and whether we happen to have an adequate understanding of its nature. Secondly, the real is the realm of objects, their structures and powers. Whether they be physical, like minerals, or social, like bureaucracies, they have certain structures and causal powers, that is, capacities to behave in particular ways, and causal liabilities or passive powers, that is, specific susceptibilities to certain kinds of change. In the transitive dimension of science we try to identify these structures and powers, such as the way in which bureaucracies can process large volumes of routine information very quickly, in virtue of their structure (hierarchical organization, specialization and filing systems, etc). Similarly, individuals, in virtue of their physical make up, socialization and education, are able to work; indeed, they have this power even when they are currently unemployed and idle. Realists therefore seek to identify both necessity and possibility or potential in the world – what things must go together, and what could happen, given the nature of the objects.

Whereas the real in this definition refers to the structures and powers of objects, the *actual* refers to what happens if and when those powers are activated, to what they do and what eventuates when they do, such as when the bureaucracy's powers are activated and it engages in activities such as classifying and invoicing, or the previously idle person does some work. If we take the example of the Marxist distinction between labour power and labour, the former (the capacity to work) and the physical and mental structures from which it derives, is equivalent to the level of the real, while labour (working), as the exercise of this power, and its effects, belong to the domain of the actual.[3]

The *empirical* is defined as the domain of experience, and insofar as it refers successfully, it can do so with respect to either the real or the actual[4] though it is contingent (neither necessary nor impossible) whether we know the real or the actual. While we may be able to observe things such as the structure of an organization or a household, as well as what happens when they act, some structures may not be observable. Observability may make us more confident about what we think exists, but existence itself is not dependent on it. In virtue of this, then, rather than rely purely upon a criterion of observability for making claims about what exists, realists accept a causal criterion too (Collier, 1994a). According to this a plausible case for the existence of unobservable entities can be made by reference to observable effects which can only be explained as the products of such entities. Both natural and social scientists regularly make such claims. For example, many linguists have inferred the existence of generative grammar from the ability of speakers to construct novel but grammatically correct sentences.

A crucial implication of this ontology is the recognition of the possibility that powers may exist unexercised, and hence that what has happened or been known to have happened does not exhaust what could happen or have happened. The nature of the real objects present at a given time constrains and enables what can happen but does not pre-determine what will happen. Realist ontology therefore makes it possible to understand how we could be or become many things which currently we are not: the unemployed could become employed, the ignorant could become knowledgeable, and so on.

Stratification and Emergence

In distinguishing the real, the actual and the empirical, critical realism proposes a 'stratified ontology' in contrast to other ontologies which have 'flat' ontologies populated by either the actual or the empirical, or a conflation of the two. Thus empirical realism assumes that what we can observe is all that exists, while 'actualism' assumes that what actually happens at the level of events exhausts the world, leaving no domain of the real, of powers which can be either activated or remain dormant. Furthermore, critical realism argues that the world is characterized by emergence, that is situations in which the conjunction of two of more features or aspects gives rise to new phenomena, which have properties which are irreducible to those of their constituents, even though the latter are necessary for their existence. The standard physical example of this is the emergent properties of water which are quite different from those of its constituents, hydrogen and oxygen. In the same way, social phenomena are emergent from biological phenomena, which are in turn emergent from the chemical and physical strata. Thus the social practice of conversing is dependent on one's physiological state, including the signals sent and received around our brain cells, but conversing is not reducible to those physiological processes. Reductionist explanations which ignore emergent properties are therefore inadequate (Bhaskar, 1975).

However, while we don't have to go back to the level of biology or chemistry to explain social phenomena, this does not mean the former have no effect on society. Nor does it mean we can ignore the way in which we react back on other strata, for example through contraception, medicine, agriculture and pollution. As we are increasingly reminded these days, but as Marx made clear in the *Theses on Feuerbach* in referring to 'sensuous human activity', we are embodied beings, and the interaction of the social with the physical needs to be acknowledged.[5]

In the social world, people's roles and identities are often internally related, so that what one person or institution is or can do, depends on their relation to others; thus, what it is to be a tutor cannot be explained at the level of individuals but only in terms of their relation to students, and vice versa. The powers which they can draw upon depend partly on their relations to one another, and to relevant parts of the context, such as educational institutions. Social systems commonly involve 'dependencies or combinations [which] causally affect the elements or aspects, and the form and structure of the elements causally influence each other and so also the whole' (Lawson, 1997, p. 64). Internal relations fall outside the ontological grids of positivism, which systematically misrepresents society by presenting such phenomena as reducible to independent individuals or atoms. At the same time we can be affected by things whose existence and position is only contingently or externally related to our own existence, by chance encounters. Individual biographies are crucially influenced by such accidents.

In virtue of the remarkable sensitivity of people to their contexts – which derives particularly from our ability to interpret situations rather than merely being passively shaped by them – social phenomena rarely have the durability of many of the objects studied by natural science, such as minerals or species. Where they are relatively enduring, as many institutions are, then this is usually an intentional achievement, a product of making continual changes in order to stay the same, or at least to maintain continuities through change, rather than a result of doing nothing. Consequently, we cannot expect social science's descriptions to remain stable or unproblematic across time and space; hence a preoccupation with conceptualization is entirely to be expected and certainly not a sign of scientific immaturity.

Causation

One of the most distinctive features of realism is its analysis of causation, which rejects the standard Humean 'successionist' view that it involves regularities among sequences of events (Harré and Madden, 1975; Bhaskar, 1975). We have already prepared the ground for the realist interpretation in making the distinction between the real and the actual, where we introduced the concept of causal powers. Objects are, or are part of, structures. 'Structure' suggests a set of internally related elements whose causal powers, when combined, are emergent from those of their constituents.[6] Thus, hierarchical structures might enable delegation, division of tasks, surveillance, and efficient throughput of work.

Whether these powers are ever exercised depends on other conditions – in the case of unemployed workers, whether they need to provide for themselves, whether there are any jobs, etc. When causal powers are activated (as when the worker works), the results depend again on other conditions (the kind of context, tools, etc). Social processes are also typically dependent on actors' interpretations of one another, though much can happen which is unacknowledged or unintended too.

Consequently, for realists, causation is *not* understood on the model of regular successions of events, and hence explanation need not depend on finding them, or searching for putative social laws. The conventional impulse to prove causation by gathering data on regularities, repeated occurrences, is therefore misguided; at best these might suggest where to look for candidates for causal mechanisms. What causes something to happen has nothing to do with the number of times we have observed it happening.[7] Explanation depends instead on identifying causal mechanisms and how they work, and discovering if they have been activated and under what conditions.

Moving in the other direction, explaining why a certain mechanism exists involves discovering the nature of the structure or object which possesses that mechanism or power: thus the teacher's power to mark pupils' work depends on his or her knowledge and qualifications and on being accepted by the school and public as legitimate; the price mechanism depends on structures of competitive relations between profit-seeking firms producing for markets, and so on. Again, the dependence of social structures on, inter alia, shared understandings is evident in these examples, in terms of the acceptance of the teacher's right to teach, and the public's understanding of the meaning of money in the case of price competition.

In other words, instead of the positivist model displayed in Figure 1.1, realism views causation as shown in Figure 1.2 (page 15).

Figure 1.1   Positivist or 'successionist' view of causation

Despite the arcane character of this kind of philosophical reconstruction, many mechanisms are *ordinary*, often being identified in ordinary language by transitive verbs, as in 'they *built up* a network of political connections'. In both everyday life and social science, we frequently explain things by reference to causal powers.

Consistent regularities are only likely to occur under special conditions, in 'closed systems'. The conditions for closure are first that the object possessing the

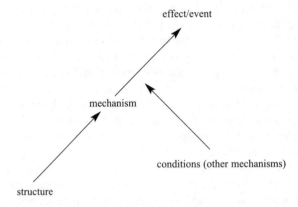

Figure 1.2 Critical realist view of causation

causal power in question is stable (the intrinsic condition), and second that external conditions in which it is situated are constant (the extrinsic condition) (Bhaskar, 1975). Such 'closed system' conditions do not occur spontaneously in the social world or indeed in much of the natural world, though often natural science can artificially produce them in experiments. In the 'open systems' of the social world, the same causal power can produce different outcomes, according to how the conditions for closure are broken: for example, economic competition can prompt firms to restructure and innovate or to close. Sometimes, different causal mechanisms can produce the same result: for instance, you can lose your job for a variety of reasons. Such regularities as do occur in social systems are approximate and limited in duration and are usually the product of deliberate efforts to produce them, through devices such as disciplinary regimes, for example, regarding the start and end of the working day, and machine-pacing of work.

Because events are not pre-determined before they happen but depend on contingent conditions, the future is open – things could go in many different ways. Yet when looking back at changes and explaining them, it is easy to imagine that what did happen was always the only thing that could have happened; hindsight can sometimes be a dubious benefit. One of the temptations of social explanation is to suppress acknowledgements of the fact that at any instant, the future is open, things can happen differently, because once something does happen it is closed.

There is more to the world, then, than patterns of events. It has ontological depth: events arise from the workings of mechanisms which derive from the structures of objects, and they take place within geo-historical contexts. This contrasts with approaches which treat the world as if it were no more than patterns of events, to be registered by recording punctiform data regarding 'variables' and looking for regularities among them.

We noted earlier that the same mechanism can produce different outcomes according to context, or more precisely, according to its spatio-temporal relations with other objects, having their own causal powers and liabilities, which may trigger, block or modify its action. Given the variety and changeability of the contexts of social life, this absence of regular associations between 'causes' and 'effects' should be expected. The causes and conditions of any particular social change tend to spread out geographically and back in time from the point at which it happened. This is particularly marked in *social* change because of memory. What actors do at a given time is likely to be affected by dispositions which were 'sedimented' at some earlier stage, often in different places. In this sense, the past and other places (now absent) are present in the here and now (Stones, 1996, p. 49). Just how much difference context makes cannot be specified at the level of ontology, for it depends on the nature of the processes of interest; as we show in Chapter 6, the latter range from the chameleon-like to the relatively context-independent or indifferent.

Frequently, two or more objects which are contingently related in the sense that each could exist without the other, are brought into contact and interact (i.e. causally influence one another). Once this has happened, certain further, new mechanisms may arise. This is sometimes called, rather confusingly, 'contingent necessity'. Thus it is contingent whether a football team is amateur or professional, but once it goes professional, then new conditions and demands necessarily come into being, such as increased need for income to cover the pay of its employees, whether it be from 'gate-money', spectators, gifts or advertising. Again, it is contingent whether it raises money by becoming a public company, but if it does, then according to the rules governing shareholders' rights, it becomes susceptible to the influence of shareholders and the threat of takeovers.

Typically, social scientists are dealing not only with systems that are open but ones in which there are many interacting structures and mechanisms. This creates the risk of attributing to one mechanism (and its structure) effects which are actually due to another. Many of the controversies of social science are about such problems, such as that regarding the respective roles of capitalism and patriarchy in accounting for the fact that women's pay is significantly lower than men's. This problem of identifying causal responsibility in complex open systems can best be dealt with by either studying examples which provide contrasts in aetiology, such as the absence of an otherwise common condition, or by asking a series of characteristically realist questions:

What does the existence of this object/practice presuppose? What are its preconditions, e.g. what does the use of money presuppose (trust, a state, etc.)?

Can/could object A, e.g. capitalism, exist without B, e.g. patriarchy? (This is another way of sorting out the conditions of existence of social phenomena.)

What is it *about* this object which enables it to do certain things: e.g. what is it about professional associations that makes them able to bid up the salaries of their members? Is it their specialized knowledge, their restrictions on entry into the profession or their domination by men? (Naturally, there may be several mechanisms at work simultaneously and we may need to seek ways of distinguishing their respective effects.)

Note these questions are about necessity, not regularity. They help us to distinguish between what *can* be the case and what *must* be the case, given certain preconditions. They involve counterfactual, rather than associational thinking; that is they are concerned not merely with what happens to be associated with what, for that may be accident, but with whether the associations could be otherwise. Thus capitalism might always, *regularly*, be found with patriarchy, but it doesn't follow from this that they *have* to co-exist as mutual pre-conditions. Patriarchy pre-dates capitalism, and it might be argued that capitalism could exist in a non-patriarchal society (Sayer, 1995). In answering these questions, much depends on how we conceptualize the objects (for example, what do we mean by capitalism and patriarchy and what is included in these?). Asking these realist questions forces us to sharpen our conceptualizations. So if we are uncertain about whether a relationship between A and B is necessary or contingent (that is, neither necessary nor impossible), asking this requires us to specify what it is about A or B that we want to interrogate regarding the status of their relations.[8] Pursuing these questions about the conditions of existence of our objects of study is fundamental to theorizing in social science (Sayer, 1992; 1995, Chapter 2).

Such judgements are fallible of course; it remains contingent whether we know necessity or contingency, but then no philosophy of science can promise 'a royal road to truth' and critical realism is no exception.[9] To some extent, researchers tend to ask such questions intuitively, regardless of whether they think of themselves as realists. However, in practice, I would suggest few researchers pursue such questions far. Moreover, orthodox philosophy of science and methods teaching actively discourages them by prioritizing the search for regularities, and prediction, regardless of the status of the regularities. As we shall see shortly, this has disastrous consequences for research.

The Interpretive or Hermeneutic Dimension

Critical realism acknowledges that social phenomena are intrinsically meaningful, and hence that meaning is not only externally descriptive of them but constitutive of them (though of course there are usually material constituents too). Meaning has to be understood, it cannot be measured or counted, and hence there is always an interpretive or hermeneutic element in social science. This is most obvious in ethnography and discourse analysis, but it is also required though often unnoticed even in the analysis of systems such as market economies, since they too presuppose that actors understand one another's actions. This means that critical realism is only partly naturalist, for although social science can use the same methods as natural science regarding causal explanation, it must also diverge from them in using 'verstehen' or interpretive understanding.[10] While natural scientists necessarily have to enter the hermeneutic circle of their scientific community, social scientists also have to enter that of those whom they study. In other words, natural science operates in a single hermeneutic while social science operates in a double hermeneutic. These circles imply a two-way movement, a 'fusing of the horizons' of listener and speaker, researcher and researched, in which the latter's actions and texts never speak simply for themselves, and yet are not reducible to the researcher's interpretation of them either.

Meanings are related to material circumstances and practical contexts in which communication takes place and to which reference is made. So while we can endorse much of hermeneutics, realism insists a) on the material commitments and settings of communicative interaction, and b) on the presence of a non-discursive, material dimension to social life.[11] Although it is common to see natural science as having all the advantages in that it has some scope for experiments and deals with objects lacking in intrinsic meaning, one can also look upon social science as having a compensatory advantage, namely that since social phenomena are dependent on actors' conceptions of them, we already have 'internal access' to them, albeit a fallible access (Bhaskar, 1979).

While realism shares with interpretive social science the view that social phenomena are concept-dependent and have to be understood, unlike interpretivism it argues that this does not rule out causal explanation, a) because material change in society has to be explained too, and b) because reasons can also be causes, in that they prompt us to do things, think differently, etc. In other words, it poses a wider conception of causation than is customary, in that it does not assume that all causes must be physical. At first sight this may seem disconcerting, but its denial is absurd, for it would entail the causal irrelevance of reasons (Bhaskar, 1979; 1989), as if, for example, when we put a cross by someone's name on a ballot paper, this had nothing to do with our reasoning regarding politics and candidates.

Actions always presuppose already existing resources and media, many of which have a social dimension that is irreducible to the properties of individuals; hence speaking presupposes a language, a language community, as well as material resources such as vocal chords or other means of making intelligible sounds; starting a bank account presupposes banks, money, and rules governing lending and borrowing. That those resources and social structures are themselves a product of actions (no structures without actions) does not mean that structures and actions can be collapsed into one another. Once one looks at them in time – remembering that they couldn't be anything other than temporal – then it becomes clear that actions presuppose an already existing set of structures including shared meanings, though these owe their existence to the fact that at any earlier time (t-1), people reproduced or transformed them through their actions, which in turn were constrained and enabled by structures existing from time t-2 (Archer, 1995).

Why *Critical* Realism?

Critical realism offers a rationale for a critical social science, one that is critical of the social practices it studies as well as of other theories. Bhaskar in particular, has argued that social science has an emancipatory potential (1986). Social practices are informed by ideas which may or may not be true and whether they are true may have some bearing upon what happens. Thus, gender relations are generally informed and reproduced through beliefs that gender is natural rather than a product of socialization, so that the disadvantages suffered by women are seen implicitly as natural too. Social scientists who merely reproduced this explanation uncritically in their own accounts so that they merely reported that gender was a product of biological difference would fail to understand gender. To explain such phenomena one has to acknowledge this dependence of actions on shared meanings while showing in what respects they are false, if they are. If social scientific accounts differ from those of actors then they cannot help but be critical of lay thought and action. Furthermore, as Bhaskar argues, to identify understandings in society as false, and hence actions informed by them as falsely based, is to imply that (other things being equal) those beliefs and actions ought to be changed (see Chapter 7).

Realism and Empirical Research Methods

Compared to positivism and interpretivism, critical realism endorses or is compatible with a relatively wide range of research methods, but it implies that the particular choices should depend on the nature of the object of study and what one wants to learn about it. For example, ethnographic and quantitative approaches are radically different but each can be appropriate for different and legitimate tasks – the former perhaps for researching say a group's norms and customs, the latter for researching world trade flows. Perhaps most importantly, realists reject cookbook prescriptions of method which allow one to imagine that one can do research by simply applying them without having a scholarly knowledge of the object of study in question.

The objects that social scientists study, be they wars, discourses, institutions, economic activities, identities, kinship or whatever, are concrete in the sense that they are the product of multiple components and forces. Social systems are always open and usually complex and messy. Unlike some of the natural sciences, we cannot isolate out these components and examine them under controlled conditions. We therefore have to rely on abstraction and careful conceptualization, on attempting to abstract out the various components or influences in our heads, and only when we have done this and considered how they combine and interact can we expect to return to the concrete, many-sided object and make sense of it. Much rests upon the nature of our abstractions, that is, our conceptions of particular one-sided components of the concrete object; if they divide what is in practice indivisible, or if they conflate what are different and separable components, then problems are likely to result. So much depends on the modes of abstraction we use, the way of carving up and defining our objects of study (Sayer, 1992, Chapter 3). Unfortunately, the bulk of the methodological literature on social science completely ignores this fundamental issue, as if it were simply a matter of intuition. Thus many kinds of social research operate with categories used in official statistics even though they are often based on bad or incoherent abstractions. Take the category 'services', for example, as in 'the service sector', which is sometimes expected to identify activities that have something in common and behave similarly, when of course it embraces economic activities as diverse as transport, hairdressing, tourism, insurance and catering and therefore are highly unlikely to do so. Not surprisingly, the category cannot bear the explanatory weight many researchers have been tempted to put upon it – for example services as the basis of 'post-industrial society' – and the conclusions of such research have therefore been inconclusive and/or misleading. It is, as Marx put it, a 'chaotic conception'. No amount of sophistication in research methods can compensate for such sloppy abstractions. Only if we give greater emphasis to problems of conceptualization and pursue the kinds of realist questions outlined earlier are we likely to avoid such pitfalls.

As we noted earlier, given the presence of multiple systems and causes in the things we study and the possibility of different causes producing the same effects, there is always a risk of misattributions of causality. Recall our earlier example of explaining the power of professional associations; it is easy to think of several possible mechanisms – the operation of a closed shop, the advantages deriving from specialist expertise, patriarchal power, the deference of the general public, and so on. There may be more than one mechanism operating in concert of course, but this is what we have to sort out if we are to make sure we are not mis-attributing causal responsibility. To do this requires abstraction, and a research design which is geared to identifying such possibilities.

Where researchers are concerned with discourses and the meaningful qualities of social practices, understanding these is not a matter of abstraction followed by concrete synthesis, but of interpretation. However, realists would add that to interpret what actors mean we have to relate their discourse to its referents and contexts. It also needs to be remembered that social reality is only partly text-like. Much of what happens does not depend on or correspond to actors' understand-ings; there are unintended consequences and unacknowledged conditions and things can happen to people regardless of their understandings.

Research design also requires thought about how we abstract. This can be illustrated by reference to the differences between extensive and intensive research designs (see Table 1.1 and Sayer, 1992, Chapter 9 for a fuller discus-sion.) These have different purposes but may be complimentary in some research projects. Traditionally, outside anthropology and perhaps history, extensive methods have been assumed to be the norm for social research. These search for regularities in the belief that large numbers of repeated observations will give us relations that are significant. One identifies a population and defines groups *taxonomically*, on the basis of shared attributes (for example, white women over 60; houses worth less than £50,000), and seeks quantitative relations among the variables. This ignores or does not directly address the *causal* groups in which particular individuals (persons, institutions, etc) are actually involved, that is the groups or networks of specific people, institutions, discourses and things with which they interact.

An intensive approach would start with individuals (again not necessarily individual people), and trace the main causal (including discursive) relationships into which they enter and study their qualitative nature as well as their number. It might not be possible to define these causal groups at the outset of the research, indeed discovering them and studying how they operate might be a key compo-nent or objective of the research. As the name suggests, extensive research shows us mainly how extensive certain phenomena and patterns are in a population, while intensive research is primarily concerned with what makes things happen in specific cases, or in more ethnographic form, what kind of universe of mean-ing exists in a particular situation. Note, however, the extensive/intensive dis-tinction is not identical to the survey-analysis/case-study or ethnography

Table 1.1 *Intensive and extensive research: a summary* from A. Sayer (1992) *Method in Social Science*, Routledge, p. 243.

	Intensive	Extensive
Research question	How does a process work in a particular case or small number of cases? What produces a certain change? What did the agents actually do?	What are the regularities, common patterns, distinguishing features of a population? How widely are certain characteristics or processes distributed or represented?
Relations	Substantial relations of connection.	Formal relations of similarity.
Type of groups studied	Causal groups.	Taxonomic groups.
Type of account produced	Causal explanation of the production of certain objects or events, though not necessarily representative ones.	Descriptive 'representative' generalizations, lacking in explanatory penetration.
Typical methods	Study of individual agents in their causal contexts, interactive interviews, ethnography, qualitative analysis.	Large-scale survey of population or representative sample, formal questionnaires, standardized interviews. Statistical analysis.
Limitations	Actual concrete patterns and contingent relations are unlikely to be 'representative', 'average' or generalizable. Necessary relations discovered will exist wherever their relata are present, for example, causal powers of objects are generalizable to other contexts as they are necessary features of these objects.	Although representative of a whole population, they are unlikely to be generalizable to other populations at different times and places. Problem of ecological fallacy in making inferences about individuals. Limited explanatory power.
Appropriate tests	Corroboration	Replication

distinction: extensive approaches might be used within a single case study; intensive approaches do not have to be limited to single cases and can use other methods besides ethnographic ones.

Intensive and extensive research have complimentary strengths and weaknesses as Table 1 suggests. Intensive research is strong on causal explanation and interpreting meanings in context, but tends to be very time-consuming, so that one can normally only deal with a small number of cases. Nevertheless, contrary to a popular assumption, the validity of the analysis of these cases and their representativeness in relation to large numbers are entirely separate matters; the adequacy of an analysis of a single case need have nothing to do with how many other such cases there are. Extensive research tells us the extent or quantitative dimensions of certain properties and relations, but these are not necessarily causal relationships and its explanatory value is minimal. Attempts to use it as a way of generating explanations are undermined by its implicit successionist theory of causation, evident in its dependence on finding regularities in punctiform data. Significantly, statistical explanations are not explanations in terms of mechanisms at all, merely quantitative descriptions of formal (not substantial) associations (Sayer, 1992).

To drive home the difference between extensive and intensive research, imagine some Martian researchers who had never seen a human body before and set themselves the task of understanding how it worked. Those of the Martians who were extensive researchers would take a random sample of specimens from all over the body and look for empirical regularities among them, claiming that this would give a 'representative' picture from which it was safe to generalize. The intensive researchers would start at a particular point – it might not matter where – but follow up the *connections* of the organ or part in question to other parts of the body, building up pictures of the body's structure and systems. Of course, it is clear that the intensive researchers would be most likely to yield explanations of the body's mechanisms, and they would not be too bothered by accusations that their work was unrepresentative of the body as a whole. Extensive research, informed by a successionist theory of causation and hence aiming to find regularities among atomistic events or variables, seeks out mainly formal similarities and differences rather than substantial connections. Intensive research seeks out substantial relations of connection and situates practices within wider contexts, thereby illuminating part-whole relationships.

Examples of Realist Research

I now want to give some brief examples of a realist approach in practice in social science.

The first, is from the research of Ray Pawson and Nick Tilley on the evaluation of public policy programmes such as crime prevention measures (Pawson and Tilley, 1997). Evaluation research is somewhat specialized in the range of questions it asks but that makes it a rather more simple kind of example of realist research than most and hence a good place to begin. Pawson and Tilley first set out a realist critique of the orthodox, quasi-experimental approach to evaluation. This is based on the search for regularities, comparing outcomes in control groups and experimental groups. In effect, it assumes a closed system in which a regular relation is expected between the cause event (the implementation of the programme) and its effects. It therefore assumes a 'successionist' theory of causation. In fact programmes are always introduced into open systems. Both the conditions for closure noted above are violated, so that any regularities are unlikely to last: the programme itself is unlikely to be stable, since it depends on how actors interpret and implement it (the intrinsic condition), and the context in which it is implemented is variable and dependent on other actors' response to it. Not surprisingly, the success rate of this orthodox approach in providing lessons which can be applied to other situations is dismal, and disillusionment has been widespread. By contrast, a realist approach assumes open systems and a generative model of causation in which the outcomes of the activation of mechanisms (e.g. crime prevention programmes) always depends on specific contexts. The policies always work through actors' perceptions and choices, and whether people respond appropriately depends on many possible circumstances which are likely to vary within and between cases, and which researchers should try to identify. Hence, contrary to the standard view of evaluation research, it is not a mechanical application of standard tools in which concrete knowledge of the phenomena being studied and previous research is irrelevant; rather scholarly knowledge of the subject is crucial, coupled with research on the particular applications and contexts.

Progress in terms of cumulative knowledge is unlikely to come from replication of orthodox quasi-experimental studies in the hope of producing universally applicable findings in terms of empirical regularities between programmes and outcomes. Instead, it needs intensive research, repeated movement between concrete and abstract, and between particular empirical cases and general theory.

In the example of crime prevention programmes, criminals have capacities and make choices to commit crimes. The policy programme embodies mechanisms such as surveillance and security measures which are intended either to deactivate the criminal's behaviour or block its realization when activated. (Note that despite the mechanical metaphor, it is fully acknowledged that they can be activated by actors' reasons.) How both sets of mechanisms work, if at all, depends on contextual conditions in which the crime and the programme are situated. Thus, for example, the success of programmes to solicit information from the public will depend on the local culture, whether it is highly privatized or relatively communal, and so on. The research therefore aims to identify and explain various combinations of contexts, mechanisms and outcomes, and given the openness and complexity of social systems, the list of possibilities is likely to be long. No mechanism or set of mechanisms, especially not those of the programme, is to be taken as a 'black box'. Their identification is not a matter of finding more specific regularities, clusters of statistical associations, for to do so would not explain the mechanisms but merely redefine the problem. Explanation requires mainly interpretive and qualitative research to discover actors' reasoning and circumstances in specific contexts – not in abstraction from them. Answering quantitative questions about the number of actors and other relevant phenomena with specific attributes may also be of interest but that is rather different from understanding the mechanisms.

This is a limited instance of realist explanation since it focuses primarily on how, and under what circumstances – if any – policy mechanisms can block mechanisms such as criminal acts, rather than on the structures and circumstances from which the mechanisms derive. Nevertheless, a critical realist analysis could go beyond this to address such matters, indeed that is what the explanatory model suggests.

A second example, based on research with Kevin Morgan (Sayer and Morgan, 1986; Morgan and Sayer, 1988), was concerned with explaining the differences in performance of firms in the same industry within and between regions.[12] The economic development of a country is invariably highly uneven, with different regions varying not only in terms of rates of growth or decline but in the types of economic activity they contain. This is the case even within a single industry operating in many regions. Attempts to explain this are normally approached through extensive research by treating firms as members of taxonomic groups, such as the electronics industry, in the hope of finding regularities in their behaviour, such as a correlation between employment growth and the availability of cheap labour. Such regularities are rarely found because of the openness of such systems. A common response to this is to disaggregate the population into more specific categories – in this case, consumer electronics, components and defence electronics, etc. Insofar as these categories correspond to different kinds of firm operating under different conditions, this may help clarify what is going on, but however small the categories or taxonomic groups, they are still dealing with parts of open systems in which both the key actors and their environments are changing continually.

At an early stage we switched from extensive research to intensive research, starting with key firms and situating them within their causal rather than their taxonomic groups. Two firms in the same taxonomic group – say consumer electronics – might operate in quite different causal groups, interacting with different institutions under different conditions. Tracing out these connections to wider causal groups increased the information load but actually made explanation much easier – it was like switching the light on – because we were explaining behaviour by reference to the concrete conditions in which they were situated, not by reference to a formal similarity to other firms in their taxonomic group. Thus, for many firms, cheap labour was not a consideration because they did not use unskilled labour, and the productivity and effectiveness of their skilled labour was more important than its cost, since they competed mainly by introducing new products and services rather than lowering the price of established goods. Moreover, in some cases, technical change altered the significance of cheap labour over time by automating it out of existence. Both the firms and the environment in which they operated changed over time, and the operation of the mechanisms depended on actors' interpretations, sometimes contested ones, so that it was important to find out how actors understood their situation. Consequently there was little sense in expecting to find enduring empirical regularities, yet using an intensive approach, asking qualitative questions about key relationships and how mechanisms work, explanations were not hard to find.

It was possible to investigate most of the major firms in the regions of interest in this manner, so at the end we could claim not only to understand a few cases but the main trends. As in the previous example of evaluation research, context was crucial; extensive research is indifferent to context because it is based on a model of quasi-experimental research in which contexts are homogenized.[13]

Those who assume that extensive research methods are the only legitimate 'scientific' approach often suppose that intensive research must lead to results that are unique and of purely parochial interest, and not generalizable. However, causal groups are not necessarily local; indeed in this research they involved global networks and markets which extensive research, with its claims to produce 'representative' results, usually ignored. In looking at objects in their taxonomic groups, one gets a representative picture of a kind, but as our Martian researcher example showed, the population of which it is representative may just be an artefact of the research, cutting across the causal groups relevant to actors. By situating actors in causal groups, intensive research provides a window onto larger entities, showing how the part is related to whole; hence it need not be of purely parochial interest.

Narratives of historical change present more demanding problems for social research. An interesting critical realist work in this context is the review of studies of postwar British politics presented by Marsh et al. (1998). Their purpose is to expose and discuss some standard problems that arise in developing narratives of political change. Above all they criticize reductionist or one-sided accounts which attempt to explain the whole in terms of a single part or theme, such as the decline of the British economy in terms of an anti-industrial culture, or Thatcherism in terms of Mrs Thatcher's personality and style.[14] Such reductionism invariably results in a misattribution of causality and a smuggling in of elements of other contributory processes under the banner of the selected part. In contrast, Marsh et al. advocate multidimensional accounts based on a synthesis of major significant elements, each of which is analysed abstractly and then combined in a movement back towards the concrete, tracing their evolution and interaction over time and space. The synthesis has to be more than a collection of factors and significant events; an account has to be given of how the various elements actually articulated.

Typical problems are suspect abstractions, such as the assumption that the state relates to the economy externally, when the state is itself a major economic actor, and a neglect of the way in which the elements identified in these abstractions evolve, changing their powers. Thus, regarding the latter problem, Marsh et al. criticize analyses of Thatcherism which treat it as fixed and unified, indeed, merely identifying a set of ideas and movements under a single name like Thatcherism may involve at best heroic assumptions, at worst a fallacy of misplaced concreteness.

Historical narratives also have to relate satisfactorily the ideational and the material. Ideas, ways of thinking, political paradigms can all produce change. For example, some commentators argue that globalization is not so much an inexorable force impinging on national governments but a discourse used by those governments to reduce their responsibilities. Whether such discourses can become effective in producing change depends on their practical adequacy, on how they relate to the constraints and opportunities of the context in which they are proposed. As realists, Marsh et al. do not reduce globalization to nothing more than a discourse, but argue that at least in part the discourse is dealing with something real. Similarly, it is not enough to cite the will and actions of key individuals and institutions as sufficient for producing change, because their effectiveness depends on how they relate to wider discourses and to the shifting and uneven possibilities of the context. Here Marsh et al. endorse the 'strategic relational approach' of Jessop (1990) regarding how actors, actions and contexts articulate.

We need to know not only what the main strategies were of actors, but what it was about the context which enabled them to be successful or otherwise. This is consistent with the realist concept of causation and requires us to ask the kinds of realist questions about necessary and sufficient conditions noted earlier, so as to decide what it was about a certain context which allowed a certain action to be successful. Often the success or failure of agents' strategies may have little or nothing to with their own reasons and intentions.

Agency and structure also have to be articulated. There are approaches which emphasize agency and are relatively silent on structure;[15] much archival research falls into the trap of reducing the relevant context to the interactions among key actors, ignoring such matters as economic change and changes in public opinion, and the structures within which agents act. Conversely, agents are written out of some accounts of Britain's postwar development; for example, accounts which frame the subject in terms of Britain's 'Anglo-US' model of capitalism, with its short-termism, high dividends, continual threat of takeovers and low levels of investment. Like so many partial accounts, this identifies something important but it leaves out political actors and is essentially economistic. Marsh et al. show that it is not unusual for narratives to shift between treatments of the historical past which are overwhelmingly structural, and accounts of the recent past and present which are voluntaristic. That this is easily done and can still seem persuasive shows both the power and dangers of narratives (see Chapter 6).

Social change is evolutionary – path-dependent yet contingent, shaped by legacies yet affected by contingently related processes or conditions. Thus the weakness of the British economy in the early 1970s, which derived from long-standing deficiencies such as underinvestment, poor marketing, lack of training and exposure to competitive markets, was exposed by the contingent event of the 1973 oil shock following the Yom Kippur War.[16] Behaviour is both selective and adaptive; again, we need to understand what it is about both its subjects and its contexts that enables particular outcomes.

Marsh et al. also draw attention to the problem of scale and boundaries in such studies. Too many analyses of postwar British politics have ignored the international setting, both in terms of connections to change elsewhere and of the presence of similar developments in other countries, such as the rise of neoliberalism. This problem is equivalent to that noted in our previous industrial studies example of defining causal groups in that it concerns the definition of the range of phenomena that are causally relevant to the development of the subject of interest.

These are just some of the problems of developing narratives of social change and an indication of a realist approach towards them. I shall have more to say about narrative in Chapter 6. Brief though the discussions of these examples have been, I hope they are sufficient to demonstrate some of the key features of critical realist research.

Conclusion

These then are some of the bare bones of a realist methodology. Many researchers operate in these ways intuitively, at least part of the time, though it is easy to stop short once one has found common associations among phenomena, without pursuing questions about their status. Many are led away from a realist approach by the hegemony of positivist methodology, with its disregard of problems of conceptualization and abstraction and its successionist theory of causation. Even research which rejects positivism may stop short of a realist approach if it rests content with finding associations among phenomena of interest without questioning whether they are associated necessarily or contingently.

A common aspect of all critical realist research is the priority given to conceptualization and abstraction, for how we 'carve up' and define our objects of study tends to set the fate of any subsequent research. Realists seek substantial connections among phenomena rather than formal associations or regularities. In explaining associations, they seek to distinguish what must be the case from what merely can be the case. Explanation of the social world also requires an attentiveness to its stratification, to emergent powers arising from certain relationships, and to the ways in which the operation of causal mechanisms depends on the constraining and enabling effects of contexts. Realists also recognize the concept-dependence of social phenomena and the need to interpret meaningful actions, though since reasons can be causes, this is not something separate from or alternative to causal explanation.

In sketching these features of realist research I have left on one side many fundamental issues such as the nature of signification, truth, objectivity, the situated nature of knowledge, and many others. These are discussed at length in Chapter 2.

Notes

1 This objection is discussed more fully in Chapter 2.

2 Strictly speaking, these are features of what Bhaskar termed 'transcendental realism', which is primarily a philosophy of and for natural science (1975). Critical realism, is a variant or development of this concerned with social science.

3 Language exists at both the level of the real - as generative grammars and vocabularies - and the actual - as speech. (Personal communication - Norman Fairclough).

4 Some accounts of these concepts give the impression that the domain of the empirical can only refer to or express a subset of the actual, and not the real, so that structures and powers are treated as unobservable. Unactivated powers or potentials are obviously not observable, but the structures in virtue of which they exist may be (the idle workers' body, for example); observability is not restricted to what changes or moves, for at least some structures can be observed.

5 The complexity of the implications of this combination of embodiment and emergence is especially important for sorting out some of the problems raised in the recent debates about essentialism (Chapter 4).

6 Not all social structures are big or supra-individual, like bureaucratic structures or class structures. There are also intra-individual and internalised structures, such as cognitive structures.

7 Imagining that it does is an example of what Bhaskar terms an 'epistemic fallacy', in that it transposes what is an ontological matter - concerning what exists (causes) - into the epistemological matter of how we develop reliable knowledge, for example by requiring repeated observations (Bhaskar, 1975).

8 Some critics of realism have complained that it is not always clear whether a relationship is necessary or contingent. This is sometimes the case, but where it occurs it shows that we have yet to arrive at a satisfactory understanding of the situation in

question, and further work on conceptualization of key objects may be necessary before we can decide whether the elements are internally or merely externally related. Like any philosophy of science, the role of critical realism is just as 'an underlabourer and occasional midwife', as Bhaskar puts it, not a substitute for substantive theory and research. Further confusion may have resulted from a slippage between two different senses of 'contingent', that is, as 'neither necessary nor impossible', and 'dependent', as in x is contingent upon y. While it is possible to combine these two, virtually opposed meanings, I prefer not to, and I restrict my use of the word to the first of these two senses. One can do this while recognizing that all phenomena, whether contingently related or not, have their respective causes and conditions: contingent does not mean 'uncaused'.

9 Some critics seem to expect otherwise. Thus Archer (1987) cites my statement that it is contingent whether we know necessity or contingency as if that was a fatal problem for realist philosophy.

10 It seems to me that Bhaskar's concession to anti-naturalism is played down unnecessarily, as if there was some loss of status in departing from the methods of the natural sciences (Bhaskar, 1979). The hermeneutic dimension is minimized too in Andrew Collier's account of realism (1994a, p. 247–8), indeed he comes close to denying that meaning is constitutive of social practice. This is unfortunate as it weakens realism's appeal for those whose main research efforts are in interpretive work. For realists, methods have to be appropriate to their objects, and there is no need to cling to naturalism more than is appropriate. For the fullest realist analysis of the interpretive dimension of social science, see Stones (1996).

11 The role of referents is often overlooked in postmodernist discussions of signification so that meanings appear to have no connection to them - see Chapter 2.

12 This research followed in the tradition of industrial research established first by Massey and Meegan (1982). For a debate regarding the relative appropriateness of intensive and extensive methods in relation to similar topics, see Keeble (1980) and Sayer (1982). For a more recent and excellent example of a realist approach in the same research field, see Nick Henry's work on industrial districts (Henry, 1992).

13 Many basic statistical methods were largely developed in experimental studies (for example, of horticulture) where these conditions could be artificially produced.

14 Similarly, they reject as a recipe for misunderstanding the ideal of an instrumentalist explanation of the kind common in neoclassical economics which prioritizes parsimony in explanation.

15 To some extent the emphasis given to structure or agency depends on the kind or research question being posed (see Stones, 1996).

16 The dangers of ignoring the path-dependent character of development, as if any society could reach a specific state from any starting point, are evident in the ruinous failure of shock-therapy marketization in Russia.

PART II

POSTMODERN-REALIST ENCOUNTERS

Introduction

One way of defining postmodernism, close to that proposed by Zygmunt Bauman (1995), is as 'modernism coming to terms with its limitations'. This it undoubtedly needs to do, though the process started long ago and most of the founders of social science had decidedly mixed feelings about modernity, if not modernist social science. Critical realism itself might be interpreted as a product of successive critiques of a complacent and overly confident modernism in social science, and its radical underestimation of the complexity, diversity and multiple meanings of the social world. Although postmodernism tends to be anti-realist and realists tend to be modernists, I agree with Rob Stones that critical realism should not reject postmodernism but acknowledge that some elements of it may be valid, particularly this problematisation of modernist categories and structures of explanation (Stones, 1996). Strategically, the main mistake made by critical realists in academic debate is to have ignored rather than engaged with poststructuralist and postmodernist thought.

Stones sees critical realism as opposed both to this complacent kind of modernism and the dominant 'defeatist' version of postmodernism – defeatist because it reacts against the failures and problems of modernism by giving up all hope of distinguishing better from worse explanations, let alone true or false ones (Stones, 1996, p. 2). However, he accepts as generally positive the postmodernist emphasis on the diversity of the world and the plurality of perspectives on it, and on the difficulty of obtaining reliable knowledge. I also have a suspicion of those modernist accounts of the social world – from both the Left and the Right of the political spectrum – which reduce it to a few basic structures and are oblivious to the complexity, openness and ambiguity of social action. Examples which spring to mind might include the crassness of rational choice and public choice theory, or of the class reductionism of some applications of Marxism. It is not that none of these has anything to offer as a partial explanation of behaviour, rather that they are so often treated in reductionist fashion with little effort to acknowledge what they exclude. The greater openness to different perspectives, indeed the recognition of the perspectival character of knowledge and experience, are progressive, though realists would dispute whether this need take us in a relativist direction. Defeatist postmodernists tend to assume that because the world is so open, diverse and complex, nothing of lasting or universal application can be said about it, and because theory is so contestable and yet difficult to test, anything goes. Critical realists accept the premise but argue for a different conclusion: that notwithstanding the daunting complexity of the world and the fallible and situated character of knowledge, it is possible to develop reliable knowledge and for there to be progress in understanding.

In Chapter 2 we confront some of the main anti-realist currents popular today in social science, many of them associated with postmodernism, though most having precursors. Here we take on fundamental issues such as approaches to meaning and truth, relativism, situated knowledges, gendered dualisms and different concepts of objectivity. In so doing, this chapter is intended to serve as an introduction to critical realism for sceptics who identify with these positions.

Chapter 3 is a critique of tendencies within defeatist postmodernism to flip from untenable positions associated with complacent modernism to positions which largely reverse their signs and hence turn out to be equally untenable. The primary 'pomo-flips' are from naive objectivism to idealism, from grand narratives to local knowledges, and from ethnocentrism to cultural relativism. In each case, critical realism offers a third way.

Chapter 4 examines a favourite target in contemporary social theory – 'essentialism'. This has become a multi-purpose pejorative term, being applied to an extraordinary diversity of ways of thinking, from biological reductionism to ethnocentrism and foundationalism. I attempt to analyse these diverse meanings, arguing first that while many of the targets of the anti-essentialist critique do indeed deserve to be criticized, there is little justification for a blanket refusal of any use of essentialist reasoning. In what might be termed a further pomo-flip, it has been common to replace the restrictive social ontology of essences with an implicit ontology of social ephemera. Against this I argue that realist ontology can embrace both the more enduring and the more ephemeral features of social life.

2

Realism for Sceptics

Critical realism is a philosophy of and for the social sciences. It is mainly concerned with ontology, with being, and has a relatively open or permissive stance towards epistemology – the theory of knowledge (Outhwaite, 1987). However, such is the influence of various kinds of idealism and relativism in recent social theory that realists increasingly find that they must first answer the epistemological questions these anti-realist positions raise before they can get their main case heard regarding ontology and explanation. There are radical disagreements between the two sides over the nature of meaning and truth. Many contemporary discussions of meaning are posed entirely in terms of the relation between signifiers and signifieds, with no mention of referents. The concept of 'objectivity' provides fertile ground for talking at cross-purposes, with some critics attacking it as an ideal. It is increasingly common to find attempts to substitute the sociology of science for the philosophy of science, and to treat knowledge as a function of power. From a different set of perspectives, feminist criticism of 'malestream' science has also brought the social and situated character of science to the fore and has at times questioned the basic values of science and reason, both in terms of their epistemic status and their social correlates or situation, though whether this leads to anti-realist conclusions is debatable. Realists have generally only paid lip service to the social and situated character of knowledge and have underestimated the influence of various forms of idealism in contemporary social theory. This chapter is intended to confront such issues. Since many of them overlap there is some redundancy in the argument, but it is important to confront the various guises in which idealist and relativist thinking occurs and demonstrate how critical realism can resolve their characteristic problems.

We begin with what may be the most common target of scepticism – the applicability of the basic realist proposition of the independence of the world from our knowledge of it to the *social* world: if the social world is socially constructed and significantly concept-dependent, how can it be treated as independent of the researcher's knowledge? Secondly, in response to the turn to discourse, we examine the problem of meaning or signification. Whereas naive objectivism and realism reduce this to a matter of reference, and idealism reduces it to intra-discursive relations in abstraction from reference and practice, critical realism argues that meaning is a product of both intra-discursive and referential relations.

Thirdly, we confront the thorny issue of 'truth', and what it might mean. While contemporary idealism tries to evade or dismiss the matter, critical realists argue that the issue is inescapable, but provide a different theory of truth from those of both naive realism/objectivism and relativism.

Fourthly, given the contemporary popularity of relativism in postmodernist thought, we examine it more closely and comment on attempts to relativize or bracket out questions of the truth of discourses. Fifthly, we also consider the claims of feminist standpoint point theory regarding the situated character of knowledge and address another theme of feminist interventions, the problems posed by gendered dualisms in 'malestream' thought.

Sixthly, we turn to an issue which runs through many problematic approaches to philosophical problems in social science, the meaning of 'objectivity' and 'subjectivity'. Here I argue that these terms have three different meanings which are independent yet typically confused, thereby causing chaos in many arguments over objectivity.

Finally, as a way of summing up, we illustrate the contradictions of anti-realism by reference to the work of a prominent social constructionist, Jonathan Potter.

How can the Basic Realist Principle Apply to Social Science?

On the face of it, while many might readily accept that the physical world is independent of our knowledge of it, the idea that the phenomena studied by social science exist independently of our knowledge seems implausible, indeed as is particularly clear in subjects like the study of education or management, the researchers are likely to encounter the influence of their own theories *within* their object of study. It is therefore tempting to reject the realist position and argue that since social phenomena are concept-dependent, since they include social science itself, and since theories can influence social practice as well as respond to it, then the social world cannot be independent of our knowledge of it. Moreover, if reflexivity is increasing in social life, then social theory comes to have a growing influence on it, so that it becomes still less a question of testing social theory against an independent reality, and more of dealing with a hall-of-mirrors effect, in which our theories are confronting themselves or reflections of themselves, so that any distinction between subject and object has melted away, and relations between them are replaced by ones of intertextuality.[1]

The analogy of multiply refracted images seems to be particularly appropriate for thinking about the way in which social theories not only direct our ways of seeing but in various forms confront our gaze wherever we look. It acknowledges the continuities and interactions between lay and scientific discourses and recognizes the possibility of social scientific claims having a self-fulfilling character. Also, in view of the beleaguered position of much of social science in wider society, it has the added attraction of emphasizing its influence. Yet despite these attractions, closer examination of the situation shows that the subject-object interactions merely become more complicated, and the realist proposition of the intransitivity of social phenomena as objects of social research stands. The hall-of-mirrors analogy is appealing, but it conceals several distinctions and universal features of social life.

Firstly, look again at our statement of the position: '…since theories can influence social practice as well as respond to it, then the social world cannot be independent of our knowledge of it.' Who is the 'we' making claims about 'our' knowledge here? Notice how it conflates the knowledge of the researcher with that of those under study. Even if the researcher and the practices under study do both depend on shared concepts, it does not follow from this that the practice is influenced by the researcher. In studying contemporary political discourse I may use the same concepts as politicians, etc., but that does not mean that the political discourse is a product of my analysis. The political discourse exists as it is regardless of whether I study it and whatever I think of it. Even if the researcher spends years researching some social phenomenon, interpreting it in various ways, s/he may still have no discernible influence on its object of study. Certainly some social theories can be influential – usually when they provide a social technology or latch onto and articulate some important but previously unarticulated structure of feeling in the wider society – but let's not kid ourselves: much of the time social scientists' work only influences a handful of peers.[2] And often where an academic reading is followed by similar articulations in lay society, this is not because academics have influenced events but because the scholars have anticipated a change which would have happened anyway even in the absence of their anticipation. To be sure, social theory can influence practice, but to assume that the hall-of-mirrors effect is universal would often involve us in mistaking the processes that social scientists describe and predict for their own products. Furthermore, in many cases, most obviously in history and the study of other societies, the concepts used by the researched and the researcher are *not* the same.

Secondly, one of the illusions of the hall-of-mirrors effect is produced by a (per)version of hermeneutics which assumes that because we can only interpret other discourses via our own, then we are not in fact studying independent discourses but rather our own discourse, or at least some kind of intertextual compound made from countless sources. This is an exaggeration, resting on the all-too-common reduction of mediation or construal to production or construction. This would reduce interpretation and communication to soliloquy.

Thirdly, that social practice is concept-dependent does not mean that it is identical to the concepts on which it is dependent: to imagine that it is, involves a combination of 'identity-thinking' or inverted foundationalism and wishful thinking – 'the world is what our concepts say it is'. Social practices are influenced by peoples' concepts of them, but that does not make the latter true of the former in some absolute sense. If all knowledge is fallible, the lay knowledge on which social practices depend cannot be exempted. While the concepts used by actors, whether implicitly or explicitly, are necessary for an explanation of their situation, they are not sufficient, for they are likely not only to be flawed but to mask or misrepresent certain aspects of what happens (Gellner, 1968). Again, to deny this implies a kind of foundationalism. The same goes for concepts which originate in social research and have diffused into wider society. They are not only likely to undergo modification as they are absorbed into different conceptual frames, but in any case they too are not identical to the practices which they inform and describe.

Fourthly, not all social research involves interaction and dialogue between the researcher and the researched through interviews, questionnaires, participant observation, where the answers given by the researched are likely to be influenced by the researcher. Plenty of social research is done without this inter-action, not least because dialogue is often impossible, inappropriate or unneces-sary. Even where there is dialogue and the answers are thus a product of the researchers' questions as well as the interviewees' experiences, then insofar as they are artefacts of the research question *rather* than the practice or situation under study, then that suggests a certain *independence* of the latter from the former. Our interviewees give us answers which are influenced by our research framework, but it does not follow from this that when they go back to their nor-mal lives, they think and act differently, though that of course is a possibility, and perhaps one which critical social science would like to encourage.

Fifthly, it is essential to note the abstraction from time in the hall-of-mirrors account, resulting in the telescoping of what are usually lengthy processes of influence and response. If we ignore the duration of a concrete recursive process in which A influences B and then B's response influences A, which in turn influences B, then it is little surprise that it is hard to distinguish A from B. Social structures and practices are concept-dependent, but they are usually most depen-dent on concepts of actors in the past, not today, and not necessarily those of today's social researchers (Archer, 1995; Harré, 1998). Consequently '(s)ocial objects exist intransitively at the time any social scientific analysis of them is initiated, whatever the eventual effect upon them induced by such an inquiry' (Lawson, 1997, p. 200).

Despite its initial appeal, in bypassing all these circumstances, the hall-of-mirrors analogy turns out to be facile, inviting various forms of idealism, foun-dationalism and wishful thinking. To be sure, it would be equally bad to fail to recognize the extent and influence of the interplay of concepts between lay and academic spheres in social life, but this does not mean that, in thoroughly undialectical fashion, subject-object relations and distinctions just collapse.

Meaning, Reference and the Death of the Object

A commonsensical or naive objectivism/realism might attempt to root meaning in a 'vertical' relation between terms and their referents. However, an extension-alist theory of meaning such as this, i.e. one that attempts to identify it with the objects to which a particular term refers, independently of the internal relations of discourse, fails because it does not address how we identify and make sense of the referent. Even our simplest experience of particulars is always already in terms of available descriptions. Yet the realization that this is so does not license the conclusion either that language is not influenced by the extra-discursive world or – inverting naive objectivism – that language gives reality its shape

(Tallis, 1988). The relations between language and the world are much more complex and elusive than any of these formulations imply, not least because the relationship can only be thought about from within discourse; we cannot step outside the latter to see how it relates to its referents.

In recent years in social theory, referents and the act of reference have received little attention, for, following the work of Saussure, it has been widely overshadowed by a preoccupation with the 'horizontal' relation between signifiers (equivalent to words or images) and signifieds (equivalent to concepts), together forming signs, in abstraction from any relation to referents. The elimination of the referent – the death of the object – is, of course, consistent with the turn to discourse and away from materialism in social theory. It inevitably obscures the role of language in practical life; not only meaning, but the world itself, become products of the play of differences across these networks[3]. Yet the abstraction from reference and referents is not one that can be sustained, and any discussion of meaning cannot avoid at least alluding to them[4], indeed the allusion often appears in the form of an elision of the distinction between the signified and the referent (Giddens, 1979, p. 17; Tallis, 1988, p. 69). However, there is a way of avoiding these idealist and naive objectivist extremes.

The relation between signifier and signified is conventional in character: there is no reason why a particular sound or image should stand for a particular concept, why the concept of what you are doing now, for example, should be called 'reading'. As Fairclough puts it, '[T]he relationship of words to meanings is many-to-one rather than one-to-one, in both directions: words typically have various meanings, and meanings are typically "worded" in various ways' (Fairclough, 1992, p. 185), though as he points out, this is an oversimplification, because different wordings change meanings. Because meanings are not given prior to being worded in various ways, signifieds cannot exist independently of words or other signifiers. Moreover, in seeking to define any particular term, we have to follow the differences among related signs. Thus we find that meaning is not to be located at any specific point but is continually 'deferred' across the network.[5] How we make sense of one subject or concept depends on the concepts we use to interpret it, as do these on still others, and hence on any number of other texts that we have read. Interpretation is therefore characterized by 'intertextuality'. In view of this, it is easy to be persuaded that meaning must be radically unstable, even though in everyday life, at least in its practical aspects, meaning seems fairly stable.

Critical realism can and must accept that meanings are not locatable at single points in the network, but are rather formed through the play of difference within the network. Nevertheless the acceptance of this point needs qualifying by reintroducing the referent into the discussion. If we correct for the omission and add the referent into our representation of the signification process, we get a triangle – see Figure 2.1 (Ullmann, 1962).

The signifier transmits the locutionary force in communication, though not in isolation but through differences from other signifiers; the referent is that which we speak or write about, be it something physical or a discursive object like a story; while the signified, which, as Bhaskar notes may involve analogies,

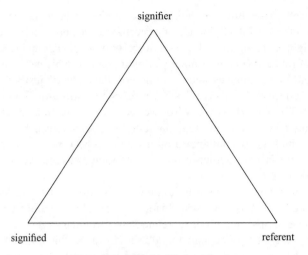

Figure 2.1 The signification triangle

metaphors and metonymies, enables conceptualization, albeit again, always through its relations of difference to other signifieds. The signification process takes place through networks of such triangles, and what is a signifier or signified in one triangle may become the referent of another. Meaning, on this account, is still constituted through difference, though not *only* through difference. Moreover, the generation of meaning and the success of acts of reference are influenced by context (Nellhaus, 1998).

People refer in the course of engaging in social practices – referring is tied to practical activity and is situation-dependent, implicitly if not explicitly. While the act of reference is generally treated as a passive relation between language and the world and always discursive in form, we should remember that we also intervene materially in the world, and we make what Bhaskar terms 'practical reference', picking things out physically, indeed we can know how to do this without being able to reflect much about it discursively (Bhaskar, 1991, Chapter 7). Whether the reference is practical (physical) or conversational, the referent is detachable from the act of picking it out. This is consistent with the realist proposition of existential independence, and with fallibilism. Moreover, we are also influenced by physical processes extra-discursively, even if we can only come to know them discursively – for example, as in catching a virus. We are involved in the world, as one of its forces.[6]

The relation between a particular sign (signifier-signified) and referent is again purely conventional, as the possibility of referring to the same thing in different languages shows. The same entity can also be validly called many different things within a single language – 'a person', 'a neighbour', 'an uncle', 'a librarian', etc. However, some terms, such as 'the economy' may have referents which do not seem to correspond to pre-existing natural kinds or occupy determinate stretches of space-time. Still others, such as 'but' and 'or' do not have referents at all. In addition it should be remembered language is not merely descriptive or propositional, but also has performative and expressive roles.

At first sight, the arbitrary relation between individual sign and referent might seem to reaffirm belief in the seemingly arbitrary and unstable nature of language, as if we could communicate and do things on the basis of just any jumble of words, and indeed this non-sequitur has been central to postmodernist idealism (Assiter, 1997, p. 61). However, when we look at *combinations* of related signs (which is how they are always *used*, implicitly if not explicitly), their relationship to referents can be shown not to be arbitrary and not necessarily unstable, though even here there is not a point-to-point correlation between words and world (Tallis, 1988, p. 106).

Consider an example, such as a discourse on health services, including terms like 'hospitals', 'doctors', 'nurses', 'patients', 'beds', 'operating theatres', etc. Each of these terms is arbitrarily related to particular referents in that the latter could always be called something else. However, this does not mean that the relationship between their referents is arbitrary, or that the relationships between the signifieds within such a discourse are arbitrary, so that the relationship between 'doctors' and 'patients' is equivalent to that between 'doctors' and 'horse-jumping' (Giddens, 1979; Tallis, 1988). Such terms never make reference on their own but always within wider referring expressions – such as 'the patient is in the hospital' – whose components are themselves dependent on their location within wider webs of signs. Moreover, the use of such expressions in communication usually also draws upon tacit knowledge to a significant degree. There is thus no isomorphism between language and reality in which the former is structured like the latter, for sense is not tightly correlated with physical characteristics. Language is not about bits of matter or whatever but about the sense the world makes to us. Nevertheless, it does not follow that there are no relatively stable meanings, or, remembering that meaning does not inhere in single signs in isolation, that their relation to the world is arbitrary.

We make reference through the play of differences among signs, but equally, the development of such networks of signs depends on reference (including references to other discourses) and practical involvement in the world. Whether the patient is in the hospital is not reducible to a matter of discursive definition, for once one has provided definitions (within a wider discourse, of course), one is still left with the empirical question of whether the thing defined as 'patient' is in the thing defined as 'hospital'. The discourse-dependence of reference does not mean that we can never distinguish between successful and unsuccessful references, though in some cases where we lack appropriate means of differentiation – such as deciding whether there is a God or not – it may indeed be impossible. Insofar as we can discern failed reference – a presupposition of any fallibilist theory of knowledge – and insofar as observation is only theory-laden rather than theory-determined, then inferences can be made about the different causal status of relations between phenomena such as doctors, patients and horse-jumping. We can also still acknowledge the scope for other meanings or interpretations of such terms, including more imaginative ones deriving from associations and analogies, which are likely to be less stable. And as we have noted already, the terms themselves may be metaphors, such as 'operating *theatre*'; the fact that a signified is a metaphor does not prevent it making successful reference, though some metaphors work much better than others in this respect.

Since this account does not rely on treating individual units of meaning as intelligible in isolation, without any dependence on wider networks of sense-relations, it is therefore not 'logocentric', as postmodernists suppose must be the case with realist accounts of reference (Assiter, 1997, p. 32; see also Quine, 1961, p. 42). As Tallis points out, for the idealist, the fact that the Inuit have many words for snow while the bushpeople of the Kalahari desert have none is merely a function of their different languages and has nothing to do with any extra-discursive reality (1998, p. 64). Similarly, for idealists, it is only in virtue of language that the boundaries of objects such as tables or liberalism differ in their clarity (Tallis, 1988). However, those who claim that reality is a discursive construct don't believe what they say, for their practice – for example avoiding extra-discursive dangers, such as oncoming cars – shows that they cannot make the world a slave to their discourses (O'Neill, 1995). Idealists also don't believe what they say in rejecting reference, for they always make reference to discourses other than their own, often in the very act of denying that reference is possible. As Tallis argues, '(I)t is, to put it mildly, rather implausible that language should be available to refer to itself and, in particular, to its own limitations *and to no other referent in the world*' (1988, p. 125–6, in original).

While our realist account of signification argues that meanings are not as unstable as postmodernism implies, it would be strange, indeed inconsistent, for realists to deny any instability. Many meanings are contested, and it would be absurd for an activity or discourse so dedicated to contesting meaning to overlook this fact. Creativity and major scientific advances depend on shifts in meanings and they should be valued accordingly. But there are other kinds of speech or writing, such as the instructions given to pilots by air traffic controllers, when the fixity of meanings, and the constancy of the objects and practices to which they refer, is crucial. Without a realist analysis of signification practices that acknowledges the independence of referents and their properties and inter-relations from discourse – absolute in the case of inanimate objects, relative in the case of human social phenomena – the success and stability of reference in social practice is unintelligible.

It is no surprise that the preoccupation with the undecidability of meaning should come from scholars who study *literature* (Tallis, 1988, p. 126). Or rather, it is surprising that so little has been made of this fact by social scientists seduced by the thesis. The distinctive feature of literature is precisely its detachment from everyday practice; it is predominantly a kind of communication that has purposes other than the achievement of some immediate practical end, though of course there are some exceptions. Even when everyday communicative action is interpreted by literary theorists, the practical contexts and ends in terms of which it operates tend to be bracketed out. Communication in everyday life is embedded in ongoing practices and material and discursive contexts (Giddens, 1979). Here we would do well to note that Wittgenstein's emphasis on forms of life does not involve a retreat from the object to the idea; for him, to know a language is to be able to participate in the material forms of life within which it is expressed, and which it expresses (Norris, 1997). Practices, including talk and writing, can be interpreted in many ways, and as texts, their meaning can never be bounded and stably defined. But part of the function of communicative action and associated material acts is to indicate which of those many possible meanings apply in a given situation.[7] When we read a final demand for payment of our electricity bill and the accompanying threat of disconnection, we could play endless parlour games running through diverse constructions of what this text says, showing off our ability to construe it in imaginative ways. Nevertheless, which of the many possible meanings is supposed to apply, is usually pretty clear; if it isn't, it might register when the lights go out.

Finally, a common assumption about realists is that they cannot countenance ambiguity, whereas postmodernists celebrate ambiguity and see a multiplicity of interpretations as a positive, rather than a problematic feature. However, I would argue that we can and must recognize ambiguity in social life, but not mistake this for a licence for just any interpretation, Some social situations are objectively ambiguous. An army parade on Remembrance Day is a case in point, for it combines a recognition of the horrors of war ('Never again, ... ') with a glorification of the army and perhaps war itself. But to interpret an event as ambiguous or having multiple meanings is not to admit just any interpretation (for example, a Remembrance Day parade is not a wedding or a rock concert), for not all interpretations can do justice to the particular ambiguities of a situation. Paradoxically, if we are to do justice to ambiguities we cannot interpret them just any way.

Truth and Practical Adequacy

While the above discussion dealt with reference and meaning, it left open the question of the truth status of propositions about the world. It has become increasingly common in social science either to avoid the word 'truth' or to put it in scare quotes, so that authors can signal their scepticism about the concept. There are good grounds for being sceptical about it, though there are bigger problems in imagining we can dispense with any concept of truth. The scepticism arises from a realization that we cannot escape to an Archimedean position from where we can see how discourse and reality, statements and their objects, compare, and from a recognition that the world can only be known under particular descriptions or within particular discourses, which can differ dramatically. Under these circumstances, and bearing in mind that knowledge and the world to which it refers are mostly different kinds of things, what could it mean to say we know the truth about something? And how would we know we had arrived at the truth? Naive ideas about 'reality checks', about finding some simple formula for discovering the truth and guaranteeing 'realistic' theory must be abandoned. History makes fools of those who claim to have at last discovered the truth in some absolute, ultimate sense, because even if their claims are not directly falsified, the concepts in which they are framed may be succeeded by different, more powerful ones. There are some claims – for example, that our blood circulates in our bodies – whose truth it is hard to imagine ever being challenged, but even here there might still be a possibility that, say, 'circulation' could be superseded by a better description. At the other extreme there are other claims, particularly regarding how texts or discourses should be interpreted or read, for which it sometimes seems doubtful whether it is appropriate to speak of an interpretation being true of its object. Even if we ask, instead, how we distinguish better from worse interpretations, answers are elusive. Such matters are particularly important in social science, given that many aspects of society are textual or text-like and therefore need to be interpreted. However, although some social scientists specialize in interpretive work, not all social practices and relations are textual or text-like, and most have a material aspect which is usually of some importance, such as the body, resources, physical environment, and mobility. I will address what 'truth' might mean in relation to claims about these first, before coming to interpretation.

Anti-realists such as Rorty (1980) suppose that realism – and also epistemology in general – must be foundationalist ventures. However, as we have noted, to acknowledge the mind-independence of the world is to undermine, not to support, hopes of some privileged relation between discourse and the world. Nor do realists need to invoke an Archimedean standpoint, for not only is it unattainable but there is no contradiction involved in accepting both that there is a world existing independently of our thoughts and that we can only know what it is like from within discourse.

It is important, however, to see that the existential independence of our objects of study from whatever researchers may think about them – mostly absolute in natural science, relative in social science – doesn't mean that such objects have no *influence* on our thinking. It does not entail the object-independence of the mind. The relation is asymmetric and the influence is always mediated by language, though that A is mediated by B does not mean that A is B's product. Although all observation is conceptually mediated[8] what we observe is not determined solely by concepts, as if concepts could antipate all empirical questions, or as if theories were observation-neutral[9]. Without this conceptually mediated influence or feedback, it is hard to see how knowledge could be shown to be fallible. Even if, in the manner of the Quine-Duhem thesis, we allow that in principle it is always possible to accommodate discrepant observations in a conceptual system by making appropriate adjustments to the system, in practice, as we have seen, the elements of the systems are (conventionally) tied to determinant practices and objects. This means that in changing the framework to eliminate any and every problem there is a risk that we will upset those parts of the system which currently work well, causing more problems than we solve, although one day we may be able to devise a framework that provisionally resolves all the problems encountered thus far.

It is common to associate realism with correspondence theories of truth as opposed to conventionalist theories of truth. The latter define truth, in relativist fashion, as whatever a community, scientific or otherwise, agrees it is. What counts as truth is intersubjectively agreed upon, and therefore there is a sense in which truths are indeed conventions. However, the matter does not end there, for, as the realist will quickly add, the conventions are not *arbitrary*, since not just any convention will work as a basis for (intersubjective) action and expectations. This is why, in practice, conventionalists, like anyone, avoid contravening conventions that are important to their well-being, such as the convention that one should drive on the left in Britain or the convention that live wires are dangerous to touch. If there were nothing more to truth than convention, then we could prove this by flouting with impunity any conventions about what is the case.

On the other hand, regarding correspondence theories of truth, it has to be acknowledged that correspondence is an awkward and elusive notion. Given that we cannot apprehend the relationship between knowledge and the world directly but only via discourse, and given that knowledge and its objects are usually radically different, then it is hardly surprising that it is difficult to find a way of conceptualizing correspondence. At one level, it seems straightforward and obvious that we want theories that 'correspond' to their objects. But what might 'correspond' mean here? If we mean 'mirror' or 'reproduce', then these are bad metaphors, for as we have already seen, the relation between knowledge and its referents is not at all like that of mirroring an object or reproducing or representing a copy of it. If we don't understand something, then it is no help whatsoever to have a mirror image or exact copy of it, for we will be none the wiser. On the contrary, what we need is something *different*, namely a *discourse*. The relationship in question is one of unlikes, not likes. (If the object is itself a discourse, then, similarly, an exact replica of that discourse would add nothing that we didn't already know: again, what we need instead is a different discourse.) However, note that, contrary to a common mistake, just because knowledge and its referents are usually different, it does not follow that there can be no relationship between them. If we are to allow a notion of correspondence, it must involve conformability and intelligibility rather than replicability. Realists do *not* need to suppose that knowledge mirrors the world; rather it interprets it in such a way that the expectations and practices it informs are intelligible and reliable. Knowledge claims involve practical commitments, that if one does such-and-such, certain things will result. Thus the claim that the money supply is the prime governor of the rate of inflation implies that if the government prints large amounts of extra money, inflation will result. If the effects are different from those expected then we are led either to doubt the claim or suspect that counteracting forces neutralized the expected effect.

There is a common way of summing up the relationship between realist and conventionalist (or, more accurately, instrumentalist) standpoints on truth, which is that realists say useful knowledge is useful because it is true, and instrumentalists say knowledge that is called true is so merely because it is useful. On the latter view, as Rorty argues, calling what works 'true' is merely a way of patting ourselves on the back, and hence quite redundant. But we can also say more than that certain beliefs are merely useful, and indeed, particularly in science, we want to know why such beliefs are successful – what it is about the world which makes them so. They are not made useful merely by a collective act of will. The question is not only what works, but what it is about the world which makes it work.

To say that certain propositions are true is not to say they are beyond improvement. It is not only that they may later be shown to be false but that, even if they are not, they may be shown to be partial rather than complete, or integrated within a wider conceptual scheme that is flawed. Thus many results of science are superceded not because they are simply false but because they can be replaced or augmented by propositions located within conceptual schemes which explain more than earlier ones. For example, consider the succession of properties used to describe the essence of particular minerals, which have developed from references to colour and taste, to hardness, to chemical composition, to atomic weight (Harré, 1972). The reduction of the issue to a simple black-and-white question of (absolute) truth or falsity does no justice to the complexity of the relation of practical knowledge to its referents. In view of this, as I have argued before (Sayer, 1992), truth might better be understood as 'practical adequacy', that is in terms of the extent to which it generates expectations about the world and about results of our actions which are realized. Just how practically adequate different parts of our knowledge are will vary according to where and to what they are applied. The differences in success of the same beliefs in different contexts and different beliefs in the same context suggests that the world is structured and differentiated, and has some degree of stability, so that while some things are transient, some are not. The practical adequacy of our beliefs about the world may be highly selective and uneven; thus we can acknowledge that Stone Age astronomers had a remarkably good predictive understanding of the movement of the stars but little idea of what stars are. That a theory is practically adequate in relation to one set of practices and questions does not mean it will be similarly adequate with reference to another set. Science and theory are dedicated to expanding the areas of success, to increasing practical adequacy, or, as Stones puts it, following Craig Calhoun, achieving 'epistemic gain' (Stones, 1996). While current knowledge of the stars has greater practical adequacy as we have defined it, it is likely that in comparison to future generations' knowledge, the practical adequacy of our own knowledge of the stars will also be shown to be highly selective.

We might note in passing here that whether practical knowledge does any good is a separate question. To say that certain beliefs are practically adequate is not to assume that behaviour informed by them can only bring us good. Repressive or dangerous practices must have some practical adequacy, conforming to something, if they are to work: they must at least be selectively practically adequate. Often, scientifically informed practices have a mixture of good and bad effects. The danger of ideological beliefs is not that they are completely untrue, for if they were ineffectual they would pose no threat, but that the particular form of their selective practical adequacy has bad consequences. This is vital to bear in mind in response to the contradictory tendency of postmodernist deflationary accounts of science to be dismissive about the practical adequacy of science while emphasizing its bad effects in practice.

An 'out-of-gear' conception of knowledge (Collier, 1994a), that is one that sees it as being both immune to extra-discursive influence and incapable of affecting the world – like a car engine decoupled from the transmission system – makes it impossible to understand how science (or any other knowledge) can have any effects, good *or bad*. That science can have bad as well as good practical consequences shows that, at least some of the time, it is in-gear, though if the consequences are bad this may suggest that scientists and others have overlooked or not understood in what ways it is in-gear.

So far, we have dealt primarily with the denotative function of language in describing and explaining the world, and ignored its performative function in creating its objects.[10] There is an important lesson in Foucault's work regarding the way in which it is possible for particular discourses not merely to describe people and situations externally but to 'construct' or at least mould them as particular kinds of subjects. In such circumstances, there is a sense in which power and knowledge are implicated in one another, forming 'regimes of truth'. Although the picture Foucault presents of social science and the 'psy-disciplines' is arguably overly negative, his work serves as a forceful warning regarding their dangers and of the often far from beneficial influence of natural science on societies' self-understanding, social relations, technology and the environment. Discourses in society can be performative as well as descriptive because they are embedded in material social practices, codes of behaviour, institutions and constructed environments. As Raymond Williams (1962) put it, discourse and practice may be 'reciprocally confirming'. However, the objects of natural and social science are not equivalent in this respect: while the knowledge produced by both natural and social science influences society, the objects of natural science, such as the rocks that geologists study, are what they are, regardless of how they are categorized, though of course they can be changed by physical manipulation, albeit only according to their properties. *Social* science does not merely discover and name practices which already exist but can be implicated in the construction of practices, thereby bringing new ones into being. It is this difference between natural and social science which makes the relativism (rightly or wrongly) associated with Kuhn (1970) different from that associated with Foucault.

However, matters can't be left at that, for apart from the question of whether such performative creations are good or bad, it is obvious that not just any ideas can successfully be performed, enacted and imposed. Indeed the very power of regimes of truth, if that's what they are, depends on developing practices which are successful in their own terms and on the difficulty of constructing alternative performances or regimes of truth. Foucault's statement that '[I]n fact power produces; it produces reality; it produces domains of objects and rituals of truth' (1977, p. 194) is either a tautology (power is only acknowledged where it produces reality, and truth is only acknowledged where this happens) or a misleading exaggeration, for many objects are not socially produced and not just any social arrangement can be created, even by the powerful.[11] Since what can be constructed depends on the properties of the 'materials' (including people, institutions and ideas) used in the construction, there is still a sense in which performativity depends on practical adequacy, although again it may be a very limited, selective practical adequacy – one that may ignore or suppress the activation or exercise of some our powers in order to activate and construct others.

In acknowledging performativity we don't have to accept exaggerated claims for how far people can be changed, 'constructed' or 'constituted'. By treating people in certain ways, they can come to conform to those treatments. In this regard it is better to avoid the metaphors of 'construction' and 'constitution', as in 'certain persons are constructed or constituted as x', when what is meant is that 'the effect of treating certain persons as if they were x, can *in varying degrees*, depending on the situation, succeed in making them x'. For both explanatory and practical purposes it is important to be able to retain the capacity to differentiate between a treatment of something as if it were x that has little or no success in actually making it like x, and one which is largely or wholly successful in so doing.

This problem of an implicit voluntarism in which any discourse can construct what it refers to is also invited where discourse and practices are conflated. To separate them we need not deny that discourse is itself a practice, merely that practice is nothing more than talk; discursive practices are a *subset* of social practices (Fairclough, 1992). Discourses invariably have conditions and effects (both ideational/textual and material) that differ from those that they acknowledge and intend. Consequently, corresponding to the distinction between the transitive and the intransitive, thought objects and real objects, we need a distinction between discourses and their effects. Conflating discourses with their effects, assuming that performativity involves producing not only effects but the exact effects intended or stated, are kinds of identity thinking (Hull, 1997). There is little difference between the empiricist kind of identity thinking in which thoughts are presumed to mirror the things to which they refer, and the constructionist kind in which things are as they are thought, or 'constructed'. Furthermore, even though the intention behind the concept of regimes of truth may be to challenge the will-to-power, conflating discourses and practices has the effect of exaggerating that power, and hence underestimating the possibility of knowledge challenging it.[12]

Finally, there is the question of truth or practical adequacy in relation to interpretive understanding. 'What is a good interpretation?' is one of the most difficult questions social researchers and philosophers of social science have to face, and as Stones argues, potentially it poses a challenge to hopes for clear, decisive empirical conclusions (Stones, 1996).

Intrinsically meaningful phenomena such as cultural values are likely to be more open to different interpretations than are material objects such as buses or buildings, even though such constructions are concept-dependent; insofar as the primary function of the latter is practical, there are certain things which they can and cannot do, whereas values are more elusive. As Aristotle noted, we should not expect more precision than the object allows. We should not expect something like cultural values to be unambiguous and determinate any more than we should expect a lump of granite to be malleable and indeterminate. There is a continuum from practical understanding, for doing familiar things such as paying bills, where meanings are straightforward, to highly open, associational thinking, such as that involving cultural values, where a wide range of lay interpretations are likely. In social science, depending on our interests, we can be concerned with any part of this range.

A different way of thinking about interpretive understanding is to regard it not as a matter of finding more or less true or adequate or authoritative interpretations, but as a matter of adding to the range of interpretations, thereby enriching an ongoing creative conversation. This is indeed what some exercises in interpretation are like, and rightly so, but they do not displace the need for social scientists to find interpretations of social action which attempt to identify what actors understood by them. That this can only take place via the interpreters' own pre-understanding does not mean actors' understandings can be absorbed into those of researchers; a researcher's own reading will not necessarily double up as a good account of the view or reception of the discourse or action by lay actors.[13] At times, social scientists' analyses of discourses, actions and images are likely to be as different from actors' understandings as an art historian's interpretation of a painting is from a layperson's. If researchers fail to acknowledge this difference, then they will unreflexively pass off their own understanding – perhaps primarily a product of competition among academic peers – as that operative amongst lay actors. Of course, actors may not be aware of everything that is going on and therefore a difference between lay and researchers' accounts may be quite justified. However, researchers need to ask themselves if this 'surplus' is indeed addressing unacknowledged conditions, meanings, and unintended effects actually present in a particular setting or whether they are developing their imaginative interpretations regardless of the original practical context, largely for their own and peers' edification.

Critical realism proposes a middle way between, on the one hand, pessimistic views according to which no interpretation can be shown to be better than any other, and on the other hand, positivistic views which either fail to see the problem or see it as minor. We need to remember that interpretive understanding or verstehen is a normal and indispensable part of everyday practice, indeed social life depends on its being reasonably successful for much of the time. As we saw earlier, what reduces the range of possible interpretations, whether in everyday life or social science, is the situation of communication and action in determinate practical contexts.[14] Accounts of interpretive understanding or hermeneutics which divorce it from these practical contexts are likely to conclude that there are no good or bad interpretations, just different ones. Even if we take one of the most contestable meaningful aspects of social life – identities – then these are not, as the discursive turn tends to imply, simply matters of discursive construction or the play of difference within discourse. Rather they relate to determinate characteristics and acts, to what actors, groups, societies have done. These acts, of course, are open to differing interpretations, but the latter in turn have some things in common – the interpretandum – over which they differ. Here, it is worth remembering what an identity parade is for – to establish the identity of an (alleged) criminal, that is, 'whodunnit?' Who killed or did not kill someone is not simply a question of discursive construction, though our thoughts about the answer are always in the medium of particular discourses. The identity of a murderer can still be interpreted in various ways, but they relate to what the person so identified has done. It is not merely a matter of discourse.

Relativism

> Everything I have said and done in these last years is relativism by intuition... From the
> fact that all ideologies are of equal value, that all ideologies are mere fictions, the mod-
> ern relativist infers that everybody has the right to create for himself his own ideology
> and to attempt to enforce it with all the energy of which he is capable. (Mussolini, cited
> in Veatch, 1962)[15]
> There is no such thing as truth. Science is a social phenomenon and like every other
> social phenomenon is limited by the benefit or injury it confers on the community
> (Hitler, cited in Daniel, 1962, p. 118)[16]

As anyone who has taught the philosophy of social science will know, one of
the most striking features of the last 30 years of post-empiricism is the recurrent
appeal of relativism. After the initial wave of relativism following the decisive
interventions of Kuhn (1970) and Feyerabend (1993) in the philosophy of natural
science, a second wave has developed in social science with the rise of postmodernism and poststructuralism.[17] Today, relativist tendencies often take the
form of attempts either to relativize truth as a construction of particular communities or dominant groups, as in Foucault's concept of 'regimes of truth', or to
'bracket out' questions of the truth or practical adequacy of the beliefs of those
we study, as for example in many approaches to the sociology of science (Wade
Hands, 1997).

Critical realism *accepts* 'epistemic relativism', that is the view that the world
can only be known in terms of available descriptions or discourses, but it rejects
'judgemental relativism' – the view that one cannot judge between different discourses and decide that some accounts are better than others (Bhaskar, 1986,
p. 72).[18] The two most common defences of judgemental relativism invoke the
theory-laden character of observation – as if this meant theories could not be
falsified by observations – and incommensurability between competing theories.
Regarding the former, that observation is theory- or concept-laden does not entail
that it is necessarily purely theory-determined. It is hard to see why observation
would ever be necessary in science or everyday life if our concepts already specified everything about what could be observed. Regarding incommensurability, as
Bhaskar argues (1979), if two discourses lack a common referent then there is
nothing for them to disagree about and no need to make a choice between them,
any more than we need to choose between astronomy and economics. If, on the
other hand, they contradict one another, they cannot be totally incommensurable,
since there must be some terms in common which are in contradiction. As
Collier argues, the psychological thesis that we cannot understand other, radically
different discourses, or understand them at the same time as we retain our own
beliefs, is highly implausible (Collier, 1994a). In practice, some kind of translation or mutual understanding is usually possible between members of different
discourses. Moreover, there is the paradox that in order to specify where exactly an
example of incommensurability lay, we would have to make such a translation, thus
demonstrating commensurability (Davidson, 1984; Norris, 1993). In practice, the
exaggeration of the problem of incommensurability, making what is a difficulty
appear as an impossibility, looks suspiciously like a way of protecting favoured

discourses from external criticism. Contrary to initial appearances, relativism encourages closed rather than open minds.

In addition to these problems, there is the long-noted paradox that consistent relativists can have no objection to doctrines which are blatantly anti-relativist, since the only way to reject them would be to renounce their relativism. As we show in Chapter 3, further contradictions are thrown up by cultural relativism, as when, for example, fear of ethnocentrism makes the relativist abstain from criticism of other cultures which may themselves be virulently ethnocentric.

Whatever the philosophers and social theorists have argued, among students who are attracted to relativism, the most common motive is a fear of absolutism, a fear that accepting the possibility of distinguishing truth from falsity will require one to pronounce the beliefs of others as false.[19] Relativism appears to have the virtue of being egalitarian and open-minded, avoiding implications that others are 'falsely conscious'. Even if one rejects an absolutist view of truth and proposes, as I have done, that absolute truth is either meaningless or unattainable, but that one can nevertheless often distinguish better from worse ideas, some relativists seem to find this unpalatable too. Effectively, this kind of relativism assumes that because everyone is or should be regarded as equal, the epistemological status of their beliefs must also be equal. However, as the quotations heading this section indicate, relativism does not entail such open-mindedness, and it can be used consistently in the most illiberal of ways. Indeed, in view of the popularity of Nietzschean associations of truth as will-to-power, liberal relativism can provide a convenient mask for what might be called 'Mussolini relativism'.

Furthermore, regarding 'false consciousness', objectionable though such a notion may seem, it is inescapable, for its refusal involves a performative contradiction: 'you are falsely conscious in believing in the possibility of false consciousness'. Every time we argue with someone, we presuppose the possibility of either party being wrong, i.e. falsely conscious. Our intuitive benign relativists would not want to insist that they are always right, but if they are to acknowledge that they are capable of being wrong (i.e. falsely conscious), then they must acknowledge that the same goes for others. The principle of equality applies to the moral worth of persons, not to the epistemological status of their empirical beliefs: although we might properly regard sociologists and chemists as equals as people, a sociologist's knowledge of chemistry is not equal to that of a chemist, any more than a chemist's knowledge of sociology is equal to that of a sociologist. Thus, social and moral equality does not entail epistemological equality.

Relativizing truth, as in Foucault's use of the concept of 'regimes of truth', is always likely to be self-undermining, for if truth is no more than a set of beliefs which are imposed by the dominant authorities, and used to construct its objects, then where does that leave the author's own account? Why should we take Foucault's own accounts seriously? On the other hand, it is not only self-undermining but self-protective, for if truth-claims are merely conventional, then they cannot be refuted. Yet we cannot escape making judgements of truth or practical adequacy. If we accept the proposition that there are or have been regimes of truth, do we not imply that *that* proposition is true – in the sense we have advanced – of the situation? Foucault says that '[B]y truth I do not mean "the ensemble of truths which are discovered and accepted" but rather "the ensemble of rules according to which the true and false are separated and specific effects of power attributed to the true"' (Foucault, 1980, p. 132). But this fails to escape more standard meanings of truth because of course we need to know the truth about the ensemble of rules for distinguishing the true from the false in a particular discourse. Universal relativization involves a performative contradiction which invites ridicule – 'there is no truth beyond whatever anyone defines as the truth – and that's the truth!' Even if we were to say that our own knowledge was also merely a function of our social position it would imply that this was true. The only way we can relativize truth is selectively, by exempting some beliefs, including our own, from the relativization.

In the absence of any qualifications regarding such exemptions, it is bound to be unclear whether references to regimes of truth, with their connotations of authoritarian imposition of ideas, are critical or agnostic. If *all* knowledge is the product of regimes of truth then they can hardly be said to be a problem. If, on the other hand, we are meant to understand their existence as problematic, then this implies that they are in some sense regimes of either untruths or else unacceptable truths insofar as the constructions of the regimes have bad consequences. Furthermore, to characterize what actors believe to be true as a product of regimes of truth involves adopting a perspective that is, in all probability, at odds with how the actors themselves would think of the situation. It therefore does not actually succeed in remaining agnostic about questions of truth and falsity but amounts to a critical judgement on the truth or falsity of their beliefs. Evasions of this critical implication amount to what Habermas has termed, in his critique of Foucault, 'crypto-normativity' (see also Larrain, 1994). Again, universally relativizing truth as a function of power leads to incoherence.

Crypto-normativity involves what might be termed 'adolescent iconoclasm' – a view of the world which assumes that the most cynical account must automatically be the best. It reduces epistemological authority to a matter of social authority, so that 'the capacity to describe, define and explain societies ... is rooted in the authority of certain discourses over others' (O'Brien and Penna, 1998). While science is not a power-free zone and some views may owe their dominance to it, it is absurd to suppose that knowledge is nothing more than whatever powerful groups choose to dictate. This is an absurd inversion which is easy to counter by asking why not just any ideas can have authority over others. By the same token, Martina Navratilova's technical expertise and domination in tennis would be reduced to a matter of her social authority in a game which favours certain social groups.[20] On this view, inquiry is reduced to persuasion or force and we never pursue questions whose answers we haven't already decided upon (Mäki, 1995). To be sure, what people *think* is the case can be a matter of assertion or negotiation, but what *is* the case is generally not – otherwise wishful thinking would always work. The fact that it so often does not, even where it is the wishful thinking of the powerful, shows that epistemic authority is not reducible to social authority.

The agnostic option of bracketing out questions regarding the truth or practical adequacy of the discourses under investigation has become popular, particularly in sociology. Bracketing out can be merely a kind of selective, *strategic* relativism. It does not require us to believe that there really is no way of deciding on the relative adequacy or truth of different discourses; it just involves a decision to suspend rather to exercise judgment about actors' beliefs in the particular research in question. There may indeed be cases in which social scientists don't have to decide on the truth or epistemic status of the beliefs of those whom they study, though they always have to decide what is a true or practically adequate account of the beliefs the researched hold, regardless of whether the beliefs themselves are true. However, often researchers cannot avoid making a judgment of the latter, at least implicitly. This is because in trying to say what is going on in a social situation, we have either to endorse actors' own accounts of what is going on or offer a different – and hence implicitly critical – account of our own. Moreover, those actors' accounts inform behaviour which produces effects, though not necessarily those supposed by the actors. In pointing out these unrecognized effects, we again find ourselves offering an implicitly critical account.

Attempts to relativize or bracket out the question of the truth or practical adequacy of a particular kind of knowledge can function as a form of escapism. Consider the following pair of responses to discussions of epistemology, both from research students in social science:

1   I'm not interested in whether ideas are right or wrong, true or false. I'm interested in where ideas are coming from and what their authors are about. So long as I can work that out I'm satisfied for then I can know how to judge them.
2   I have my values and I just need to know what the various competing ideas are so I can judge them according to my values.

Such positions seem particularly to appeal to those who are either struggling with or reluctant to engage with philosophy of social science, for they appear to allow an escape from all its arguments, a way of bracketing out its concerns. They also involve sociological reductionism, that is, reducing ideas to their social origins, as if there were no question of whether they were true.

The first can only be coherent if it is strictly a limited, strategic form of relativism, for in order to decide where various ideas come from, we have to decide what are the better - or more true - accounts of where they come from, and what those ideas are. Sociologists of knowledge can hardly bracket out the question of the truth of their own accounts. The second response appears to be open and honest in that its proponents say they intend to lay their cards on the table and be open about their values: 'As an x-ist I believe such-and-such.' On the one hand it gives the appearance of being able to rise above the fray, on the other, it appeals to subjective foundations. The appeal to values is perhaps intended as an argument-stopper, as if values were beyond critical appraisal, as if they were just what we have, as beyond reason. Also, being *'personal* values', the implication is that to criticize them would be a kind of violation of what is private. Despite the apparently radical character of this position, it reproduces rather than challenges the fact-value, reason-emotion, science-ideology dichotomies of positivism.[21] The appeal to values could also protect the racist, the mysogonist, the homophobe, etc. from criticism too. Would it be acceptable for racists to defend racist science on the grounds that it was based on their values? Of course, it may indeed be based on their values, and it may be helpful to check this and find out where they are coming from, but it still leaves the question of whether their beliefs are good/justified/right/true/misleading.[22] As John O'Neill notes, this kind of appeal to values suggests a romantic hope of becoming strong self-creative beings able to escape external judgments and criteria (1998, p. 91).[23] Appealing to one's own subjective values as arbiter is simultaneously a way of hiding dogmatism (a 'god-trick') behind apparent modesty ('it's merely my view'), and arrogantly evading philosophical argument.

Situated Knowledge and Standpoint Theory

Recently, the concept of 'situated knowledge' and concerns with questions of power in deciding what constitutes knowledge have been major themes in feminist literature on epistemology (for example, Harding, 1991; Haraway, 1991; Grimshaw, 1996). Knowledge has not merely a general anthropocentric character but bears more specific social markings such as those associated with the particular contexts in which it develops, including the gender, race and sexuality of its authors, as well as the media and technologies of visualization. However, those in dominant positions, notably the white, western, male, middle-class heterosexuals who dominate science, tend to presume that their knowledge is disembodied, unmarked by their position and character, and that it is of universal applicability, when in fact they are passing off their own particular, situated view as universal. It is argued in effect that the dominant claim to see everything, while themselves remaining unseen – a kind of 'god-trick' – assumes that their position has no bearing upon the content or status of their knowledge (Haraway, 1991). They regard embodiment and situatedness as threats to objectivity, as something which must be transcended, or at least limited purely to 'the context of discovery' (in which ideas are developed) and not to 'the context of justification' (in which they are evaluated). Such assumptions have increasingly come under fire.

Feminist theory has often exposed how what was previously thought to be context-independent knowledge bears the marks of its social origins. (See, for example, Haraway's analysis of changing approaches to race, 1997.) Science in its transitive dimension is itself a social practice conducted within determinate social relations, and embedded within a culture or cultures. Metaphors in lay discourse, such as those of nature as female, seep into scientific discourses, though scientists and their audiences may not even notice their presence, especially if both come from the same social background (Harding, 1991). Given the social selectivity of the scientific community – characteristically white, male, heterosexual and affluent – then assumptions that are prejudicial to the interests of those excluded from the community are likely to enter social science, perhaps unnoticed, and a 'view from above' is likely to prevail. Such facts bear upon not only 'the context of discovery', but 'the context of justification' of scientific ideas. This is not to say that just any idea can be confirmed as long as it is consistent with what the dominant scientific community believe. Nevertheless, even allowing for the possibility of falsification, this still leaves plenty of room for social influence, in most cases the influence of the dominant. Denial or ignorance of the situated character of knowledge leads to what Harding calls 'weak objectivity', while taking into account standpoints and the way in which observation is mediated leads to 'strong objectivity'.

Such an approach to epistemology is open to competing pulls. In recognizing the situatedness of knowledge, it is tempting to move towards a relativist position, in which the validity of various different knowledges is assumed to be purely relative to their specific context, so that comparisons of their validity are impossible. However, as Haraway argues (1991, p. 191), the relativist's equanimity in the face of different and often conflicting knowledges involves its own kind of 'god-trick': it is a way of being nowhere while claiming to be everywhere equally, involving a denial of responsibility and critical enquiry. Alternatively we could attempt to bracket out questions of their validity. However, feminist 'standpoint theory' responds differently, arguing in anti-relativist fashion that some positions or standpoints have epistemic advantages over others. Reversing the usual valuations, it is generally argued that the dominated and marginalized – those in subaltern positions – have certain advantages in terms of understanding society, in that they are able to see things which are invisible to the dominant groups (Harding, 1991), and this despite – or perhaps partly because of – their exclusion from access to the privileges and resources, including intellectual resources, enjoyed by dominant groups. Just how strongly this claim can be made is debatable, for if it is made too strongly, then it treats the views of the subaltern as privileged, thus merely shifting, rather than challenging foundationalism.

Deciding on practical adequacy is itself a social practice, one affected by the social position of those involved and social relations among them. Here I want to argue that we can accept that this is the case without falling into a form of relativism or sociological reductionism which sees truth as merely a cover for sectional interests. This is in accord with Donna Haraway's search for a way of having '*simultaneously* an account of radical historical contingency for all knowledge claims and knowing subjects, a critical practice for recognizing our own "semiotic technologies" for making meanings, *and* a no-nonsense commitment to faithful accounts of a "real" world ...' (1991, p. 187) and finding 'enforceable, reliable accounts of things not reducible to power moves and agonistic, high status games of rhetoric or to scientistic, positivist arrogance' (p. 188). Critical realists should be in agreement with such sentiments.[24] While science and answers to questions regarding practical adequacy are likely to be influenced by social situation and by wider lay ways of thinking, these are not necessarily the only determinants. Again, not just any convention will stand up – some claims and predictions do not work out, some explanations are clearly incoherent, not everyone can be fooled all the time. Indeed, anyone who argued for a strong sociological reductionism would, of course, have to presuppose that they themselves had escaped it in order to identify it; only a qualified or moderate sociological reductionism could avoid this contradiction.

In a convergent way, Pierre Bourdieu – who has been called a 'perspectival realist' – argues that most social scientists unreflexively allow the special features of their own social position to be projected onto those they study, and that considerable effort and methodological sophistication is needed to avoid this (Bourdieu, 1984, 1993). Realism does not require some kind of denial of 'subjective' influences or standpoints and researchers' social context. On the contrary, it requires us to examine those standpoints so as to guard against forms of projection and selection which misrepresent our objects. Realist social science requires reflexivity. We are always in some position or other in relation to our objects; the important thing is to consider whether that influence is benign or malign.

Haraway's emphasis on the selectivity and particularity of vision – and indeed different kinds of vision – are compatible with a critical-realist emphasis on the selectivity of conceptual schemes and on the difference between the real (that which exists) and the empirical (that which is experienced): the latter provides only limited and mediated 'takes' on the former. This can be accepted without imagining that mediation means determination so that the media construct rather than construe their objects. Knowledge is always selective.

Yet there are also some further qualifications to make regarding the implications of situatedness. Firstly, to note that a particular kind of knowledge comes from a particular culture or is associated with a particular subject position, does not entail that it is valid for or applies only to those who belong to the same originating social group. Acupuncture is Chinese in origin but it can also work on non-Chinese people, just as western medicine can work on non-western people. Similarly, French social theory cannot be discounted as only applicable within France! To be sure, there is no view from nowhere – all knowledge is social, situated, and contextual. But it does not follow from this that truth claims can only be applicable to the particular groups who propose them.

Secondly, the problem is not that knowledge bears the marks of its social origins – for we could hardly expect it not to – but where the marks it bears are problematic in relation to understanding the object in question. In other words, recognizing such influences is not an invitation to ad hominem or ad feminam arguments, but to ones that show in what respects the metaphors and priorities present in the theories or accounts misrepresent their object. If, for example, a study of politics reflects men's social position while presenting itself as universally applicable and gender-neutral, then the problem is not that it is socially influenced, but that the particular kind of influence is misleading. And the problem is not merely that it is a masculine view, but rather that it is not only masculine but inadequate in some respect.

Thirdly, without a concept of misrepresentation and error, which requires an acceptance of the realist assumption of an independent reality about which we can be mistaken, then criticisms of 'malestream' social science and the like are reduced to complaints about who is making the truth claims, not about whether they are true. The problem with malestream social science is not that it has its own conventions (every science does), but that those conventions have so often proved mistaken about the world, and mistaken in a way that encourages inequality, domination and social exclusion. To criticize malestream science for passing off its special, sectional viewpoint as if it were universal, is effectively to say that this is not how the world is or has to be. And if that is the case, the way the world must in some way be independent of the malestream view of it.

Fourthly, discourses, prevailing ways of thinking and social contexts are constraining and enabling, but they are not prisons. The limitations of standpoints are real but should not be exaggerated. A strong version of standpoint theory is problematic because it implies a misplaced essentialism in assuming members of particular social groups will necessarily have a certain standpoint, for example, a 'women's standpoint' (Assiter, 1997, p. 90). People in any particular situation are open to a number of influences, and therefore can have more than one subject position and be located within networks that include people different from them. Education, in its root Latin sense, means 'leading out', or seeing beyond one's familiar horizons. We are not necessarily prisoners of our situation or habitus but can attempt to change them, though this can be extremely difficult. Knowledge is not exclusively or narrowly related to context: those who are unhappy with correspondence theories of truth should be the last to expect such a correspondence to context. Knowledge is discursive and discourse is intertextual and borderless. It is therefore never easily tied down or restricted to particular social contexts, even though it will almost certainly bear their traces in some form. Sandra Harding's idea of developing 'a scientific account of the relationships between historically located belief and maximally objective belief' (1991, p. 142) therefore expects too much of correspondence to context. To some extent it may be possible for researchers to see beyond their own circumstances, though it is not easy. Thus Marx was able to see beyond his own social position, though with hindsight we can now recognize that there were still many things he could not see, and that his thought still bore the marks of his own social position, particularly in terms of gender, if not class. Communication presupposes the possibility of sharing experience, of learning from others. If our interlocutors' experience and knowledge are already identical to our own, communication is redundant. Communication therefore also presupposes some degree of difference of situation and experience, though extreme differences make it difficult. Sometimes, others may be able to speak to us from a considerable social distance. We are not locked into closed worlds of meaning, as Jean Grimshaw puts it (1996); communication is more open-textured and open-ended than standpoint theory implies. Moreover, standpoints, like identities, are complex, since they are relational, so that not everyone in a particular social category will share the same standpoint.

It is nevertheless clear that the current range of standpoints represented in social science is too narrow, not only on egalitarian grounds, but on epistemic grounds in that it cannot be expected to provide much understanding of the full spectrum of social positions. For both reasons, even though it is necessary to avoid exaggerating the influence of standpoints, we need a more inclusive and representative scientific community, and one which is less divorced from wider society. Ideally – and it is an important ideal – we might wish that scientific and other knowledge communities were like those of Habermas's ideal speech situation, i.e. democratic, open and free of domination, whether hard and blatant or soft and subtle, so that the only force within them was the force of the better argument. In practice, this is far from the case. Maximizing opportunities for criticism of scientific research may offset some of the problems, but the criticism will be limited if most of the participants belong to the same narrow social group.

However – and this is the fifth point – as Alison Assiter argues, while Harding is right to 'claim that excluding representatives of certain groups cannot help the advancement of knowledge', the converse – that including them will necessarily guarantee progress – is overstated (Assiter, 1997, p. 86); the standpoints of the subjugated are not innocent or exempt from critical re-examination (Haraway, 1991, p. 191). In this context it is as well to remember critical social science's traditional wariness of unexamined commonsense knowledge. We can accept that we need to take note of previously excluded and unheard voices, for they are likely to lead to new knowledge, but there is no warrant for giving them an epistemic privilege which we would deny to socially privileged groups. Furthermore, those in socially dominant standpoints also have certain advantages as regards what they can see. Which standpoint is more valuable will depend on what we are trying to explain.

Sixthly, while particular standpoints are not necessarily parochial, since they are located in wider networks of communication (Haraway, 1991), wider or more global views are not necessarily merely local views masquerading as universal knowledge, for we should not rule out the possibility of synthesizing the views from several standpoints. Thus, Amartya Sen, who argues in similar fashion for a 'positional objectivity' as 'an objective inquiry in which the observational position is specified' notes the possibility of developing broader or 'transpositional' views, not by ignoring positionality or situatedness, but by building on a range of positional views (Sen, 1992, cited in Nelson, 1995, p. 42).

To summarize, knowledge is indeed situated but whether the social influences present in a particular kind of science lead to more or less practically adequate results and have good or bad effects is an *a posteriori* question, and the answers are not determined by the social position of those who answer it. Given the specificity of standpoints and their effect on how we see and think, realists should accept the need for reflexivity in considering their influence (Stones, 1996, pp. 68–70). While it is wise to be on our guard about sectional myopias and biases, it would be as wrong to dismiss research by white males on *a priori* grounds as inevitably distorted as it would be to dismiss research by black females on such grounds.

Gendered Dualisms?

It has been common in recent years to argue against 'malestream' social science and philosophy by drawing attention to an alleged structure of parallel dualisms which are implicitly gendered, and in each of which the first term is treated as superior (for example, Haraway, 1985; Le Doeuff, 1989; Pile, 1994). Thus:

science - ideology
reason - emotion
mind - body
fact - value
public - private
objective - subjective
masculine - feminine
superior - inferior

I don't doubt that something like this preferential structure, with its derogatory views of the feminine, is common and important in contemporary thought, both lay and scientific. However merely identifying this structure on its own doesn't amount to an argument for or against anything, though it can play upon the guilt of men. There are initially two kinds of question that can be posed about it:

1   Is this indeed how knowledge has been structured?; and
2   if it is, what, if anything, is wrong with it?

Regarding the first question, Jean Grimshaw shows that while such a preferential structure has often been used by malestream science, there is no aspect of the right-hand side of the structure that has not been defended at some time by male philosophers. It is absurd to associate philosophy as a male-dominated discipline exclusively with a defence of the left side and a derogation of the right (Grimshaw, 1986). But if we allow that the preferential structure has at least been common, if not overwhelming, especially in science, how should we answer the second question? If the structure of dualisms is damaging and should be challenged, in what respects is it wrong and what exactly should be challenged? Often we are not told, but there are three possible kinds of response.

First, we can question whether the left side is superior to the right side, as is generally assumed. Thus, one response of opponents of malestream science is to invert the valuation, so that the right side is elevated over the left, personal experience is valued over scientific knowledge, emotion over reason, etc. Of course, such inversions or other challenges to the dominant valuations need to be argued for. Nor can one avoid the arguments merely by reference to the way the structure is gendered, as if it were self-evident that anything masculine is bad and anything feminine good. On the whole, I find it hard to think of much that is good about masculinity, but it is as misguided simply to *assume* ideas and practices are wrong because they are masculine as it is to assume that they are right because they are masculine. To argue for a different valuation of terms on either side of the list requires one to go beyond gender associations and to make a case regarding the qualities of the specific characteristics listed.

Secondly, we could question the way in which the dualisms are assumed to be gendered. *Are* science and reason masculine? Is emotion primarily feminine? Here, there are some serious flaws in the schema. In particular, while reason is undoubtedly often claimed by men to be their preserve, their behaviour often betrays the opposite. Masculinity can be that of the thug, whose characteristic response to reason is to reply with physical violence. Reason is essentially masculine? 'Fuckin' hit 'im!' And violence and physical domination of course have everything to do with the body and emotion (and probably not even emotion that has been reasoned about) rather than reason. Faced with the threat of such violence, women have generally, of course, been on the side of reason. Moreover, the association of men with reason as opposed to the body is also brought into question by the finding in Britain that girls do better than boys at school in every subject, the sole exception being, significantly, physical education. In raising such objections I do not wish to deny that there are not also powerful traditional associations between the feminine, nature, emotions and the body, rather to show that the individual terms of the binaries are gendered in a much more complex fashion than the diagram suggests.

It also needs to be remembered that even insofar as the characteristics in the list can indeed be shown to be gendered in the way suggested, it still needs to be decided whether the characteristics are merely contingently gendered like this, as a consequence of the way in which girls and boys, women and men are socialized, or whether the characteristics are part of some female or male essences, and each characteristic is inherently masculine or feminine. Again, it does not follow from answers to these questions that masculine is bad and feminine good; further arguments are needed to say why they should be valued in this or any other way.

Thirdly, and more profoundly, we can question – or if you prefer, 'deconstruct' – the binary oppositions themselves. Are emotion and values beyond reason, unreasonable even, or can they be in some ways reasonable? Who is the more rational/ reasonable – the person who is sensitive to others' emotions or the person who reacts to others without any regard for their emotions? (It is worth noting that whereas the meanings of reason and rationality seem very close, the meanings of 'reasonable' and 'rational' diverge somewhat insofar as the former, but not the latter, would generally include being sensitive to the emotions of others.) Too many attempts at radical alternatives in social science stick within the same terms as their opponents instead of challenging them. In particular, it is very common for would-be radicals who know that science is not value-free nevertheless to retain the decidedly positivist idea that values are beyond reason or science-free, defending their critical view of science by reference to their values *rather than* reason, and not by challenging the science-values binary itself. Merely to defend the right-hand side of the structure and attack the left is to remain a prisoner of the same conceptual structure as one's opponents. Much of this book argues that we cannot make much progress without deconstructing such binaries.

The shift from the first and second to the third kind of response to the preferential structure has been assisted in feminist thought by critiques of essentialism (see Chapter 4), which argue against assumptions that men and women have essential characteristics, and which avoid defending characteristics in women which are products of socialization into a patriarchal society. The meanings and practices associated with masculinity and femininity are complex and unstable and often contradictory, and of course you don't have to be a man to behave in a masculine way or a woman to behave in a feminine way. This possibility exposes the looseness or detachability of particular characteristics of masculinity or femininity from one another and from the sex of their holders. In a strongly gendered society, we can use the words 'masculine' or 'male', and 'feminine' or 'female' as surrogates for bundles of qualities conventionally associated with them. Thus a job involving long working hours might be safely described as conforming to male norms, while unpaid 'caring' work might be described as feminine. Thus social policies favouring the full-time employed or care-givers can be reasonably described as respectively favouring men and women. Insofar as progress is made in deconstructing gender, and men do hitherto conventionally feminine things and women do masculine things, the use of gendered categories as a surrogate becomes less safe. It also becomes more apparent that one cannot simply operate on a man-bad, woman-good assumption, so that behaviour could be judged favourably or unfavourably merely by association with gender (New, 1996). Instead it becomes clearer that behaviours and practices need to be evaluated in their own terms, regardless of their conventional gender associations. We might therefore say, yes, x is masculine by association, and y is feminine, but we still need to justify decisions regarding how to judge either of them in terms of considerations relevant to x and y, not gender. Thus, violence is wrong not because it is typically male, but because of the suffering it causes to people regardless of gender: one of the things that's wrong with masculinity is its association with violence, not vice versa.

Objectivity and Subjectivity: Three Different Distinctions

'Objectivity' and 'subjectivity' are some of the most ambiguous words in the vocabularies of social scientists and philosophers, causing widespread difficulties, even for scholars well-versed in social theory. This is because either term can mean at least three different things, which are commonly confused. Moreover, as I shall attempt to demonstrate, these three meanings are logically independent of one another, although sometimes users intend more than one of the senses simultaneously. Disambiguating these terms will also serve to bring together many of the points already made in a different way. Taking the adjectival form, they can be defined thus:

'Objective$_1$' -means value-neutral, indifferent or value-free, for example, 'I personally don't stand to gain or lose from the situation, so I can perhaps give a more objective account of it'. Correspondingly, 'subjective$_1$' means value-laden, as in 'I've known her as a friend for years so my views on her are subjective'.

'Objective$_2$' -as in 'the search for objective knowledge' is a synonym for 'true', or perhaps 'practically adequate'. Correspondingly, in contrast, 'subjective$_2$' implies an idea that is 'not true' or 'merely a matter of opinion'.

'Objective$_3$' -as in 'the objective properties of capital' means 'pertaining to objects', as distinct from subjects and refers to the nature of things regardless of what we or others may think about them[25]. This is opposed to 'subjective$_3$', which means 'pertaining to subjects' and concerns what we think, experience, believe or feel about something, as in 'the subjective experience of class'. This also relates to the situated and embodied character of knowledge, emphasized by feminism.

Objectivity$_3$ concerns the intransitive dimension of knowledge or science. All beliefs, whether value-laden or value-free (subjective$_1$ or objective$_1$), 'true' or 'false' (objective$_2$ or subjective$_2$), belong to the transitive dimension of science. Objectivity$_1$ and objectivity$_2$ are often conflated and confused so that it is assumed that in order to arrive at objective$_2$ (true) statements about the world, those statements must be value-free. Yet why should true or adequate statements about the world need to be value-neutral? While having strong feelings about some state of affairs might distort our beliefs about what is the case, it needn't do necessarily, for although there is indeed a danger that we may believe what we want to believe, we demean ourselves if we imagine we can't possibly accept factual statements about circumstances we find unpalatable. For example, people of contrasting political values can agree on the outcome of an election, regardless of whether they are happy with it or not. While it is advisable to interrogate our research to see if we are not engaging in wishful thinking and to make sure it is capable of acknowledging possible circumstances of which we disapprove, our values need not be a problem. Sometimes, as we saw in the discussion of stand-point theory, values may even have a positive effect by directing us to issues and aspects of situations that others miss, as in the case of feminism and gender, whereas attempts at value-freedom may just result in blindness to values that are present. However, progressive values do not *guarantee* objectivity$_2$ and repugnant values do not necessarily make it unattainable[26]. The conflation of these two senses of objectivity by advocates of the necessity of value-freedom is peculiar, because they often insist on the logical independence of facts and values; but if they are independent it makes no sense to say the absence of the latter is necessary for establishing the former. Value-neutrality and objectivity in terms of commitment to finding true statements are different things, and the former is not necessary for the latter. Objective$_2$ research may therefore be subjective$_1$.

Part of the problem with the conflation of these two senses of objectivity is the emotivist assumption that values are beyond reason, incapable of having any objective$_2$ content, and thus being antithetical to science (see Chapter 8). However, value-laden descriptions of the world, such as 'the *beneficial* effects of the education programme can be seen in the rise in literacy rates' include factual content – in this case that there was an education programme and a rise in literacy rates. Further, many terms and expressions are simultaneously descriptive and evaluative (for example, 'beneficial', 'cruel', 'abrasive'), in that they are not merely emotive expressions equivalent to 'boo' and 'hooray' but imply something about some aspect of the world, even if rather vaguely. 'Value judgements' such as 'single parenthood is *inferior* to dual parenthood' are not simply about what the speaker likes, equivalent to a statement about what one's favourite colour is; rather they make a claim about what the speaker thinks is *true*, a claim which others are likely to contest in terms of whether it is true. Consequently, evaluative statements need not be assumed to lack positive content which might be objective$_2$.

Often, critics of the orthodox view of science as value-free fail to challenge the association between value-ladenness and lack of objectivity$_2$, and fail to note that the two are mutually independent, and hence respond by arguing that if objectivity means value-neutrality, then objectivity in terms of truth is not worth seeking. This amounts to saying 'all science is ideological, only we admit it, and we will not let the facts get in the way of our favoured stories'. This is a disastrous response that plays into the hands of the defenders of value-freedom because it allows the critic to be dismissed as only interested in confirming their values, not in establishing the truth. In other words it fails to challenge the root confusion and instead just inverts the conclusion.

The distinction between objectivity$_2$ and objectivity$_3$ is more difficult. It relates to the fundamental point made at the outset about the connection between ontological realism and epistemological fallibilism. That is, to claim that objects can have qualities which exist independently of our consciousness of them (that is, objectively$_3$) is not to claim privileged access to them (that is, objectivity$_2$), in the sense of truth. On the contrary, that there is a world existing independently of thought makes the relation of thought to that world problematic rather than privileged – hence objectivity$_2$ is at best an ideal. *Claims* about objective$_3$ properties of things belong to the transitive dimension of knowledge and are fallible.

Marx often referred to 'objective conditions', in contrast to what people may have imagined to have been the case. In so doing he simultaneously drew a contrast between what actually (objectively$_3$) existed (regardless of what people thought) and what they imagined existed, and implied that he knew the truth (objective$_2$) about the former, though of course his own claims were fallible. While we might note this elision in philosophical reflection, it is hardly avoidable in practice. There are always likely to be situations where we need to distinguish what really exists (objectively$_3$) from what some imagine to exist, but doing so implies a claim to know the truth about the former (objectivity$_2$), or at least that the claim is less fallible than others. It is the kind of claim that everyone – whether avowedly realist or not – makes frequently in everyday life.

That objects can only be known through thought does not mean that there is no distinction between thought objects and real objects, or 'subjective$_3$' beliefs and what they are about (objects$_3$). To deny this distinction is to invite identity thinking, making it impossible to understand how we could ever be mistaken about anything.[27]

Non-realists reject objectivity$_3$; from the correct point that the objective$_3$ properties of something can't be known independently of our ('subjective$_3$') thoughts about them, they wrongly conclude from this that they can only *exist* if they are thought about. As we have seen, the distinction between the actual and the imagined is unavoidable, and any attempt to reject it by arguing that it is only an imagined distinction (not an actual/real one) involves a performative contradiction[28]. In our practical lives, no one can escape having to distinguish between more and less adequate (objective$_2$) claims about the world and hence having to say at some time that the world is this way (objectively$_3$) rather than what is believed to be case.

Regarding subjectivity$_3$ and subjectivity/objectivity$_2$, when we try to elicit someone's subjective$_3$ beliefs, we could say that we are trying to objectively$_2$ represent their subjectivity$_3$. Subjectivity$_3$ is distinguished from subjectivity$_2$ so as not to prejudge the truth, practical adequacy or epistemic status of beliefs. That something is my subjective belief does not entail that it cannot be true, though it may indeed be false. Subjectivity$_3$ also refers to the subjective quality of all knowledge – that it can be of and for subjects, and is situated and embodied, even though it is mostly about objects. As with subjectivity in the sense of value-ladenness (subjectivity$_1$), in noting this subjective$_3$ quality of knowledge, we say nothing about whether it is objective in the sense of true or practically adequate representation of its object. However, repressing or unreflexively ignoring this subjective$_3$ dimension is likely to mislead.

Sometimes 'objectivity' is rejected because it is seen as being detached from and external to the subjective, internal experience of being, and also supposedly value-free, thus denying the validity and importance of experience and emotions. I would agree that this kind of objectivity may be problematic, for in many social situations, what is needed is not a value-free or detached stance, but involvement and empathy, and a sense of being with others rather than observing them. But although the quest for objectivity$_2$ has its limits in such situations, it is certainly not dispensable for social science.

To summarize: there is not a single distinction between objectivity and sub-jectivity but three. They concern contrasts between the absence or presence of values, truth and the absence of truth, and matters pertaining to objects as opposed to matters pertaining to subjects. The relations between the three dis-tinctions are contingent. Thus, value-ladenness may or may not affect the truth status of propositions, and where it does it may do so for better or worse. The fact that knowledge is subjective in the sense of being of and for subjects, and situ-ated and embodied, may have positive, negative or neutral implications for its truth status. In both these cases, it is advisable to be aware of the specific forms of subjectivity. What kinds of values, if any, inform an analysis or account, and does this cause any problems or occlusions? What kind of subject position is evi-dent, and does it raise any problematic implications? Reflexivity is conducive – we can put it no more strongly – to objectivity in the sense of the developing of true or practically adequate accounts.

Finally, we can illustrate the power of this three-way disambiguation of objec-tivity by reference to Donna Haraway's discussion of objectivity and subjectiv-ity. When she writes that 'feminist objectivity is about limited location and situated knowledge, not about transcendence and splitting of subject and object' (1991, p. 190; see also Grimshaw, 1996), realists can both agree and disagree with her, depending on how they construe 'objectivity'. Insofar as knowledge is always subjective in the sense of being of and for subjects and always bears their cultural and technological traces, while contingently simultaneously being capa-ble of being objective in the sense of true, and capable of being about an objec-tive$_3$ world, then we can agree that there is a sense in which knowledge can be both subjective and objective. However, insofar as the world exists independently of our conceptions of it, subject and object are indeed split, in that the latter (object$_3$) does not depend on the former. (At times, Haraway (1991, p. 197) acknowledges the extra-discursive nature of body and world, and the possibility of accepting this without imagining that this implies they are transparent so that knowledge of them is immediate (unmediated), but her reluctance to disam-biguate means that she seems not to notice how one sense of 'objectivity' con-cerns precisely this independence.) The split is evident every time we argue that a claim about the world is mistaken, but it also exists even when a claim appears to be true, for the claim and concepts involved are not the same thing as its referent. Even in the case of propositions about discursive objects, where there is an internal conceptual relation between the proposition and its object, the rela-tion is usually asymmetric – for the discourse can usually exist without the researcher's comment on it. Because it fails to disambiguate objectivity (through blurring the distinction between the transitive and intransitive dimensions of science), Haraway's project of rescuing some concept of objectivity from strong social constructionism while retaining the latters' insights on the social character of knowledge is only partly successful. By making the distinctions suggested above, I believe critical realists can achieve Haraway's goal.

Conclusion or: How Wrong Can One Be About Realism?

Throughout this critique of popular anti-realist positions in social theory, the reader will have noticed certain common threads weaving their way through ideas regarding signification, truth, relativism and situatedness. One of these threads has been the inescapability of distinctions between what is true and false, or more true and less true, real or actual and imaginary, fact and fiction. There is no doubt that appealing to such distinctions can amount to little more than disguised table-thumping: 'We know what is real/fact, you don't.' Clearly, we need to be aware of this danger. But defeatist postmodernism challenges not particular claims about what is true or false but the very distinctions themselves, usually on the grounds that all the terms on the left of such distinctions exist within discourse and involve claims that are fallible. However, while realists of course accept that the *terms* exist within discourse, their referents may exist outside (our) discourse: *discourse and knowledge are not merely self-referential – that is why they are fallible!*

The efforts of those who, like Jonathan Potter, try to show that realism always relies on various tropes and sleights of hand for passing off what is actually socially constructed as real, are trapped within an inescapable performative con-tradiction (Potter, 1997). In arguing, for example, that one cannot counterpose questionable constructions of the world to realistic ones, extreme constructionists cannot help but rely upon the distinction they are trying to reject: effectively they are saying 'there are those (that is, realists) who *imagine* that we can distinguish between questionable accounts (what is imagined to occur but actually doesn't) and realistic, practically adequate or true ones (which show what actually hap-pens), but *actually* we can't'. Realists need have no problem with 'weak' social constructionism, that is with the idea that accounts of facts or the real are socially constructed. But 'strong' social constructionists suppose that this means that they can't adequately refer to and describe external circumstances which are either not social constructions or are the constructions of others. With every assertion – including most glaringly, those intended to tell us the facts about real-ism, indeed, with their every usage of the verb 'to be', strong social construc-tionists undermine their own position.

The confusions arise from a slippage between referents or real objects and discourse about them, between facts as states of affairs and factual statements made about them, and distinctions between more and less practically adequate statements. As their common Latin root implies, factual statements, like fictive statements, are constructions, and they are fallible. But that does not undermine the distinction for we still need to distinguish between more and less fallible descriptions, between ones whose inadequacy is already clear and those which so far have proved to be adequate.

Potter himself leaves the embarrassing question of the self-undermining nature of his work to the closing pages of his book on *Representing Reality* (1997), and wriggles, coyly admitting he has opted for 'conventional realist discourse' in identifying the nature of realism so as to make the arguments as accessible as possible (p. 229) and inviting others to deconstruct his own tropes of fact construction. While this would undermine his findings and render his method a mere parlour game, a realist account could *accept* some of his claims as good/true accounts of how rhetoric works. Why else should anyone pay them any attention? Potter cannot defend any of his claims about 'tropes' and the like without appealing to what is actually the case about them.

A recent article by Potter illustrates further just how far critical realism is from common images of realism (1998, p. 37). In this paper, Potter accuses realists of using the following kinds of rhetorical strategies in trying to debunk relativism or constructionism. Realists allegedly:

1 *Construct constructionism as something simple and unitary.* In the above I have distinguished between strong and weak constructionism, the latter being compatible with critical realism, the former not. The distinction is further elaborated in Chapter 4. Sismondo distinguishes four different varieties in his critique of social constructionist studies of science (Sismondo, 1993; see also Murphy, 1994).

2 *Avoid reflexivity at all costs.* On the contrary, as we have shown in relation to the situated character of knowledge, reflexivity is vital for any kind of objectivity. Further, realists' emphasis on the relations between theory and practice in their critiques of relativism indicates reflexivity while the vulnerability of strong constructionists to performative and theory-practice contradictions shows an extraordinary lack of reflexivity.

3 *Avoid considering empirical studies of science.* On the contrary, realists have no reason to avoid them, for they give a better account than idealized accounts of what science is *really like*: why else should we take them seriously? See Cole (1992), Mäki (1993), Millstone (1978), Murphy (1994), Sismondo (1993), and Wade Hands (1994) for realist discussions, and critiques of social constructionism in science studies.

4 *Treat scientific practice as governed by logic.* This shows Potter's ignorance of realism, for realist philosophers of science, such as Hanson, Hesse and Harré, led the way in showing the extent to which science is unavoidably metaphorical, and in demoting the role of logic in science. Indeed, Harré even coined the term 'logicism' to denote the illusion that science depends centrally and dominantly upon logic. Other realists, including Bhaskar, followed up with a critique of deductivism (deductive logic) and developed the metaphor of mechanism (see also Sayer, 1992).

5 *Elide everyday and philosophical notions of realism.* In distinguishing the intransitive dimension of science from the transitive, critical realism distinguishes the real from descriptions of it. 'Real' concerns the former, 'realistic' belongs to the realm of representations. The everyday notion tends to overlook what critical realism explicitly asserts – that the world can only be

known under particular descriptions. See Mäki (1993 and 1995) for a discussion of the distinction.

6 *Treat description as something obvious.* Following the previous point, and as I have already argued, consistent realists have to acknowledge that description is always problematic because of the independence of many objects of study from their descriptions. In his *Sociological Reasoning* (1996), Rob Stones has developed a realist analysis of description and rhetoric, which fully recognizes the role of the discursive features and devices on which Potter focuses. In *Method in Social Science* (1992), I argued that conceptualization – indispensable for description – was the most critical task in social science. See also Chapter 5 on narrative.

As I noted at the outset, (critical) realism is not what many think it is.

Notes

1 Here we might note a potential alliance between anti-realist philosophy and recent sociologies emphasizing reflexivity. However, one of the main theorists of reflexivity, Anthony Giddens, is sympathetic to realism.

2 A Ph.D thesis may be seen by as few as three or four readers.

3 See Tallis (1988).

4 Emile Benveniste criticises Saussure, arguing that his argument 'is falsified by an unconscious and surreptitious recourse to a third term which was not included in the initial definition. This third term is the thing itself, the reality. Even though Saussure said that the idea of "sister" is not connected to the signifier s-o-r, he was not thinking any less of the *reality* of the notion. When he spoke of the difference between b-o-f and o-k-s, he was referring in spite of himself to the fact that these two terms applied to the same *reality*. Here, then, is the *thing*, expressly excluded at first from the definition of the sign, now creeping into it by a detour ...' (Giddens, 1979, p. 15). Consistent Saussureans ought to try to teach their children to speak without making or allowing any reference to extra-discursive objects. That they don't, shows they don't believe what they say.

5 I am of course alluding to Derrida's concept of 'differance' here (1976).

6 This is in keeping with Marx: 'The question whether objective truth can be attributed to human thinking is not a question of theory but is a *practical* question. Man must prove the truth, i.e. the reality and the power, the this-sidedness of his thinking in practice. The dispute over the reality or non-reality of thinking that is isolated from practice is a purely *scholastic* question.' Marx, in Marx and Engels (1975, p. 422). It is also not incompatible with Heidegger's view of our basic engagement with the world in which things are encountered 'ready-to-hand', having specific relations to human purposes. Material involvement in the world is different from contemplation of it; as Charles Taylor puts it: 'We can draw a neat line between my picture of an object and that object, but not between my *dealing* with the object and that object. It may make sense to ask one to focus on what one *believes* about something, say a football, even in the absence of that thing; but when it comes to *playing* football, the corresponding objection would be absurd. The actions in the game cannot be done without the object; they include the object. Take it away and we have something quite different – people miming a match on the stage, perhaps. The notion that our understanding of the world is grounded in our dealings with it is equivalent to the thesis that this understanding is not ultimately based on representations at all, in the sense of depictions that are separately identifiable from what they are of' (Taylor, 1987, p. 477). However, insofar as our understandings are based on representations, the things represented are detachable from the representations.

7 As Stones observes, there is little mileage in Derrida's example of Nietzsche's strange posthumous note bearing the words, 'I have forgotten my umbrella', because the difficulty of interpreting it derives precisely from the fact that it lacks what normal communication provides – relevant contextual information (Stones, 1996, pp. 154–5).

8 Philosophers of science are wont to say observation is 'theory-laden' but, as Ian Hacking points out, this implies a strange notion of theory, according to which observing something like how many fingers we have, requires a theory rather than just a system of concepts (Ian Hacking, 1983).

9 See also Chapter 3, p. 70 on empirical evaluation.

10 As Collier (1998) notes, in recognizing this, there is no need to ignore or deny the denotative function, as in some poststructuralist work.

11 I shall return to the relativistic implications of Foucault in the next section.

12 Whether this is fair to Foucault himself is another issue; my intention is to criticize a certain functionalist interpretation of the relationship between power and knowledge rather than join the debate about what Foucault meant (for further discussion of Foucault himself, see McNay, 1994, and Hoy, 1986). As I noted earlier, I am primarily interested in common ideas rather than their authorship.

13 From the point of view of social research, this distinction is equivalent to that between real object and thought object in realism.

14 This is not to suppose that language is totally context-dependent. On the contrary, an essential feature of language is its ability to enable communication across different contexts. Context-dependence is generally partial (Bloch, 1989).

15 I am indebted to John O'Neill for this quotation (personal communication).

16 I am indebted to Peter Wilkin for this quotation (personal communication).

17 In either case one can argue about whether these theorists and positions are necessarily relativist, but both have been associated with relativism.

18 John O'Neill (1998) argues that in principle it is possible to be both a realist and a judgmental relativist, that is, to believe in the existence of a mind-independent reality and yet see no way of distinguishing between the adequacy of different discourses. While I accept this is a possible position, I don't think it is a good one, for as I have argued, the main reason for believing the basic realist proposition of a mind-independent reality is the experience of failed truth claims, and to accept that these occur while other empirical truth claims escape falsification entails the rejection of judgmental relativism.

19 Alan Bloom notes that most students, whether left or right wing, believe truth is relative: 'They are unified only in their relativism and in their allegiance to equality. And the two are related in a moral intention. The relativity of truth is not a theoretical insight but a moral postulate, the condition of a free society, or so they see it' (A. Bloom, 'The closing of the American mind',1995, pp. 9–18). While I have found the same motives in students' defences of relativism in Britain, I hasten to dissociate myself from the reactionary views which follow in Bloom's article – all of them non-sequiturs in relation to the above point.

20 Actually, this is a telling example, for she achieved her success in the face of considerable *opposition* to her social identity.

21 See Gendered dualisms? below.

22 I discuss ethical relativism further in Chapter 8.

23 '... in recent post-modern leftism, especially that influenced by Foucault, all forms of epistemological authority in medicine, science and other disciplines are understood as themselves forms of power. The upshot is a still more radical defence of the sphere in which individual preference cannot be challenged. Hence the degree to which social constructionists have appealed to market models of science. Hence also the odd alliance in defence of the market and consumer culture between the New Right and the post-modern left' (O'Neill, 1998, p. 95).

24 Unfortunately, in the same chapter of her book, Haraway misses the compatibility and equates realism with naive objectivism.

25 This is what Bhaskar terms 'alethic truth' (Bhaskar, 1995).

3

Postmodernism and the Three
'Pomo Flips'

> Once upon a time a valiant fellow had the idea that men were drowned in water
> only because they were possessed with the *idea of gravity*. If they were to knock this
> notion out of their heads, say by stating it to be a superstition, a religious concept, they
> would be sublimely proof against any danger from water. His whole life long he fought
> against the illusion of gravity, of whose harmful results all statistic bought him new
> and manifold evidence. This valiant fellow was the type of the new revolutionary
> philosophers in Germany (Marx and Engels, 1974, p. 37).

Faced with theoretical or philosophical positions that seem untenable, it is tempting to counter them by reversing or inverting them, for example, responding to
empiricism's belief in the rooting of knowledge in empirical observation by
claiming knowledge to be independent of observation and observation to be
wholly dependent on discourses. This strategy retains the problematic structures
which generated the problems in the first place. Thus, for example, as we saw in
the previous chapter in the case of gendered dualisms, merely reversing the evaluations of objectivity and subjectivity, reason and emotion, preserved rather than
undermined the problems. Deconstruction, often associated (rightly or wrongly)
with postmodernism, aims to go far beyond a simple inversion of dualisms to a
deep problematization of fundamental premises and categories of social thought,
though it is not a process which need lead to a rejection of those categories. For
example, as Judith Butler has argued, 'The critique of the subject is not a negation or repudiation of the subject, but, rather, a way of interrogating its construction as a pre-given or foundationalist premise' (Butler, 1992, p. 9). When the
deconstruction is done, we have to decide what kind of revised conception is most
adequate. While I think such a view of deconstruction need not be anti-realist,
much that is advanced under the banners of deconstruction and postmodernism
does involve a flip from empiricism and naive objectivism into idealism, and it is
this defeatist postmodernism that I want to criticize.

The chief characteristics of defeatist postmodernist thought of concern here
are: its suspicion of concepts of truth and falsity and of empirical testing; its
'incredulity towards metanarratives' such as philosophical systems or Marxism;

its distrust of the idea of a progressive development of knowledge having an emancipatory role; and its openness to difference and advocacy of 'local knowledges' (Lyotard, 1984). How far postmodernism represents a shift towards idealism and relativism, making knowledge relative to the holder or to particular social groups is controversial (for example, Norris, 1990), but a certain anti-realism is much in evidence in sociology and cultural studies.

Defeatist postmodernism typically defines itself in opposition to 'foundationalism', 'objectivism', and those who claim privileged access to 'the truth'. In reacting against this, it then flips over into an anti-realism which rules out any possibility of empirical/practical evaluation and makes truth relative to discourse.[1] Realists also reject naive objectivism, but as we argued in the previous chapter, this need not make us flip over into relativism or idealism, or make us doubt the possibility of scientific progress or abandon the Enlightenment project.

I shall call the former reaction a 'pomo flip', but there are other pomo flips too: from a rejection of grand narratives or totalizing discourses to an incapacitating fragmentation of the world and its discourses; and from a rejection of ethnocentrism, androcentrism and imperialism to an equally self-defeating cultural and judgmental relativism.[2] In these cases too, realism offers a third way between the polarities. In what follows, I shall discuss these three pomo flips in turn, comparing the postmodernist and realist angles. Before concluding I shall also comment on the postmodernist challenge to philosophy.

Pomo Flip 1: Foundationalism to Idealism

Postmodernists make a great deal of fuss about their rejection of 'foundationalism' and notions of (absolute) truth, and are quick to accuse opponents of assuming a 'god's-eye view' or an Archimedean point from which they can evaluate knowledge. They also oppose what Derrida terms 'the metaphysics of presence', that is, the assumption that the intentions of an author, both subjective and concerning references to real objects, are transparent, as if there were no complications to do with language and textuality. Against this, postmodernists see language and textuality as opaque and slippery, and yet constitutive of knowledge.

These are largely invented targets; it is not too inaccurate to say that almost everyone had been an anti-foundationalist for a long time, certainly well before postmodernism became popular. Contemporary realism is included in this since it is openly fallibilist, indeed necessarily so, as we have already seen. Yet defeatist postmodernists are reluctant to believe that their opponents could be anything but dyed-in-the-wool foundationalists or naive objectivists. Thus, despite realists' repeated insistence on fallibilism, Cloke et al. (1991, p. 171) assert that realism is one of a number of 'isms' that 'claim to be sole guardians of "truth"'. However, to reject foundationalism and then deny the possibility of empirical evaluation or criticism from rival discourses is to readmit a different kind of foundationalism by the back door.

So while realists and postmodernists actually agree on anti-foundationalism, they diverge on what follows from this. At worst, on the postmodernist side, we find a flip from the idea of absolute truth and absolute foundations to the other extreme of relativism/idealism. This involves refusing all talk of truth and falsity, denying any kind of relationship between thought and the world, asserting that we do not 'discover' things, but socially or discursively constitute them (Laclau and Mouffe, 1985; Deutsche, 1991), and denying the possibility of any kind of empirical test.

Thus Julie Graham writes approvingly of a kind of knowledge 'unburdened by its representational responsibilities':

> Thought processes are *sui generis* and complexly determined rather than representations or reflections of something else ... theory cannot be validated on the basis of its corre-spondence to the 'real world' ... The criteria for validating some thoughts rather than others are internal to a theory. We cannot argue that our theory has more explanatory power or greater proximity to the truth than other theories because there is no common agreed standard which could serve as the instrument of such a metatheoretical valida-tion process. (Graham, 1990, pp. 59–60)

This, of course, is said in an article in which, firstly, she *does* argue with rival theories, and secondly, she *does* assert what is and what is not the case (in reality), though it is not clear why a relativist should bother to argue anything.

We have already seen that while the notion of absolute truth (or falsity) is untenable, especially where truth and falsity are seen as categorical opposites, we cannot afford to do without some kind of differentiation between the representa-tional and practice-guiding capabilities of discourses. Thus the rejection of notions of absolute truth need not stop us differentiating between statements such as: 'No-one died in the Gulf War' and 'Thousands died in the Gulf War'. Nor need we reduce the warrant for such statements to pure agreement or power. Nor does our inability to claim absolute truth for any beliefs imply that they are therefore not objective but 'individual, subjective matters of opinion', merely matters of 'individual judgement' (Archer, 1987, p. 392; Cloke et al., 1991, p. 169). Archer and Cloke et al. thus show themselves still to be in the grip of an impoverished dualism of naive objectivism and idealism, for they can apparently see no alterna-tives other than those of absolute truth and mere 'subjective' opinion. It makes little sense to say of an old 'falsified' theory in science, such as that of Galileo, that it suffered from being merely subjective opinion, or the product of individual judgment. The ideas were not an isolated, 'subjective' opinion but were held collectively and hence were intersubjective. Moreover, they had considerable practical adequacy.

If science discovered absolute truths then the history of science would be unin-telligible for scarcely any ideas have escaped revision. Yet presumably there is also scientific progress, otherwise we would still be using quill pens and stage-coaches rather than wordprocessors and e-mail. The ability of scientists to manip-ulate nature has clearly increased enormously, even though their interventions often also have unforeseen and bad effects. Accepting that knowledge is fallible does not mean that it should be taken as all equally false or true, or equally practically adequate.

Fallibilism provides no warrant for the idea that our beliefs are unconstrained, such that people could, like Marx and Engels' new revolutionary philosopher, believe anything they liked with impunity. If they could, they would surely be infallible. This is why idealism is so dogmatic, and why, ironically, it can support authoritarianism. Herein lies one of the great paradoxes of defeatist post-modernism: while it claims to be anti-foundationalist it regards theories as immune to empirical test, whereas those whom it accuses of foundationalism believe that theories can be susceptible to empirical test! In effect, defeatist post-modernism flips from the idea of theory-neutral observation to observation-neutral theory, where, as in strong forms of social constructionism, the world is theory-determined.

This state of affairs has arisen partly because of the retention of naive objectivism's expectations of empirical testing – as a straightforward and unambiguous process, uninfluenced by theoretical understandings. However, just because it is none of these, it doesn't mean that it is impossible or ineffective. Just as assessing truth or practical adequacy is not an all-or-nothing affair, neither is falsification. In practice it is messy, provisional and often partial, and the empirical observations are theory-laden – or at least conceptually mediated – though this does not make it impossible for the theory in question to be contradicted. Take the example of the reserve army of labour thesis in accounting for women's role in labour markets. This has been largely falsified by reference to the substantial numbers of women who are employed in sectors such as local government and the health service where they are a permanent part of the labour force and are not dispensable during slumps (Walby, 1986). This does not mean that women never form a reserve army, but it will not stand as a universal explanation. This is typical of falsification in social science. It is messy (there are fuzzy areas where its applicability is uncertain), it is partial (it isn't falsified for all cases), it is provisional (maybe some of the currently permanent jobs may be abolished in the future, or maybe we shall become dissatisfied with the concept of reserve army even for cases to which it currently seems to apply). Of course, this doesn't mean that we have arrived at absolute truth, whatever that might mean, but in putting forward this explanation, and coming up with this falsification or critique of it, progress surely has been made in sorting out the relative practical adequacy of rival theories. Do we seriously want to claim that this is merely an intra-discursive or intra-theoretical skirmish, purely a matter of a change in what we choose to believe, purely a function of suasive rhetoric or the relative power of the theories' proponents, and absolutely nothing to do with social reality?

Another version of our first pomo flip concerns meaning. Having realized that words do not establish meanings singly and through reference/denotation (naive objectivism), it is concluded that they neither convey authors'/speakers' intentions nor refer to anything outside discourse at all; meanings are endlessly 'deferred' intra-discursively without reference to any extra-discursive reality, and we are free to interpret texts as we wish. Taken to the extreme, this embodies a standard contradiction of relativism, for if we are free to interpret what someone writes as we like, then we can interpret them against their intentions, attributing to them views diametrically opposed to those that they (appear to) profess, for of course they have denied themselves grounds for complaining about this.

The 'linguistic turn' in philosophy has been a mixed blessing. While it has alerted us to the constitutive role of language and textuality in understanding, it is strikingly ignorant of our ability to do things without language. Thus deaf-mute people who have never learned a language, whether verbal or signed, can still know a lot. It is therefore a mistake to restrict epistemology to the relationship between language and objects (Dews, 1984). Practice is conspicuously absent from postmodernist critiques of reference and representation, such as those of Strohmayer and Hannah (1992) or Hutcheon (1988). Knowledge is only discussed in terms of speaking and writing, never doing.

This doesn't, of course, mean that we have no need for representations as well, but just because I can only refer to sticks and stones – or male violence – in words, it does not mean that the effects I impute to these objects are actually purely the discursive effects of their concepts, as if it were the words, rather than their referents, which are capable of producing physical and psychological injury. Moreover these objects can have their effects regardless of whether we recognize them in language – unless that is, one seriously wants to entertain the idea – like Marx and Engels' new revolutionary philosopher – that we would be free from harm if we only got rid of the concept of harm.

Postmodernists are right to note the importance of naming in empowering or disempowering people, but naming is only important if it has effects in terms of practical reference, and hence makes people *act* differently. Names and concepts are important, but not as important as the things (including people and practices) to which they refer. Which should we fear more: war or the concept of war? What is needed after the 'linguistic turn' is a further 'practical turn'. There are signs of this in the philosophy of natural science, which is beginning to recognize the long-neglected role of scientists' practical interventions in physical processes (Hacking, 1983; Harré, 1986), but the time is ripe for social science to take practice more seriously too.

The issues involved in the flip from naive objectivism to relativism boil down to the question of whether we can simultaneously accept the following two propositions:

1 There is no neutral access to the world, knowledge is linguistic (by and large) and social, and language is not a transparent, stable medium, but opaque and slippery.
2 We can nevertheless develop reliable knowledge of the world and have scientific progress.

The anti-realist answer to this question is either 'no', or 'yes' on condition that the status of knowledge depends purely upon agreement or conventions about what is the case, and not at all on its relationship to the world. Thoroughly undialectical in character, anti-realism cannot appreciate that knowledge can be both social and linguistic *and* be capable of grasping something of the nature of the world (Bhaskar, 1991). Realists see 1 and 2 as compatible.

I have argued that instead of flipping from naive objectivism to idealism, realism offers a third way. However, while there are also some postmodernists who want to avoid the two extremes, and who refuse to choose between them (for example, Hutcheon, 1988; Pile and Rose, 1992), such authors not only lack any alternative but attempt to make a virtue out of this by arguing that answers cannot be expected, and that all one can do is persist with sceptical questioning. As long as they see truth as an all-or-nothing matter, as long as they confuse knowledge with its objects, and as long as they ignore practice, they are indeed unlikely to find answers, even where they are possible. Meanwhile, in their own practice, the most audacious of sceptics can't avoid assessments of practical adequacy in choosing which accounts to guide their practice.

Pomo Flip 2: Grand Narratives and Local Knowledges

One of the hallmarks of postmodernism is its distrust of metanarratives and totalizing discourses, whether major philosophical systems or grand theories such as Marxism (Lyotard, 1984), In their place, it is argued that we need more limited local knowledges, which do not claim universal applicability.

Metanarratives are seen as distinctive of modernism and 'the Enlightenment project', in which the construction of a grand, overarching system would allow humankind to rid itself of illusion and domination, and control its destiny and progress. The Enlightenment project is obviously up against it, though it is far from abandoned. Critics of the project face the contradiction that in attacking it as an illusion or false goal, they are themselves presupposing the possibility of a reduction of illusion and the possibility of a better life (Wellmer, 1972; Doel, 1992; Hutcheon, 1988), Moreover, whatever their criticisms of grand narratives, postmodernists' own narrative outstretches them all, categorizing and levelling differences with breathtaking disregard for complexity.

Totalizing discourses try to impose order on the world by constructing a 'centre' around which social life resolves (Gregory, 1989b). In the case of Marxism the centre is production and its social relations. Other structures and phenomena may be admitted but they are seen in terms of their relations to the centre. Even though Marxism's totalizing ambitions have given way to a more pluralist attitude, signalled by notions of relative autonomy, contingency, and multiple determination (McLennan, 1989), there are still major aspects of social life – gender, for example – on which even a more open Marxism has little to offer and which are consequently marginalized by it.

In contrast, the kind of social ontology favoured by some post-structuralists, is of a centreless web of heterogeneous relationships, none of which hold universally, and in which each location is unique. A web at least suggests connections and interdependence, but as we shall see, in some cases the reaction against the ontology of grand theories has put fragmentation before interdependence (for example, Deutsche, 1991: p. 13). Interesting though the centerless web ontology is, it seems dogmatic and perverse to deny that there are not some structures that are extensive or widely replicated, such as those of patriarchy and capitalism. As Fraser and Nicholson say of Lyotard's view of metanarratives,

> There is no place … for critique of pervasive axes of stratification, for critique of broad-based relations of dominance and subordination along lines like gender, race and class (1989, p. 23).

Neither ontology seems satisfactory and as Gregory observes: '…we are presently strung out between notions of totality which are plainly dis-creditable and a "politics of the fragment or conjuncture" which is largely ineffectual (1989b, p. 91–2).'

If a link can be made, as Gregory implies (1989b), between the search for order and totalizing discourses, realism cannot be implicated in this. Realism prioritizes the search for necessity rather than for order and it conceptualizes necessity as plural rather than singular, as residing in the causal powers and liabilities of objects, which may in many cases be contingently related to one another. While its ontology includes structures there need be no single or central structure (Harding, 1989). It is also receptive towards difference, though it does not see this as antithetical to explanation, as some fear (for example, Harvey and Scott, 1989). Realism therefore provides a theory of determinations rather than (pre-) determinism (Bhaskar, 1975), Moreover it stresses that in open systems, which are universal in social science, the activation of these causal powers is unlikely to produce stable regularities or order. Such an ontology fits well with the more open kind of Marxism or post-Marxism that has emerged in the last 20 years.

Both the moderation of the centred ontology of totalizing discourses, such as Marxism, and the postmodernist alternative of a centreless web can be seen as reactions to the failure of approaches which expected to find regularities at the level of events and which effectively assumed a flat ontology. But the postmodernist reaction fails to break with this assumption because it interprets the absence of those regularities as evidence of the lack of such structures. Thus, for example, if you can't read off an individual's standard of living from a Marxist concept of their class position, it is assumed that there is therefore no class structure (Sayer and Walker, 1992, Chapter 1). But on a realist ontology which is stratified, structures may have powers emergent from and irreducible to those of their constituents, and different structures can come into a variety of contingent relationships with one another to co-determine the occurrence of events, thus breaking the one-to-one relationships between structures and events found in the closed systems of scientific experiments.

Totalizing discourses are characteristically reductionist, for they treat events and processes as direct, unmediated expressions of the central underlying structures, and hence misattribute causality. In some cases – extraordinarily – postmodernists have responded to this problem by trying to dispense with causation altogether and to argue that to say that some causes are more important than others is itself a kind of essentialism (for example, Graham, 1990; Chapter 4). On this view our hair colour would have to be deemed just as vital for our survival as the functioning of our hearts. If all causes are equal, it is not clear how we could explain anything, or how one could ever hope to achieve anything (cause something to happen) by acting, for if no cause is more important than any other, then doing nothing is as effective as doing something. To say that A was caused by B, not C, is not to claim some kind of ultimate truth; like any other such claim it is open to revision, but that doesn't mean that we can remain agnostic about causal priority. Our survival depends on identifying it – not 'ultimately', but well enough to be able to meet our needs.

Realism, as a philosophy, does not provide any warrant for putting class and production at the center of social explanation, for that is a substantive, not a philosophical question. But it does support the view that some structures (mechanisms, objects or whatever we care to call them) are more important than others in shaping *particular* outcomes. This doesn't justify assuming a single centre: rather it simply supports the unexceptional idea that what is central or most important depends on what objects we are dealing with and what we are trying to explain. What is central to a child's conception of space is not central to the determination of trade balances, and vice versa. Such a view fits with a cautiously pluralist reinterpretation of major theories, but it doesn't license a prohibition on references to causal priority. Realism therefore resists the temptations of this second kind of postmodernist flip.

But there are also epistemological objections to grand narratives. It might be argued, for example, that they squeeze out rival discourses and claim a privileged access to truth. In other words they are foundationalist. What is needed, on this view, is an acceptance of 'local knowledges' whose truth is relative to particular contexts and groups. But there are several problems with this argument. Firstly, *grand narratives don't have to be foundationalist:* there can be more than one grand narrative for a particular domain (for example, liberalism, socialism and feminism for political philosophy); their proponents may be perfectly aware that foundationalism is untenable, and yet not unreasonably continue to regard their grand narrative as the best available or the least bad. As long as each one does not dogmatically refuse any claims of rival theories but tries to engage with them, then this objection to grand narratives does not stand. (However, it is of course possible that theorists could pay lip service to fallibilism and continue to be dogmatic in their evaluation of alternative substantive discourses.) Equally the contrast with local knowledges does not hold. *If all knowledge is fallible, then the critique of foundationalism is as relevant to local knowledges as it is to grand narratives.* Neither epistemology nor anti-epistemology can help us evaluate the relative qualities of grand theory and local knowledges. It is an *a posteriori* matter.

Another line of criticism concerns the alleged universality of grand narratives. The supposedly grand totalizing visions of liberalism and Marxism have been exposed as partial, particular, situated views of the world masquerading as general, universal views. Just as liberalism was attacked by Marx for representing the special interests of the bourgeoisie as the general social interest, so Marxism has in turn been criticized for representing class as the universal and over-riding structuring principle of society, while both liberalism and Marxism have been accused of embodying unacknowledged androcentric views of society (Pateman, 1987; Phillips, 1987, 1991; Soper, 1990). Similarly, within feminism too, liberal feminists have been accused of speaking only for affluent white women, and others have been criticized for the 'levelling of differences' among women (McDowell, 1991; Nicholson, 1990; Soper, 1990). These critiques are successful in pointing to cases of theories which have been presented as speaking for everyone but which, in fact, only speak for the author's social group – most notoriously, white, middle-class men.

The risks of grand narratives do not mean we should abandon all attempts at grand syntheses, ignoring big pictures and limiting ourselves to the local details. For example, with some justification, David Harvey's influential *The Condition of Postmodernity* (Harvey, 1989) has been accused of disregarding his own social positioning (Deutsche, 1991). But his attempt at an aerial view does not mean that he is trying to assume an Archimedean standpoint, outside discourse (Smith, 1992). A bird's-eye view is not necessarily a god's-eye view. Stepping back from details and choosing to concentrate on common and large features does not entail imagining one could step outside discourse to see how it compares to reality. Surely a Marxist would argue the opposite: you need to stay *within* this Marxist discourse if you want to understand the big picture! Personally, I would prefer a more open discourse, not avoiding the big picture, but attempting to compose it by synthesizing the insights of many situated knowledges.

We do not need to flip from grand narratives to local knowledges, for they are implicated in one another. If there are big global structures or systems, the view from one local part of them is likely to be very different from that at another part: the Indian tea picker and the British tea drinker are part of the same system (though they belong to different systems too), but their viewpoints are radically different. This doesn't mean to say that they can have nothing useful to say, but that what they do say would be better if their standpoint were acknowledged. Nor does it mean that their views are in fact purely local. Rather they are local views of something bigger (Haraway, 1991). And precisely because the tea picker and the tea drinker act – at least in part of their lives – within the same system, the idea that we should forget grand views of that system and develop local knowledges, discrete and self-referential, is disastrous. The tensions between the views of those in different but interdependent positions have to be confronted and negotiated. There are invariably local views within, and of, large, grand structures, but we need to discover what links up those local views, not eagerly fragment them into separate, non-communicating discourses or local knowledges.[3]

Ironically, a contributory influence in the distrust of grand narratives has been the increasing 'hybridization' of culture, which is ironic because it has much to do with the global extension of capitalism. Thanks to division of labour, to gender, class and race, individuals have for a long time had multiple identities. While this fragmentation need not be seen as pathological, it can be recognized without obliterating similarity and interconnection. (See McDowell, 1991, Phillips, 1987, 1991, and Soper, 1991, on this issue in relation to equality, difference and gender.) Rubin's plea for the recognition of the oppression of women both in its 'endless variety and monotonous similarity' is salutary; the same goes for other major social relations too (quoted in Fraser and Nicholson, 1989, p. 28). A recognition of an earlier neglect of difference need not prompt a flip in which similarity, interdependence, structure and persistence are forgotten. As long as there are similarities and connections as well as differences, it is at least possible that we can go beyond the localized voice. And as many feminist writers on postmodernism note, an obsession with difference and a picture of society as an unstable mosaic can be corrosive of solidarity and political identity, of politics as 'making common cause' (Soper, 1990; McDowell, 1991; Fraser and Nicholson, 1989).

In summary, grand views are as needed as ever, but the challenge is to develop them in a way that synthesizes – though neither undemocratically nor uncritically – the standpoints of the many rather than speaking only for a minority.

Pomo Flip 3: Cultural Relativism Writ Small

Several decades ago, anthropology reacted against its ethnocentric beginnings by adopting cultural relativism, according to which the knowledge of other cultures was to be treated as beyond the scope of external criticism. In Gellner's phrase, a position of 'contextual charity' was adopted; it was assumed that whatever looked irrational to the outsider could be shown to be perfectly rational once placed in the appropriate context and seen in the local culture's own terms (Gellner, 1970).

Totalizing discourses or grand narratives are reminiscent of ethnocentrism since they marginalize and disqualify voices other than those of their authors (Slater, 1992). Although postmodernist thought has been effective in exposing this imperialism/ethnocentrism/androcentrism, it is again in danger of flipping over into an equally untenable position of a cultural relativism, this time applied not only to other cultures but to particular groups within any culture. In place of a paternalistic and imperialist presumption to speak for others, we have an extreme deference towards others, a reluctance to speak for them, even where doing so might help, thereby making us 'reluctant utopians' (Soper, 1990).

If we have two people, A and B, belonging to different cultures, social groups, or of different gender or ethnicity, A's interpretations and criticisms of B *may* indeed be ethnocentric or otherwise misguided; that, of course, is always a significant and often dangerous risk. For example Stokes warns that Maori geography is not that of outsiders, and that the qualifications of a non-Maori geographer may be more of a hindrance than a help in understanding it (cited in Cloke et al., 1991, p. xi). Such warnings should make non-Maoris more careful about how they interpret Maori culture, but they should not make them grant Maori understandings some ultimate privilege or foundation that non-Maoris would not claim for themselves. If our own knowledge cannot be given any privilege – even about our own situation – and hence must be attentive to criticism, so must the knowledge of others, even if they belong to a different culture. To suppose otherwise is thoroughly inconsistent: as Gellner (1970) puts it, it leads to the contradiction of being a liberal at home and a conservative abroad – or an anti-foundationalist at home and a foundationalist abroad. It is one thing to grant respect to the knowledge of others, but quite another to grant them immunity from external criticism (Taylor et al., 1992).

It has been claimed that the powerful have most to fear from relativism. Insofar as they claim to monopolize the truth, the point seems convincing, but relativism can also serve the interests of the powerful admirably, for they can use it as an excuse to ignore the criticism of those they oppress or exclude, on the grounds that its 'truth' is purely relative to a different discourse to their own. Such a privileging of supposedly local knowledge therefore cuts both ways, for at the same time as it protects particular sets of ideas, it denies them any influence on others (Hartsock, 1989). Too often, postmodernists fail to see that relativism is the flip side of foundationalism, so it is no surprise that it can produce similar effects. In other words, fragmentation plus relativism equals 'ghettoization'. Relativism is no friend of feminism, anti-racism or any other kind of critical social theory.

Gellner (1970) also pointed out a further absurd consequence of the contradictions of relativism, regarding cases where the understandings of others change radically. Over 20 years later, the proponents of local knowledges are in danger of repeating the same error. Suppose that we, belonging to culture A, are told by members of culture B that they now reject their former beliefs as false. For example, a former Communist Party member in Russia may quite sincerely reject his or her previous political beliefs as false. If we take the relativist line, then we are confronted with a crushing dilemma, for it obliges us to accept their beliefs, and yet to accept their current beliefs is to deny their former beliefs, and vice versa! We obviously cannot say that the past political beliefs were correct when they were held and wrong when they were disavowed. Such are the absurdities of a theory of truth as wholly conventional and socially or culturally relative. We may have to judge, even if we are outsiders.

Note how illiberal and insulting it is for members of A to assert that members of B who have come to prefer certain beliefs of A as superior to B's must be mistaken; they are dupes, fodder for suasive rhetoric, victims of a stronger will-to-power. Challenging this does not require us to deny that some changes in B are indeed a result of mere power rather than rational persuasion and unforced acceptance. But it would actually be more liberal for members of A to allow the possibility that their own knowledge is sometimes superior, for ironically to refuse this may be to imply that B is inferior or misguided in cases where B comes to favour A. Moreover, unless we assume such a possibility, there is no point in arguing for anything, even relativism, though as already noted to argue for relativism is to encourage anti-relativism too. Once again, the contradictions of relativism bite back at every turn.

It might salve left-liberal consciences to assume that the knowledges of A and B or any array of language/cultural/social communities or groups have equal cognitive status, that they have equal explanatory powers, such that they are equally successful in informing, guiding and interpreting successful practice. Indeed, even to query such an assumption might be taken as shocking, as evidence of ethnocentrism, cultural imperialism and dogmatism, etc. But the reverse is the case, for such a cognitive equality principal would run into the usual relativist dilemmas. Thus the consistent proponent of the equality thesis would have to grant equal status to racist and fascist beliefs, and to affirm the ethnocentrism of other societies. By contrast, as a nonrelativist, a realist need have no qualms in rejecting racism and fascism, partly for moral reasons and partly because they can be shown to have inferior cognitive status – they are based on misleading accounts and explanations of human society, ones which are inferior to non-racist theories.

Finally, while this kind of A versus B model is useful heuristically for sorting out the dilemmas of relativism, it is only a starting point, one that needs to be immediately qualified. For it obscures the fact that A and B usually overlap and are themselves divided internally and 'decentred.' Local knowledges have been increasingly intermingled and are set within global systems. Fascism and racism are not neatly restricted to particular societies. As the discussions of equality and difference in feminism illustrates, particular groups invariably tend to be cross-cut and differentiated by others. We therefore need to avoid projecting the absurd fiction of autonomous academic discourses onto social reality. Differentiation and interdependence, yes; fragmentation no.

The Alleged Death of Philosophy

Postmodernist thought sees itself as challenging philosophy (Dear, 1988; Gregory, 1989a), though of course its arguments against philosophy have a decidedly philosophical character. Postmodernists argue that philosophy has assumed a god-like role, supposing to direct and sit in authoritative judgement upon scientific and everyday knowledge, when in fact it is on the same level as any other kind of knowledge (Rorty, 1980). However, popularizers of postmodernism have often mistakenly reduced philosophy to epistemology and epistemology to foundationalism. This obscures the fact that philosophy has been a rather modest enterprise in recent decades (Baynes, et al., 1987). Epistemology, if defined as the search for ultimate foundations of knowledge, has been dead for some time; scepticism is as old as philosophy, and epistemology defined more broadly but more modestly as the study of knowledge shows no sign of giving up. Critical realism is a philosophy but its main focus is on ontology, not epistemology (Outhwaite, 1987), and it is anti-foundationalist. It is explicitly more modest in its goals than postmodernists would like to believe, aiming primarily to 'under-labour' for social science, and acknowledging its dependence on the materials/knowledge available to it in society (Bhaskar, 1979). This, however, does not prevent it from providing *immanent critiques*, taking on areas of controversy and difficulty by starting from areas of agreement and success, or from inquiring into the preconditions of successful practices. It is self-defeating for sceptics to try to reject this strategy by refusing to acknowledge any points of agreement and success because a) this leaves them no grounds from which to doubt anything, and b) because they have to suspend such doubt in order to live.

Another line of attack focuses on the inescapably metaphorical and rhetorical character of all discursive knowledge, including that of science. Those kinds of science or philosophy which have tried to escape from reliance on metaphor and rhetoric into pure reason or logic have been known to be incapable of doing so. Even to speak of 'logical rigour' is to employ a metaphor, beyond which we cannot proceed. Moreover, language is opaque. We can never make it a completely transparent medium of representation however much we try, and reason, logic, rigour and concepts of truth can't be given any absolute grounding.

The unavoidability of metaphor need not be seen as a problem for science and it has been acknowledged for some time in realist philosophy (Harré, 1961; Hesse, 1974). Scientific progress is very much about improving the metaphors we use so that our interventions in the world are more successful. Moreover, to point out the irreducibly metaphorical and rhetorical character of knowledge does not mean that logic, or protocols of reason, just disappear. They remain indispensable as ever: no flip from reason to rhetoric is needed.[4]

While postmodernist critiques of philosophy do have some point, it should be noted that in their critiques of substantive accounts in social science, postmodernists are not slow to deploy philosophical arguments when it suits them. Charges of 'totalizing discourses' or logocentrism sound rather impressive, if not intimidating, and it is especially important to go into the arguments behind them rather than merely parroting these terms. Otherwise academic debates may become debased to the point where, instead of engaging with the substantive accounts of others, one simply disqualifies them by accusing them of assuming some privileged vantage point or foundationalism. Even if anyone did claim such a privilege, simply pointing out the philosophical error allows them the fallback position that their account, even if fallible, was at least the best available. To counter such a claim, one would have to move to a critique of the substantive content of the account. Since antifoundationalism is virtually universally accepted, it doesn't have much use as a critical weapon. One can hardly criticize a theory or an account for being fallible, for not being the ultimate truth, if it could not be otherwise.

Conclusions

I have argued against the postmodern tendency to flip from naive objectivism to relativism and idealism, from totalities to fragments, and from ethnocentrisms to new forms of self-contradictory cultural relativism. A realist approach shows us that we can escape from these alternatives. The Modernist project – and more specifically, critical social science – don't need foundationalism or notions of absolute truth. They can be not only better understood but furthered through a critical realist interpretation. The new kinds of idealism and relativism that have infected postmodernist thought offer no support to critical social science, to anti-racism and feminism.

Let us update Hume's taunts against idealism: we will see how idealists – all those who bracket out reality, who imagine that knowledge is purely a matter of rhetoric and power, those who want to throw out reference and representation along with any concept of truth – fare when the meeting is ended. Truth being apparently purely a matter of convention or power and purely internal to theory and nothing to do with representation of some external 'reality', it will of course be easy for the anti-realists to change the conventions and leave through (the so-called) solid walls rather than through the doors of realist orthodoxy. And to add a dash of Bachelard, we shall see the difference between the nocturnal philosophies of the idealists and their diurnal realism, when at the end of the meeting, they sheepishly leave by the door.

Notes

1 This reaction is reminiscent of that made by many in the 1960s upon encountering the arguments of Kuhn and Feyerabend against logical empiricism. In place of paradigms, we

have discourses, in place of the critique of neutral observation languages, we have the critique of the 'metaphysics of presence', in addition to doubts about scientific progress, we have a wider critique of the 'Enlightenment project', and so on.

2 A fourth pomo-flip, not discussed here but common in post-structuralism, is the extraordinary switch from deterministic interpretations of the subject (which of course invite one to wonder who the subject is who can think their decentring) to voluntaristic resistance and performativity (McNay, 1996; Norris, 1993).

3 Furthermore, local knowledges include universals and universal claims, no less than grand narratives; universals are not restricted to the latter. I am grateful to John O'Neill for this point.

4 Norris (1990, 1991) argues that some of the leading figures associated with deconstructionism defend this distinction and are themselves rigorous. Note that some authors use 'rhetoric' to refer just to suasive rhetoric, and some to this plus logic and reason. It is therefore important to know how the term is being used.

4

Essentialism, Social Constructionism and Beyond

It has become common to see references to 'essentialism' in social scientific literature, and they are overwhelmingly derogatory, indeed it has been widely noted to have become a term of abuse which silences or short-circuits argument, being irredeemably tainted by association with racism and sexism (Schor and Weed, 1994; Assiter, 1997; Nussbaum, 1992, p. 205). There are many essentialisms and critiques of essentialism, relating to different issues and originating in different contexts, some of them highly sensitive ones. Critiques of essentialism construed as biological reductionism or determinism in relation to gender and sexuality have been especially prominent in feminism. There is also 'cultural essentialism', for example, concerning identity. This refers to discourses and practices that label and relate to particular groups of people in ways which suppress difference and homogenize and fix them, not merely stereotyping but either pathologizing or wrongly idealizing them. Many poststructuralist and postmodernist critiques of essentialism draw upon Derridean arguments and foreground discourse, and are common again in some feminist, anti-racist and post-colonial literature (for example, Williams and Chrisman, 1993). Poststructuralist critiques of essentialism have also been developed in political theory (Laclau and Mouffe, 1985) and with respect to political economy (Hindess, 1987; Tomlinson, 1990). In development studies, the accusation of essentialism is usually directed against what is taken to be ethnocentric and non-relativist thinking (Nussbaum, 1992). Finally, there is what Jane Martin has termed methodological essentialism – the limitation of methodology to a single kind, rejecting any attempts at generalization (Martin, 1994). To make matters more complicated, many anti-essentialists have been influenced by more than one of these lines of critique.

Whichever of the above debates we are involved in, essentialism is unavoidably a philosophical concept, one whose definition and critique quickly gets us into arguments which are as old as philosophy itself. If there is anything common to all the critiques of essentialism in social science, it is a concern to counter characterizations of people, practices, institutions and other social phenomena as having fixed identities that deterministically produce fixed, uniform outcomes. Whether they are talking about cultural identity, economic behaviour or gender and sexuality, anti-essentialists have argued that people are not creatures of determinism, whether natural or cultural, but are socially constructed and constructing. In contrast to homogenizing, deterministic and repressive discourses, anti-essentialism therefore appears to be emancipatory. At the same time, several critics of essentialism acknowledge that, at the limit, insofar as we always have to categorize, essentialism is unavoidable, or that at least, it is sometimes necessary to employ essentialist descriptions for strategic purposes (Fuss, 1990; Schor and Weed, 1994; Spivak, 1987). Only a relatively small number of theorists actively defend any kind of essentialism in its own right (for example, Assiter, 1997; Dodd, 1994; Malik, 1996; Martin, 1994; McLennan, 1996; Nussbaum, 1992; O'Neill, 1995).[1] These developments represent a remarkable shift in radical academia. As Gregor McLennan notes, whereas, in the 1970s, radicals used to attack pluralists for failing to recognize the underlying structures or essence behind superficial appearances, the criticism has now been inverted; postmodern pluralism in the guise of anti-essentialism is resistant both to notions of generative structures and of relatively clear-cut social divisions, asserting instead difference to the point of implosion into 'de-differentiation' (McLennan, 1996).

I want to comment on several of the debates, but to do so, I can only make my case clear by moving from a discussion of concepts of essence to the social science issues; in particular, some ground-clearing regarding issues such as causality is needed in order to discuss biological reductionism. I shall argue that some things have essences and some – for example, gender or ethnicity – do *not*. While some kinds of essentialism are certainly mistaken and even dangerous, hence deserving to be anathematized, others are not, and indeed are an important resource for critical social science. At the same time, while we can't do without something like a concept of essences, we need to get beyond the stark alternatives of essentialism and anti-essentialism and work with a richer ontology. I shall also argue that 'social constructionism' – often opposed to essentialism – is unsatisfactory with regard to ontology, epistemology and its conceptualization of nature and society, and is as open to reactionary interpretations as it is to progressive ones.

Given the diversity of definitions of essentialism and anti-essentialism, particular anti-essentialists will not recognize their positions in all of the arguments I put forward. Also in view of the heat generated by some of the debates, it is necessary to ask that, where anti-essentialist readers feel arguments are being attacked which they do not hold, they should feel pleased rather than angry, because this obviously means that on those points they have nothing to worry about. In any case I am interested in the various arguments themselves, not in identifying authors. If the term 'essentialism' has been anathematized, then no useful debate can take place until such reactions are suspended.

Essences, Sameness and Difference

In philosophy, essentialism is generally taken to be the doctrine that objects have certain essential properties, which make them one kind of thing rather than any other. In addition to these essential features they may have other accidental properties. The essence of water can be defined as H_2O; whether it is in a bowl or a kettle is a matter of accident rather than essence. The essence of chess is its rules; whether the chess pieces are wooden or plastic, or whether the chess players are left-handed or right-handed, makes no essential difference. The ability to communicate and share experience might be held to be an essential feature of human beings while wearing jeans is not.

Several points should be noted straightaway about this concept of essence. Firstly, despite the fact that essentialism is often counterposed to social constructionism, essentialists can happily include things such as institutions or languages, which are obviously socially constructed, as having essences on this definition. Secondly, essentialists need *not* assert that all members of a class are identical in every respect, only that they have *some* features in common. It is therefore not necessarily guilty of homogenizing and 'flattening difference'; it all depends which features are held to be essential, and it is a substantive, empirical question – and not a matter of ontological fiat – whether such common, essential properties exist. A possible suspicion regarding this last point is that categorizing differences as 'accidental' must involve treating them as unimportant relative to the essential features, when in political terms they may in fact be highly important. However, while this is a possibility, such judgments of relative importance are not entailed by the philosophical definition of essences; for example, a claim that there are essential properties shared by humans does not necessarily render 'accidental' differences, such as those of particular cultures, unimportant, indeed it may be the essential similarities that are trivial.

Thirdly, there is another reason why asserting sameness need not involve denying difference (and equally, asserting difference need not involve denying sameness). Since the whole point of attempting to categorize is to specify what, if anything, is common in the midst of diversity, the search for common properties, including essences, *presupposes* diversity. As Jane Martin points out, any categorizing or naming calls attention to similarities, so that at the same time as language involves a play of difference, it also masks difference (Martin, 1994). Conversely, the only point of asking to know the difference between two or more things, is if they also have something in common. The nature of the difference between various groups of people is more interesting than the difference between people and toothpaste partly because the former have some things in common.

The upshot of these last two points is that what is problematic is not the assertion of sameness (or difference) per se, but *mistaken* claims about particular kinds of sameness (or difference). We should be concerned about assertions of non-existent commonalities or denials of significant differences, and equally about assertions of insignificant differences and/or denials of significant commonalities. Thus racism involves both kinds of error – on the one hand spurious claims about differences which actually have no significance, and on the other denial of differences which are significant, through the stereotyping characteristic of cultural essentialism. However, as we have just seen, blanket *a priori* injunctions against sameness or difference are absurd for they always unknowingly presuppose what they attempt to deny.

Notwithstanding these defensive points about essences, sameness and difference, there are also problems with the concept of essence. One of the difficulties is revealed when we move from simple objects, such as, water, to complex ones, such as the human body or social institutions, which might be said to have complexes of essential features, and in the case of social phenomena, ones which vary over time and space. In these latter cases, it is unclear at what scale or level their essential features are supposed to exist. Regarding people, essentialists might refer to what is essential to their belonging to a particular social group, or to what is human about them, or to the essential properties of the body, or its constituents, such as its cells. In other words, talk of essences is often intended not to capture the basis of every aspect of an object, but merely to say that a specific property is essential or necessary for some specific behaviour or outcome – for example, it might be claimed that an assumption of truth-telling is 'essential' for communication. While the distinction between essential and 'accidental' properties is useful, it leaves open the question 'essential in relation to what?' Moreover, we might also be inclined to argue that some properties are *more* essential than others; the only useful sense we might make of such a claim would be to say that A is more essential than B if a wider range of behaviours depend on A than on B; thus my heart is more essential for all the things that I do than is my little finger.

A further fundamental problem with the concept of essence is that it is called upon for two different purposes which are not necessarily compatible. One purpose is to identify the essence of an object in terms of properties that supposedly determine – or are indispensable for – what it can and cannot do; these are its 'generative' properties. Thus, it might be argued that it is in virtue of the essential features of bureaucracies, such as their division of labour and hierarchical structures, their formalized procedures, etc., that they can process large amounts of routine work quickly, but find it difficult to provide flexible responses to unforeseen circumstances. The other purpose is to refer to those features of an object which enable us to distinguish it from other kinds of object; these are its distinguishing or identifying properties.

Sometimes, the two aspects largely coincide: the capital-labour relation might be said to be the essence of capitalism both in the generative and the distinguishing sense, although even here there are also some other generative features of capitalism, such as industrialism, which are not unique to it, and hence not distinctive (Sayer, 1995). In other cases, there may be no significant overlap between the two aspects – scarcely any generative properties of an object may be unique to it and its distinguishing features may not tell us much about what enables it to do whatever it does. Thus, urban sociologists in the 1970s and 1980s effectively concluded that there was no capitalist urban essence because the processes which generated capitalist cities (for example, capital accumulation, property development) were hardly unique to cities, merely more concentrated than elsewhere[2] (Castells, 1977; Saunders, 1986; Sayer, 1983). However, as we shall see, this still leaves the question of whether merely to reject mistaken claims about essences – such as those to do with the urban or with 'race' – or to dispense with notions of essences altogether.

If a group of objects referred to by a common term (be they people, institutions or practices) do not have any universally shared attributes, then clearly they do not have a common essence. If they do have some shared attributes, this alone does not mean these are essential rather than accidental, even if they occur in 100% of cases. 'Associational thinking', which assumes that what happens to go together must go together, is therefore analytically feeble. If we are to understand the structure of any object of study, we need to distinguish those features that merely happen to coexist – and perhaps interact – but could exist apart, from those that could not exist without a certain other feature. To work out which obtains, we would have to find or create test cases, or ask counterfactual questions to determine the features whose absence makes a far-reaching difference to their 'host' objects, and the features whose absence leaves the other attributes largely intact. Thus, all capitalist societies have private property, money, capital accumulation, industrialism and patriarchy, but it does not follow from this that the first four features could not exist without the fifth[3]. What matters is not finding an essence in the sense of a single feature or structure of features that both distinguishes the object from other types and covers all its important generative powers – which, as we have seen, is improbable – but simply working out which attributes or relata of an object or situation can only exist with others, which can exist without them, and what their generative powers are[4]. Thus, while the industrial and patriarchal characters of concrete instances of capitalism are not what distinguishes it from state socialism, both are enormously important.

One advantage of acknowledging this common non-correspondence of distinguishing features and generative powers is that it helps us avoid disabling dualisms. Thus, instead of attempting simply to counterpose the human or the social to the animal, or mind to body as mutually exclusive terms, we can recognize that not all the generative powers of the referents of each term are unique to it and hence consider the continuities or similarities between the classes (see Benton, 1993).

Finally, at this point, it should be noted that we often categorize without identifying essential properties common to all members of a class. Often the reason for defining a class of objects is that its members merely have 'family resemblances' – that is 'a complicated network of similarities overlapping and crisscrossing: sometimes overall similarities, sometimes similarities in detail' (Wittgenstein, cited in O'Neill, 1995). Such cases are legion in social science; for example, the debate over the nature of Fordism and post-Fordism is more likely to identify family resemblances than essences, for if we associate Fordism with moving assembly lines, mass production, large hierarchical organizations and Taylorism, many of the organizations commonly described as Fordist lack some of these features (Amin, 1994).

In view of these problems, a possible provisional conclusion is that although there might be occasions on which its use is unproblematic, the concept of essence is expected to do too much work. I shall argue that if, instead, we use the realist concept of causal powers possessed by objects (including people and social phenomena) – that is, powers or dispositions that are generative of behaviour, we can avoid implying that any object has a *single* essence and avoid raising expectations that we can simultaneously deal with the different question of what is unique or specific to a particular kind of object.[5] Thus people have not one but many causal powers and not all of them are unique to human beings, nor are those which are unique to them necessarily any more important than those which are not, nor do humans all have exactly the same causal powers.

Against Essentialism or Against Misplaced Essentialism?

Treating the members of a class as sharing the same essential properties is particularly risky with respect to social phenomena. Probably the most commonly cited and criticized instances of essentialism have concerned gender, whose relational, diverse, positional and shifting character defies any identification of a fixed essence. Thus, the attribution to women of 'feminine intuition' – as if it not only clearly existed but was part of women's essence rather than a local, accidental or contingent feature of the way many women are socialized – is a more specific example of this false essentializing. Often such descriptions not only homogenize and fix what are actually contingent and variable characteristics but also either pathologize or wrongly idealize them.

These criticisms are often further associated with arguments to the effect that hard categorical boundaries conceal fuzzy, complex, shifting transitions, with the distinctions often being the subject of social struggle. In particular, familiar bi-polar distinctions such as those regarding sexualities suppress difference and hybridity. Clearly, the problems are not merely semantic but ones that can damage lives, for such discourses inform, and are objectified in, practices which institutionalize and often pathologize particular groups or behaviours. This kind of critique therefore has important emancipatory potential. Thus bell hooks notes the progressive implications of the critique of essentialism for anti-racism, allowing the 'affirmation of multiple black identities, varied black experience...' against racist stereotyping (hooks, 1991 (1993), p. 425.) It illustrates how suspicion of categorical analyses can be progressive, for example by replacing complacent categorizations of men and women with a problematization of their constitution and interdependence, and by drawing attention to how certain supposedly universal and inclusive concepts actually extrapolate from a particular social location, suppressing difference and marginalizing others. In addition, the critique opens up questions of who has the power to define and categorize in ways which fix and homogenize people, when they actually could be, and often are, different. Morever, the process of 'de-differentiation', supposedly distinctive of postmodernity, can be seen as a practical refutation of cultural essentialism.

Yet if we refer back to our philosophical distinction between essential and accidental properties, then the problem might be construed as one of mistaking peoples' accidental properties, for their essential properties. Clearly this interpretation of the problem does not involve denying that there are any essences; on the contrary, it is concerned with their correct identification. In the same vein, essentialists might agree that certain categorizations are misleading, on the grounds that they incorrectly conflate different kinds of object, with different essences. The problems of essentialism can therefore be countered in two contrasting ways: firstly, by rejecting – in the manner of 'anti-essentialism' – *any* allusion to essential properties; or secondly, by correcting particular attributions of essences which are deemed to be mistaken.

However, the 'all-out' kind of anti-essentialism is often justified by appealing to instances of the second kind of criticism; typically it is assumed that because, say, gender and identity have no essence, *nothing* has an essence. While I agree with the premise of this argument, the conclusion does not follow from it. We could, for example, argue that gender has no essence but that minerals, species, contracts, bureaucracies or the game of football do. Further, it should be remembered that essentialism does not assert that the members of a class are identical, only that they have the same essential properties: in other respects, in their accidental properties, which might involve quite important characteristics, they may show considerable variety.[6] Thus, as we shall see, instances of essential sameness at one level or 'ontological stratum', such as that of biological processes, need not of course preclude difference at the level of the social.

If we choose to reject essentialism in general, the debate widens out to encompass broader issues of ontology, that is of providing a general understanding of the nature of being, and also epistemological arguments, usually involving accusations of foundationalism. Thus broader philosophies, particularly of social constructionism and realism, become implicated. I shall argue that these ontological and epistemological extensions to the more restricted criticisms of misplaced essentialism are generally misguided.

Ontology: Strong and Moderate Essentialists, and the Charge of Reductionism

Strong and Moderate Essentialists

Although there might be 'strong essentialists' who believe that everything has an essence – a set of properties which make each thing that thing and nothing else – it is also possible to be a moderate essentialist[7], arguing as above that, while some things – for example, water or capitalist enterprises – have essences, others – such as conversations or gender – do not. It is dogmatic and illogical to insist that because examples of context-dependent and positional phenomena, such as gender and identity, are impressive, we must insist on a restrictive ontology which makes *everything* of this kind and refuse any claim that some things do have essences. Conversely, it would be equally dogmatic and illogical to argue that because objects such as water or bureaucracies have essences, everything does. Moderate essentialism and criticisms of cases of misplaced essentialism are therefore quite compatible.

Critics of essentialism often assert that it invokes not merely essences, but unchanging, eternal ones (for example, Fuss, 1990; Rattansi, 1994)[8]. This helps to load the dice against essentialism, but there is no reason why all essences should be of this kind (Assiter, 1997). The essential properties of members of animal species undergo physical ageing processes and over longer periods they can evolve new essences. Some things that are widely regarded as essential characteristics of humans, such as the ability to communicate, have to be acquired. To say that an object or a social relation has an essence, which makes it that kind of object or social relation rather than any other kind, is not to rule out any change within it. But neither does this make all objects, natural or social, like leaves in the wind, vulnerable to the slightest change of context or actors' interpretation or discursive construction. Here we run into the limitations of the basic terms of the debate: how durable must a quality be, and how big a range of behaviours must it enable, before we call it an essence? Or conversely, how much change can a thing undergo or how much diversity and instability can it exhibit before we conclude that it has no essence? If the only choice is between either regarding objects as having essences fixed for all time or conceptualizing them as merely transient or even ephemeral, and as having no integrity or particular form, then most social phenomena, which lie in between these extremes, will be occluded.

It helps to understand how essences or causal powers can change if it is appreciated that they are not wholly unconditional. The creation and reproduction of the essential features of animals, or of the capitalist economy, in terms of capital accumulation, ownership and non-ownership of means of production, and so on, is not automatic but conditional upon the existence of other things, such as oxygen, food, money and communication. Thus, change in these preconditions can bring about change in the essential features or natures of the objects, so that they diversify, attenuate or disappear. However, this conditional nature is often limited, so that essences are indifferent to a vast variety of phenomena and contexts and hence can often retain their identity across large regions of time and space. There is surely a continuum from highly durable, relatively context-*in*dependent objects, such as the elements, through biological phenomena which can survive varying degrees of environmental change, through those social institutions, such as capital-labour relations, which can survive in a wide but not unlimited variety of contexts (effectively by reproducing their own preconditions or favourable contexts in new places), through to highly relational context-dependent phenomena, such as post-colonial identities, which lack essences (see Chapter 6; Williams and Chrisman, 1993). Obviously, it is easier to generalize about the former objects than the latter, and less of a problem to be essentialist about them.

For some critics (for example, Harvey, 1996), essentialism appears to be associated with a non-relational ontology in which all objects are discrete and merely externally related to one another, like pebbles on a beach. However, it is possible to conceive of relational essences in some cases, as in the essence of friendship or of master-slave relations, in which the identities of the relata are interdependent[9] (O'Neill, 1994). Indeed essentialism has also been associated with a view of the world as formed wholly through relational essences, and with a totalizing view in which social relations are conceived as totalities governed by a single determinative principle (Hirst, cited in Barrett, 1991, p. 63). But there is no need to associate essences with such perversely restricted ontologies. A more inclusive ontology, in which the world is understood to be composed of both internally and externally related phenomena, some with durable essences, some not, and with no single determinative principle, would accommodate more comfortably the variety of concrete phenomena which social and natural science and lay knowledges, at their present level of development,[10] claim to exist. I will return to further ontological issues to do with essences and causation shortly.

Essentialism as Reductionism

A further variant of anti-essentialism targets reductionism. Ali Rattansi defines anti-essentialism as 'a manoeuvre cutting the ground from conceptions of subjects and social forms as reducible to timeless, unchanging, defining and determining elements or ensemble of elements – "human nature", for example, or in the case of the social, the logic of the market or mode of production' (1994, p. 30). While this definition would not necessarily threaten moderate essentialists, the examples and the mention of reducibility introduce an additional and quite different dimension. Long before the term 'anti-essentialism' was coined, it had been common to criticize reductionism – the practice of explaining the behaviour of concrete (that is, many-sided) objects by reducing them wholly to (or reading them off from) just one of their abstract (that is, one-sided) constituents (Sayer, 1992). However, while Rattansi is surely right to deny that we can understand concrete behaviour, such as what people actually do in markets, purely by reducing it to what an abstract theory of markets tells us, he also appears to deny that the phenomena identified by the theory of the logic of the market, such as price incentives, are even a contributory element. In other words, he appears to be throwing out not merely reductionism but the distinction between the abstract and the concrete as defined above, and along with it, explanation. This is rather like rejecting the abstract theory of gravity on the grounds that planes can fly.

Reductionism is certainly still a major problem in social science, but it is not to be confused with abstraction and positing causal powers or dispositions, indeed it is hard to imagine how we could understand the multi-dimensional character of concrete social phenomena without drawing upon or constructing such abstractions, and postmodernists are no more able to avoid them than anyone else. Criticism – some of it from postmodernist quarters – of the violence of certain key modernist abstractions is salutary (Stones, 1996), but since we can hardly avoid abstraction, the answer is to do it more carefully, not dismiss it as unavoidably reductionist. Most explanation involves abstraction and assessing the relative importance of various conditions and processes. Even the most extreme contextualist is selective, and is unlikely to attribute, say, the political instability of the Middle East to the weather there. As Gregor McLennan notes '… some degree of essentialism is simply unavoidable. The disputes are usually over which essences we should accept as important, not whether essences can be dispensed with' (1996, p. 67).

Epistemological Associations: Foundationalism, Social Constructionism and the Derridean Connection

Foundationalism

Another way in which some anti-essentialists load the dice against essentialism is by defining it as assuming that essences are 'transparent' and identifiable with certainty (Fuss, 1990). By this manoeuvre, the ontological doctrine of essentialism is tarred with the epistemological brush of foundationalism (and likewise anti-essentialism is conflated with anti-foundationalism).[11] This is the source of many rejections of essentialism and more generally of realism, but it is a non-sequitur because a claim that the essence of x is y need not involve a claim to absolute truth, whatever that might mean.[12] The epistemological status of a claim that something is or has an essence is no different from that of a claim that a relationship is contingent; both are in principle fallible, both may be more or less practically adequate ways of understanding the world. Equally, the incontrovertible point that knowledge is situated, perspectival and discursive does not entail that its referents cannot have essences or that none of them can be extra-discursive.[13] Of course, the former confusion may derive from the fact that part of the meaning of essence might be that it is an *ontological* 'foundation' of something else – my genes as a 'foundation' for my size, for example – but whatever we believe to be an essence, it does not provide us with an ultimate, absolute epistemological foundation for anything. Essentialism in the philosophical sense is an ontological doctrine; it leaves open the epistemological problem of the 'truth' or reliability of our knowledge; we should avoid the 'epistemic fallacy' of transposing ontological matters into epistemological ones (Bhaskar, 1975).

There is, then, no inconsistency in believing that there are essences or at least generative powers and that our descriptions or definitions of them are fallible (but often provisionally practically adequate) interpretations or 'social constructions'. Belief in essences does not arise from some kind of imagined transparency or privileged access to definitive descriptions but rather from the fact that if our practice is guided by just any categories or claims about essences that we happen to dream up, we soon meet with failure if not disaster; not just anything goes. To say that essences are 'given' can be fatally ambiguous, for it could mean, a) that they exist independently of our recognition of them; or b) that their 'true' description is automatically and directly given to us. a) does not entail b) Nor does the negation of b) entail the negation of a) The otherness, the obduracy and unpredictability of the world suggests that it has certain properties regardless of whether we happen to understand them. As the enormous amount of practical and mental labour involved in science shows, it is often extremely difficult to find adequate ways of conceptualizing essences.

Social Constructionism

As we noted earlier, essentialism is often countered by social constructionism. In its weak form, the latter merely emphasizes the socially constructed nature of knowledge and institutions, and the way in which knowledge often bears the marks of its social origins. In its strong form, it also claims that objects or referents of knowledge are nothing more than social constructions.[14] Realists can happily accept weak social constructionism, while noting that the social character of knowledge does not mean that it cannot successfully identify real objects (including social constructions) which exist independently of the researcher. Knowledge, though situated, can, in some sense, be objective (Haraway, 1991).

The irony of strong social constructionists accusing essentialists of foundationalism is that 'transparency' should surely come easily to those for whom the world is nothing more than their own social construction, whereas for critical realists and essentialists, the world is relatively inaccessible precisely *because* it is not reducible to, or a construction of, our concepts of it. If our knowledge were infallible, if things always worked out as we expected, there would be no reason for supposing that there was a reality that was not merely our construction. Moreover, that we always already have to have some way of conceptualizing the objects that we register does not entail the solipsistic conclusion that they could not predate our apprehension of them.[15] The epistemological position of fallibilism or anti-foundationalism therefore fits more comfortably with realism than with a strong (idealist) version of social constructionism.[16] There are also further ironies: what could be more modernist than the idea that the world is our social construction? And – with respect to nature – what could be more conducive to triumphalism?[17]

Similarly, it is no objection to essentialism or realism to point out that our concepts of essential features of certain objects have changed; revised ideas about essences are still ideas about essences.[18] In this regard is also worth noting that scientific change regarding essences is often not a simple matter of falsification but of reconceptualizations which often supplement rather than displace earlier conceptualizations. Similarly, much theoretical debate in social science involving questions like 'What is the state?' are effectively trying to revise and improve the conceptualizations of the generative powers and distinctive features of their objects.

Social constructionism is inevitably most appealing in social science, since its objects are also social constructions which are concept-dependent. Yet even where socially produced or constructed phenomena, such as institutions, are concerned, they still often come to have a substantial independence from the 'constructions' – in the sense of interpretations, or descriptions – which external observers such as social scientists have of them. Even to insiders, the objectification of an institution in real resources and relations means that not just any interpretation will be practically adequate, either as a representation or as a guide to action. *Of course* knowledge and social phenomena are socially constructed; but that doesn't mean external phenomena (including existing material social constructions) cannot influence our interpretations. Nor does acknowledging that we are studying social constructions mean that many social phenomena cannot have a structural integrity that limits and enables what they can do; in other words recognizing their socially constructed character is not a licence for a kind of voluntarism which makes them merely discursively revisable (Malik, 1996).

There is a fatal double elision in strong social constructionism – firstly of the difference between the act of material construction and the acts of construing, interpreting, categorizing or naming, and secondly between actors' and theorists' interpretations/constructions[19]. Both actors' and theorists' interpretations/constructions are revisable, but revisions of the latter can take place without any revision of the former, unless the theorists actually influence the actors. Islam is a social construction, but it is not *my* social construction, and though I may make constructions *of* it, it is likely to remain independent of these particular constructions, though it may be influenced by some wider 'western' interpretations of it. In practice, intertextuality is not unbounded. That there is a possibility of the observer or theorist actually influencing, rather than merely externally interpreting, the object does not mean that the latter becomes nothing more than the observer's construction. More simply, that A influences B does not mean B is A's construction (O'Neill, 1994).

Social constructionists often deny the charge of idealism and acknowledge the existence of a real world independent of their 'constructions' (for example, Laclau and Mouffe, 1985; Yanagisako and Delaney, 1995), but the use of the hopelessly misleading metaphor of construction invites idealist slippage, for it evades the question of the relationship of our social constructions to the nature of their referents. They might further insist that social constructions such as institutions are real, but if they also assume that they must be identical to what their constitutive discourses construe them as, then they slip back into idealism by transposing foundationalism into social ontology by projecting it onto actors (Gellner[20], 1968). If researchers' knowledge is fallible, so must actors' be. That knowledge or discourse can have objective effects does not mean that its understanding of its referents is objective or adequate. We have no alternative but to attempt to assess the relative practical adequacy or objectivity of different social constructions. Thus Ronald Reagan once tried to challenge the social construction of 'battered women' by calling them 'runaway wives'. The only way the latter social construction can be challenged is by defending the realism, objectivity or practical adequacy of the first social construction: they really were battered. Of course, in practice, social constructionists do, in effect, argue that certain social constructions are mistaken or unrealistic – for example, with reference to 'race' – but only by trading on a collectively misrecognized realist assumption that there is something independent of our constructions about which we can be mistaken.

Finally, social constructionists might try to outflank essentialists by pointing to the fact that essentialism is itself a social construction. They are right, of course, but this poses no challenge – indeed, imagining that it does reproduces the basic error of strong social constructionism, for it does not follow from this fact that what essentialism refers *to* – essences – are all necessarily social constructions. Some are, for example, those of artefacts, though they usually exist independently of *researchers'* constructions/interpretations of them, while others, for example, water, are no-one's constructions. Furthermore, our material constructions are always constrained and enabled by the intransitive properties of the materials and agents.

Derridean/Anti-Essentialist Affinities

There is an influential affinity between anti-essentialism and Derridean views of meaning (for example, Assiter, 1997; Fuss, 1990; Gherardi, 1995; Schor and Weed, 1994). While the former refuses the possibility of objects having enduring cores, the latter's refusal of the 'metaphysics of presence' makes a similar point about meaning. But even though the meaning of a term is indeed never discrete and self-contained but always derived from and deferred through the play of difference among wider networks of terms, this does not necessarily render it fundamentally unstable or ambiguous in practice. That there are relatively stable objects and differences between them, and that some descriptions are able to make practically adequate, intersubjective, stable reference to them, is a condition of possibility for both language and practical social life in general, and for this reason alone, some kind of 'essentialism' is inescapable (Stones, 1996, 25–6).[21] When postmodernists manage to turn up together at a pre-arranged venue and time to discuss the instability of meaning, their actions presuppose a large measure of stability and common understanding, and the (extra-discursive) existence of the venue itself. Indeed, without successful stable practical reference, which requires stable referents, we would not be able to agree on what was unstable. Even if reference is unstable, it does not follow that referents are.[22]

There are certainly important discursive objects of study – in particular questions of identity such as 'Englishness' – whose meanings are not bounded or fixed but positional and subject to interminable reconstruction or reinterpretation.[23] But of course these elusive objects are not the only kind of thing sociologists study. Some have a decidedly categorical character: we may interpret the end of a fixed-term employment contract in various ways, but it unfortunately lacks much indeterminacy; there are several definitions of homelessness, but who would care to argue that it is merely a discursive construction? The practice or referent is usually more important than its concept. There are many occasions when, as Foucault himself remarked, our 'point of reference should not be to the great model of language (langue) and signs, but to that of war and battle' (1980, pp. 114–5). Social phenomena have many qualities which are not at all text-like, though this does not make them transparent. To argue for a relatively stable ontology is not to underestimate the difficulty of social understanding. Indeed, the difficulty of developing interpretations and explanations derives not only from the impossibility of permanently fixing meanings within single, self-sufficient concepts, or of the lack of autonomous, self-present subjects. It also derives from the otherness of the object, the referent, and the fact that it is so often *not* our construction – either because it is not a social construction at all, or because it is a material or conceptual social construction made by others, or one made by us but which differs from our conception of it – and hence something we have to struggle to make a construction *of* in our discourse.[24]

Essences, Causation and Determinism

One of the attractions of anti-essentialism is its opposition to determinism as incompatible with emancipation, or indeed, politics. In some cases, anti-essentialists have even rejected causality on these grounds (for example, Graham, 1990). By contrast to causality, discourse, though implicated in power relations, appears to offer more scope for freedom, creativity, and performativity. Against this, I shall argue that we cannot understand any kind of change – not even that produced by discourses – without implying causation, but that to make sense of causation, we need to dispense with determinism. Indeed, as we shall see subsequently, emancipation is inconceivable *without* causality.

There are two kinds of dubious assumption which support the association between causality and determinism: a) that causality is a matter of empirical regularities, and b) that causes can only be physical, so that reasons or discourse cannot be causal. I shall examine these in turn.

Causation and Regularity

The association between causation and determinism derives from the assumption of a regularity conception of causality, in which a necessary condition for identifying causality is a regular relationship between cause event and effect event, such that given the former, the latter always follows. Thus the absence of regular conjunctions between events (or stimulus and response) is adduced as evidence of the absence of causation. As in earlier debates, this assumption is made not only by positivists, but by many anti-positivists too (Bhaskar, 1979).

This assumption generates insurmountable problems: if causality is a matter of regularity, how are unique or irregular events, such as the dismantling of the Berlin Wall, caused? If the world is already determined by a host of regular causal relationships, how can people ever intervene in the course of events in a way which is not already pre-determined? Anti-essentialists, such as Hindess (1987), are therefore right to attack strong versions of essentialism which incorporate 'regularity determinism', but they wrongly assume that there are no other accounts of causation.[25]

These problems can be eliminated if we reject the regularity theory and adopt a critical realist conception of causation[26]. A cause is whatever is responsible for producing change. Whether they use causal terminology or not, accounts of change that suggest how it was it produced cannot avoid invoking causes. They seek to identify properties that enable an object to produce or undergo distinctive kinds of changes, and indeed are a *necessary condition* for doing those things. In virtue of their physiological and cognitive structures, human beings can communicate but not fly, they can kill one another, reproduce, and assume or acquire an astonishing variety of identities. We could refer to these properties as 'essences' (of the generative kind) but given the problems noted earlier regarding the tendency to expect the term to serve the different function of distinguishing between different kinds of object, it is better to reconstruct the explanation in the more modest terms of critical realism, as a matter of positing structures which have particular causal powers capable of producing the behaviour in question. Similar arguments can be made for the causal powers of social structures; the power to extract rent depends on structures of land ownership (Sayer, 1992).

This account of causal powers does not imply any determinism. While we could exercise causal powers, such as our ability to kill other people, we might not ever do so. It is one thing to say someone has a causal power, for example, the power to bear children, in virtue of a certain (physiological) structure; but quite another to say whether that power will (or should) ever be activated or exercised. And if such powers are exercised, the results are not thereby pre-determined; they depend on context, on the contingent presence of other objects with their own causal powers or ways of acting. There are also of course individuals who could not do some of these things even if they tried, because they were not born with, or have lost or have not acquired the necessary causal powers. Thus, whereas 'essence' implies a sameness that can be problematic, we can talk of causal powers without implying that every individual has exactly the same ones.

There are therefore four barriers to determinism. Firstly, whether causal powers – such as the ability to bear children – exist depends on the contingent presence of certain structures or objects. Secondly, whether these powers are ever exercised is contingent, not pre-determined. Thirdly, if and when they are ever exercised, their consequences will depend on mediation – or neutralization – by other contingently related phenomena. A fourth possibility is that natural and social causal powers themselves (and not merely whether and in what circumstances they are exercised) can be changed. Often, as in the case of gene technology, there is a micro regress, in which we find that what was once considered to be a unitary generative essence or causal power, can actually be physically divided into a part (the newly identified causal power) which is responsible for what we had previously attributed to the whole, and other parts which play a different role. Yet such technologies still have to accord with the properties of the objects they manipulate.[27] Again, this is why it usually takes considerable scientific labour to find ways of making technology work. Natural science is not merely about interpreting the world but about intervening in the world and doing things to it (Hacking, 1983). Science is of course also a social construction, but insofar as it is goes beyond reflection, then like any material process or act of construction, its results are influenced by the properties of both the materials and the tools used in the construction. And as we noted earlier the causal powers (essences) of social phenomena need not be fixed but can be changed through socialization, education, practice, struggle, and so on.

For all four reasons, we can only make sense of causation by abandoning determinism in the sense of an assumption that what happens in the world is wholly predetermined. At the same time, we don't need to throw out any notion of determination and flip over into imagining that anything can happen, anywhere. There are certain things that objects – including people, as they are constituted at a certain time and place – can and cannot do, and changes in these causal powers are often difficult to achieve.

Finally it should be clear from the above that seeking a causal explanation for something need not mean trying to find an ultimate, singular, 'first cause'. As Michèle Barrett notes, poststructuralism challenges causality by providing a critique of the search for the origin – the 'founding moment' – that will explain anything (Barrett, 1992, pp. 202–3). This critique, derived from Derrida and Foucault, is an extraordinary view of causation[28], for what contemporary account of causation would deny that causes of changes can be multiple rather than single, or that causal processes can be repeated and ongoing rather than compressed into a single founding moment? Some human causal powers, like the ability to ride a bike, may become permanent once 'installed', even if they are rarely exercised or sometimes obstructed when exercised. Others, such as an ability to assume a particular identity or speak a foreign language, can only be maintained by regularly exercising them. Again, it is absurd to adopt restrictive ontologies which imply the denial of such diversity. As long as social scientists seek to explain change, whether it is the disciplining of the body or world trade movements, they cannot avoid identifying causes – usually multiple rather than single.[29]

Reasons or Discourses as Causes

The second reason for anti-essentialists' resistance to causality concerns the assumption that the only kind of causality is physical causality, which has apparently nothing to do with what is distinctive (essential?) about social phenomena, namely their discursive or intrinsically meaningful character. In these respects, anti-essentialism resembles the position of interpretivism in earlier debates in the philosophy of social science concerning understanding versus explanation and on whether reasons could be causes. It also repeats many of their problems in new forms.

Again, the regularity theory of causation, as assumed by strong essentialism, is part of the problem because it makes the physical world completely (pre-)determined, in which case, the social world, including intentional action, cannot have any effect on the physical world – a surprising conclusion!

> If the intentional level, at which we cite reasons for actions and offer justifications and criticisms of beliefs, is merely a redescription of movements which are already sufficiently determined by antecedent physicalistic causes, then the *causal irrelevance of reasons* for the states of the phenomenal world of bodily movements and physical happenings (including the production of sounds and marks) immediately follows. (Bhaskar, 1991, p. 53)

If we want to reject the behaviourist view that reasons, beliefs, intentions, etc., are merely redundant redescriptions of physical processes which are purely physically determined, then we need to get rid of the dogma that causes can only be physical.[30] Those who dismiss discourse as 'just talk' are usually rightly reminded that it can have real effects: but then if it can have effects, it must also be capable of being causal, that is, capable of producing change. Likewise, if, in some sense, knowledge is a form of power, it must also be capable of causing change. We need both to *understand* reasons or discourse in general, and assess to what extent (if at all) they cause change.

Finally, treating reasons and discourse as capable of being causes is consistent with emphasizing the *performative* aspect of discourse, as opposed to its representational or denotative aspect or alternatively, as opposed to discourse as the 'house of being'. If performativity is '*that aspect of discourse that has the capacity to produce what it names*' (Butler, 1994, p. 33, emphasis in original), then it must be causal. Similarly, if the 'sedimentation of meanings' has any effects (for example, on identity) then again they must be causal. Those who reject talk of causes as essentialist and instead assert the play of difference and 'repetitivity' within discourse[31], but then treat the latter as responsible for the patterns and processes of social life, also implicitly readmit causation by another route.

Determinism and Emancipation

As we have seen, an attraction of anti-essentialism is its opposition to determinism, and its assertion of the socially constructed nature of the world. Yet if it reacts to regularity theories of causation by throwing out causation instead of the regularity assumption, if it ignores the possibility that reasons or discourse can be causal, then it simultaneously rejects the means of understanding how we can be architects rather than bees.

It might seem that freedom requires a refusal of, or escape from, necessity or causation, and that real freedom lies in being able to redescribe ourselves and the world through new discourses. But the freedom to redescribe ourselves is worthless, unless the discourse is performative, that is causal. For changes in discourse to be causally efficacious or successfully performative, and not just by accident, we must know something about how the determinations we want to avoid work, and how they can be subverted, blocked and replaced by more wanted and perhaps novel determinations, and we must make appropriate causal interventions. Without causality any concept of responsibility, agency or freedom is meaningless, for we can only be responsible for what we can influence (Bhaskar, 1989, pp. 163–4). 'It is not a matter of disengaging ourselves from the world so that it gets no grip on us – for by the same token, we would get no grip of it' (Collier, 1994a, pp. 192–3). Idealism makes discourse both inconsequential and all-powerful: inconsequential because it refuses to acknowledge that it can be causal and that its causal efficacy depends on how it relates to extra-discursive processes; all-powerful because it also makes it seem that we can re-make the world merely by redescribing it.

While strong essentialism not only fixes essences but takes them to predetermine actualities or outcomes, critical realism or moderate essentialism seeks to identify causal powers or essences without presuming that they must be fixed, and conceptualizes them as *potentialities* not as actualities. In order to be transcendent beings, we must have particular (emergent) powers (to do with the construction of meaning, for example) that enable us to develop new identities. Other animals cannot liberate themselves and become something new because they lack these powers. People, as language-using, meaning-creating beings, are able to change themselves, their social relations and their environments, and hence are able to transform the ways of acting, relating and thinking that hold at any particular time. This is an *essential* feature of human beings.[32]

Biological Reductionism

For more than a century, Marxists, liberals, feminists and anti-racists have attacked the practice of attributing to nature what is due to social convention, as in the naturalization of gender differences. Anti-essentialists or social constructionists have since taken this critique in a different direction, and one which I shall argue is retrograde.

Particularly in discussions of sexuality, 'essentialism' is often construed as biological reductionism, in which particular forms of behaviour are deemed to be expressions of an underlying natural essence, and social determinations are denied. Biological reductionism is an instance of what we have termed strong essentialism, in that it assumes a one-to-one correspondence between causal powers (including essences), and behaviour, and treats social phenomena as reducible without residue to a biological substratum. It therefore shifts everything onto the nature side of the society/nature distinction and interprets our social being as purely animal-like. Strong social constructionism responds to biological reductionism by inverting this reduction, pulling everything onto the social side. In the case of sex-gender relations,

> [w]hilst providing an 'anti-essentialist' account of the body, social constructionist approaches propose such an arbitrary link between the body and sexual identity (sex-gender) that it is difficult to explain why it is a female body which is inscribed with an inferior feminine identity. (McNay, 1996)

Since they fail to challenge their enemy's mistaken belief that natural powers are deterministic rather than potentials and constraints, they can only defend a realm of social determination by excluding nature and positing a socially constructed realm in which biological constraints are either absent or inconsequential.

There has thus been a shift from criticisms of the naturalization of forms of social oppression to what seem to be attempts to write out nature as an extra-social or extra-discursive force altogether (Butler, 1989, 1994; Fuss, 1990; Foucault, 1978, p. 101)[33]. However, while anti-essentialism might appear to liberate those whose oppression has been legitimized by being represented as naturally grounded, if it also denies that we have any particular properties as human beings, as organic bodies, then it loses all critical purchase on any oppressive exercise of power, particularly through torture, mutilation or abuse (Soper, 1995a, p. 138). This is disastrous for emancipatory movements. For example, in

> denying that there are any instincts, needs, pleasures or sensations which are not simply the effects of culture but impose their own conditions upon its 'constructions', then it is difficult to see what sense we can make of the notion of feminist reclamations of the body or selfhood from the distorting and repressive representations to which they have been culturally subjugated. (Soper, 1995b: p. 23; see also her 1995a, Chapter 4).

While the humanist doctrine of ethical naturalism – that the nature of the good can be derived from our nature as human, social beings – does not adequately deal with the conventional or 'socially constructed' character of values and the striking diversity of cultural norms, a total rejection of it undermines any criticism of oppression because it cannot say *what* oppression is bad *for*, or what it does damage *to*. It does not help to refuse talk of nature as essentialist because it is not nature that is the main source of the problems which progressive movements oppose, but rather oppressive cultural practices which wrongly invoke nature in their defence (Soper, 1995a). Yet again, the peculiar enthusiasm of anti-essentialists for jumping from tackling limited substantive issues to acts of ontological vandalism generates absurdities.

It is not unreasonable to argue that some acts are wrong because they involve damage to biological and psychological powers which are important for human flourishing and happiness, or indeed for the flourishing of other species; for example, lobotomy or clitoridectomy can be argued to be wrong on the grounds that removing organs or parts of them deprives their victims of important biologically based capacities, which contribute to human flourishing and happiness. Moreover, harm can also be done to humans and other species not only by direct injury to their causal powers but by preventing the use of those of powers whose exercise is necessary for flourishing, as in the case of sensory deprivation or factory farming. While the exercise of these powers is invariably socially medi-ated, many of the powers are not themselves social constructions, and those that are presuppose biological powers in the way that talking requires a larynx.[34] If there is no biological substratum enabling us to feel pleasure or pain, then they become mere discursive constructions, things which we talk ourselves into believing we have, but which wouldn't 'exist' otherwise. But if this were the case we could equally persuade ourselves they don't exist through discursive denial. The torturer could claim that the pain he inflicts is merely discursive, socially constructed – and that therefore it can't be opposed by invoking damage to our biological powers. Thus, despite the fact that social constructionism is generally deployed in support of progressive causes, its support for them is weak and it could equally be used to justify reactionary and repressive practices. In fact, as Martha Nussbaum argues, if social science is to be critical of oppression, it must be essentialist insofar as it has to invoke common, extra-discursive human capacities for suffering (Nussbaum, 1992).

As our discussion of causality showed, those who wish to argue that the body has certain essential properties, or at least causal powers, do not need to suppose that this entails a one-to-one relationship between a single biological essence and a single kind of behaviour, without any social mediation or construction. We have many biological powers, they can be activated and mediated in a vast number of ways, and hence the range of sexualities and other activities of which people are capable is wide, but like any social constructions, behaviours draw partly upon non-social materials, including the body, and are constrained and enabled by their properties.

To account for nature-society relations in a way that avoids biological reduc-tionism without denying natural powers, we need firstly to disambiguate 'nature', and secondly to outline a 'stratified ontology'. Regarding the first, as Kate Soper argues, any useful discussion of what is natural needs to take note of the fact that two very different concepts of nature tend to be deployed in this context: one which treats humans and society as part of nature, and one which treats nature as apart from the human and the social. In the former, realist sense, 'nature' refers

> to the structures, processes and causal powers that are constantly operative in the phys-ical world, that provide the objects of study of the natural sciences, and condition the possible forms of human intervention in biology or human interaction with the envi-ronment. It is the nature to whose laws we are always subject, even as we harness them to human purposes, and whose processes we can neither escape nor destroy. (Soper, 1995a, pp. 155–6)

While this realist concept of nature is concerned with what is common to the human and non-human worlds, it is inadequate on its own for understanding how they differ. Here we need a different, 'metaphysical' concept, in which '"nature" is the concept through which humanity thinks its difference and specificity. It is the concept of the non-human ...' (Soper, 1995a, p. 155). It is therefore central to attempts to define the human, the artificial, the social and the cultural *in contrast* to nature. The metaphysical concept is always problematic if it is set up in simple and total opposition to the human for it then denies what the realist concept of nature highlights, and obscures the many ways in which humans have impacted on outer nature. However, as Soper argues, as long as we are interested in what is specific about human beings and their society, then we shall always need some version of the metaphysical concept.

To be able to understand the specificity of the social while acknowledging the validity of the realist concept of nature, we need to recognize how the social can be both dependent on and irreducible to – or emergent from – the material processes studied by the natural sciences (Bhaskar, 1979; Collier, 1994a). When certain objects combine, new emergent properties arise. Water itself has properties quite unlike those of its constituents; it is a product of two highly inflammable gases, yet can itself be used for extinguishing fire. Our brain cells are a necessary condition of our ability to think, but individual brain cells do not have this ability; thinking is an emergent property or power. Our thoughts and actions presuppose certain chemical transformations in our brains but are not reducible to them; in answering someone's question we are responding to the question not their brain chemistry. Thus, biological, chemical and physical powers are necessary conditions for the existence of the social world but the latter has properties – particularly, or 'essentially', communicative interaction and discourse, which are irreducible to or emergent from these ontological strata. If we couple this stratified ontology with a critical realist analysis of causation, in which, as we saw earlier, the existence of a causal power is not uniquely and deterministically linked to a particular outcome, then it becomes possible to see that the acknowledgement of a biological (and other physical) substratum of social life need not be seen as denying variety and agency at the social level.

Without an appreciation of emergence and the open nature of biological and social systems, and of the existence of two different concepts of nature, unsatisfactory resolutions of the relationship between the biological and the social are inevitable. Thus with regard to sexuality, it is certainly common for reactionary attitudes to be supported by claims about what is and isn't natural, as in the homophobic claim that homosexuality and lesbianism are 'unnatural', or 'crimes against nature'. But what are the best lines of argument against this? One strategy is to associate it with essentialism in the form of biological reductionism. Thus Sarah Franklin writes:

> What is 'essentialist' about this claim is, of course, the assumption that there is one essential form of human sexuality which is the only acceptable form of sexuality because it is the only natural expression of it. What is argued against this view is that human sexuality is not based on a 'natural' essence (for example, biologically determined) but is instead *socially constructed*, taking different formations in different cultural and historical contexts. (Franklin, 1993, p. 30, emphasis in original; see also Dollimore, quoted in Soper, 1995a).

However, a *consistent* essentialist – strong or moderate – is obliged to accept all human behaviours as consistent with nature in the realist sense. It is contradictory to argue that behaviour is biologically determined or influenced, and then turn round and say that some kinds of behaviour are nevertheless 'unnatural'; nothing that happens in the world can be 'unnatural'.[35] The huge diversity of social forms shows that the laws of nature are very permissive. But then if it is absurd to say that any behaviour of which people are capable is unnatural, it is also strange to say that something like sexuality is *not* natural or unnatural *but* socially constructed. It is *both* natural and socially constructed. More accurately, we could say that like any kind of social behaviour, sexuality presupposes biological powers but is emergent from them, and involves culturally specific (though contested) practices, norms and identities.

Of course, those who refer to behaviour as 'unnatural' are actually expressing a particularly unthinking kind of disapproval of it. In popular discourse, what is held to be 'unnatural' is actually merely 'unconventional', or rather a convention which some find unacceptable. Instead of illuminating the relationship between the biological and the social, social constructionism merely inverts biological reductionism, so that what is both social and within the bounds of nature in the realist sense is treated as a matter of convention having nothing to do with nature. Ironically, strong social constructionism inadvertently reproduces and revalidates the hierarchical dualisms of mind and body, reason and nature. There is no 'clean break' between the natural and the human or the social, the latter emerges from within nature in the realist sense but is not reducible to it; moreover, the social is not unique to humans (Benton, 1993).

Conclusion

To summarize: Anti-essentialists have attacked a diverse mix of targets; some of the criticism has been legitimate and some not. In view of this, anathematizing all these alleged ills under the same name is decidedly unhelpful, and what is needed is careful discrimination between them. 'Strong essentialism' is always wrong. There are many cases in social science and lay knowledge of misidentified generative powers and mistaken assumptions about the homogeneity and fixity of certain classes of people or practice, and such errors can be dangerous. Whether separately or in combination, these problems are often identified as problems of essentialism per se, thereby prohibiting all talk of generative powers or structures and all universals, when they would be better treated in less grandiose terms as particular mistaken conceptualisations. Misplaced essentialism is a common sin, but essentialism – at least the moderate, non-deterministic version – doesn't have to be misplaced, and indeed is often necessary for explanation and for *critical* social science. Moderate essentialists can acknowledge that some important social phenomena do not have essences, without concluding that nothing has an essence.

However, the concept of essence is, in any case, overly restrictive and we do not have to limit ourselves to choosing between an ontology of essences, or one of endless difference or ephemeral, entirely context-dependent, relational forms. We can retain a concept of generative or causal powers without assuming that such powers are necessarily essential in the sense of distinguishing their bearers from others. It would also not be inconsistent to acknowledge difference while retaining the concept of generative or causal powers. In rejecting strong essentialism's deterministic relation between causal powers and events and acknowledging contingency and emergence we can recognize that shared generative powers or essences vis-à-vis one set of possible behaviours (for example, our physical metabolism) is quite consistent with variety at another ontological level (for example, culture). While many specific accusations of (misplaced) essentialism are on target, there is no justification for dogmatic claims to know in advance that nothing can be explained by reference to essential properties or widely distributed structures, or universals.

Social science requires both the interpretation of meaning or discourse and causal explanation, and the two combine where reasons are causes or discourse is performative. There can be both sameness and difference and recognition of the former need not be merely a reluctant concession to political expedience, as in 'strategic essentialism'. Essentialists and realists can happily accept that knowledge and other social phenomena are socially constructed. However, 'strong' social constructionism is founded on an epistemic fallacy in confusing its social constructs or interpretations with their material products or referents, and in confusing researchers' constructions with those of the people they study. Its response to biological reductionism merely inverts it, replacing biological determinism with a social determinism, or, as Perry Anderson puts it, 'subjectivism without a subject' (cited in Soper, 1986, p. 142). Finally, we would be better off without kindred dogmas, such as that generalizing methodologies will always be wrong, that we can never have anything in common with our others, and that no needs could ever have any origin in universal human characteristics (Martin, 1994; Nussbaum, 1992).

Notes

1 I would suggest that Kate Soper's work also defends some versions of essentialism, though interestingly – perhaps as a matter of tactics – she avoids using the term essentialism (Soper, 1986; 1995b).

2 While they did not use the term 'essence', their search for a definition of the urban amounted to seeking the same thing.

3 For further discussion of both the general point and this particular example, see Sayer, 1995, Chapters 2 and 3. Note that acknowledging that capitalism could exist without patriarchy in no way implies that patriarchy is any less important a feature of social life than capitalism. This kind of structural analysis does not apply to discourse, though it may apply to discourse-dependent material, practices and artefacts.

4 I have avoided explaining this in terms of the distinction between necessary or internal relations and contingent or external relations (as in Sayer, 1992) because of the danger of a confusion between the two diametrically opposed meanings of 'contingent' as 'neither necessary nor impossible' and 'dependent'. Obviously it is *only* the first sense of the term that is relevant here.

5 For expositions of critical realism, see Bhaskar (1979); Collier (1994a); Sayer (1992); Stones (1996).

6 In view of this, it would not be absurd for an essentialist to complain about stereotyping of something with respect to its accidental features.

7 For a different, but compatible kind of moderate or weak essentialism, see O'Neill (1994).

8 At the same time, Fuss argues that essentialism cannot be entirely avoided. However, she sees it as always problematic.

9 Whether friendship and master-slave relations are good examples of relational essences is, of course, debatable, but the argument of this paper does not depend on it.

10 Ontological arguments are not transhistorical and prior to substantive sciences and lay knowledges, but are always dependent on them (Bhaskar, 1979).

11 Judith Butler inverts this equation of essentialism with foundationalism by opposing 'foundationalism' which 'presumes, fixes and constrains the very "subjects" that it hopes to represent and liberate' (Butler, 1989 p. 148). In other words, she terms what we call essentialism, foundationalism.

12 Another reason for dismissals of realism probably derives from the recent influence on some social science of literary criticism, which has a different usage of the term. *Literary* realism, unlike *critical* realism, is equivalent to 'empiricism' and 'foundationalism' in that it assumes the real can be directly or immediately accessible.

13 Thus, despite Haraway's professed rejection of 'realism', her discussion of objectivity and the situated and perspectival nature of knowledge is compatible with *critical* realism, and indeed helps develop it (Haraway, 1991; see also Stones, 1996).

14 For a similar distinction between strong and moderate or weak social constructionism, see Dittmar (1992) and Dickens (1996). For a critique of strong social constructionism in psychology, see Greenwood (1994).

15 See Geras' critique of Laclau and Mouffe regarding their attempt to acknowledge an external reality and to assert that objects are discursively constituted (Geras, 1990).

16 Although anti-essentialism as an ontological doctrine and social constructionism are often allied together, the former need not entail the latter. The belief that nothing has any fixed essence and that everything is always contextually and relationally determined, does not entail that the world is a social construction or that objects are discursively constructed, though of course some might be.

17 Though, of course, in practice, its implied triumphalism would fail because of its denial of the independent powers of nature.

18 As we saw in Chapter 2, the history of natural science shows a succession of attempts to define the essences of minerals, and there is no reason to believe that further definitions will not be added in future.

19 In her *tour de force* on nature and sexual politics, Kate Soper illustrates the contradictions generated by the vocabulary of 'construction' or 'production' of bodies in Foucault and others (Soper, 1995a). The existence of situations intermediate between interpretation and material change or construction, such as when a new interpretation prompts new kinds of action, does not mean that there is no difference between the two, any more than dusk requires us to abandon the distinction between day and night.

20 Gellner's critique was directed against the generation of idealist social science that preceded social constructionism – interpretivism, but is equally salutary now.

21 Note how common it is to discuss signifier and signified while ignoring the referent or eliding the difference between signified and referent (Assiter, 1997).

22 I am aware that Derrida's statement that 'there is nothing outside the text' should not to be taken as a denial of an extra-discursive realm.

23 Even something as contestable as identity is unlikely to be wholly unrelated to often fairly stable material circumstances. The body can function as a text, but the meanings of the text often have something to do with the nature of the (extra-discursive) body; why else does the sight of large, calloused hands with swollen joints make us assume their owner has had a life of hard, manual labour? People can contest their identity discursively but if their material situation including their social relations remains the same, the claimed new identity might reasonably be said to be spurious. You can proclaim yourself free when in fact you are still in chains: not all social constructions work out.

24 A concern with differentiation, if not with certain versions of 'difference', has no necessary connection to social constructionism. A social constructionist could, without contradiction, claim that there were just a few simple, internally homogenous classes of socially-constructed object, like 'man' or 'woman'. Conversely, an essentialist could

accept that objects come in a vast variety of types (for example, the huge range of ethnicities) while still believing that each type had its own essence.

25 For example, Barry Hindess's rejection of essentialism assumes that it can only mean that the mere existence of essences is sufficient to produce particular effects (Hindess, 1987, p. 149). Bhaskar terms this assumption of a one-to-one relationship between causal powers and effects 'actualism'.

26 (Harré and Madden, 1975; Bhaskar, 1979, Sayer, 1992) Aristotelians have a similar account of causation which also avoids determinism (O'Neill, 1994).

27 The erosion of the boundary between organism and technology presents no problems for this kind of realist analysis, but rather presupposes these points.

28 Similarly quaint is the idea that causal concepts must be teleological. Possession of a causal power does not mean that it necessarily will eventually be exercised, or if it is exercised, that it will not be modified or blocked by other mechanisms.

29 Nor need the lack of satisfactory causal accounts of certain complex phenomena, such as catastrophes in complex systems, prompt us to deny causality; as Andrew Collier puts it, unanswered causal questions are just that, not necessarily evidence of the absence of causality (Collier, 1994a, 127).

30 As with any causes, reasons, particularly as dispositions, may be unexercised. When they are exercised, their effects may be modified or nullified by other mechanisms. That reasons can be causes is presupposed by the distinction between the real reasons and the imagined reasons for an action, for in describing them as the real reasons we can only mean they are the causally efficacious reasons, as distinct from professed but non-efficacious reasons (Bhaskar, 1991).

31 Note the ironic similarity between 'repetitivity' and behaviourist conditioning.

32 Or as Sartre put it, 'man is the being whose essence is to have no essence'. This point, though with labour as the prime enabling force, is also central to Marx's conception of human nature.

33 When cross-examined in interview Butler acknowledges the existence of biological limitations but with an extraordinary reluctance to concede that anything follows from this (Butler, 1994).

34 Of course it may be possible to construct artificial substitutes for organs such as the larynx, but these too would be social constructions constrained and enabled by the (non-social) essential powers of the materials used. The point is that a material substratum is still needed whether we classify it as organic or inorganic.

35 Of course, when this inconsistency is pointed out, homophobes generally find other justifications for their prejudices.

PART III
SOCIAL SCIENCE AND SPACE

Introduction

Throughout the greater part of the history of social science, space has generally been ignored or left implicit in both social theory and empirical research, while time has received rather more attention, evident in recurrent concern over the relationship of theory and history (Soja, 1989). One of the main developments in social theory in the last 20 years has been a growing recognition of the significance of space in social life (Giddens, 1984; Gregory and Urry, 1985). Where once such concerns were relegated to human geography and treated as if they could be ignored by the other social sciences, it has now become common, especially in sociology, to attempt to make it an integral concern of theory and empirical research. Of course, such developments are not unrelated to social changes within academia, particularly the rise of human geography from its former lowly status, which was no doubt connected to its lack of distance from the concrete and the mundane. Where once, anything to do with geographical space would have been dismissed by avant garde theory, it is now a common matter of concern in the latter, at least when discussed in the abstract.[1] For example, Foucault's analysis of power in *Discipline and Punish* places considerable emphasis on the structuring of space, the control of bodily movements, and visual surveillance, in disciplining people (Foucault, 1977).

One of the peculiarities of the literature on space and social theory is the persistence of attempts to write about this topic in the abstract when such discussions appear to be able to yield rather little beyond concepts like space-time compression and locale, and sensitizing researchers to take it into account in concrete studies. There have been numerous attempts to develop spatial social theory which find it difficult to get beyond repeated *mentions* of space, without being able to say much about what social spaces are like in terms of their spatial form or configuration.

Rather than add to this literature, my aim in Chapter 5 is to illuminate why it cannot get as far as it would obviously like to. This requires an analysis of the nature of physical space – at once ordinary and obvious and yet difficult and elusive. As to the question of whether space or geography is important to social life, I argue in effect that the answer is yes and no. In some respects, it is absolutely vital, in others it doesn't make much difference.

While Chapter 5 is primarily concerned with what can be said about space in the abstract, Chapter 6 is about the problems of concrete geohistorical syntheses. These became popular in the 1980s, with the rise of locality studies and a 'new' regional geography, provoking much debate about methodology. For some, these developments signalled an abandonment of theory for empiricism, while others saw them as self-consciously theoretically informed enterprises. There are echoes here of the old debate between idiographic and nomothetic approaches to the study of society, but I shall argue that realist philosophy enables this dualism to be transcended, and also offers insights into the related issue of the relative merits of narrative and analysis.

At the time the original version of this chapter was written, there was an emerging concern in a number of disciplines, particularly anthropology, with narrative and the construction of texts, and also with rhetoric. For the first time questions were being raised about the implications of the textual character of social scientific knowledge. Although many of the discussions of these issues have been anti-realist, realists such as Rob Stones and Uskali Mäki have argued that concerns about textuality and rhetoric are not necessarily incompatible with realism. Here I discuss the formidable problems posed by works of geohistorical synthesis for the construction of texts, for dealing with things happening at the same time in different places, and, in Marx's terms, for demonstrating how the concrete is a unity of diverse determinations.

Note

1 Here I am alluding to the usual Bourdieuian correlation between status and abstraction.

5

Space and Social Theory

For some years there have been calls for a convergence of the interests of history and social science, and critiques of the neglect of time in social theory (for example, Abrams, 1982; Adam, 1990; Bourdieu, 1977; Giddens, 1984). Recently, similar arguments have been made regarding the relationship of social science to geography and the former's neglect of space. Human geographers have insisted that the spatiality of society is not simply an output of social processes but is constitutive of social forms themselves and hence makes a significant difference to the nature of societies (for example, Gregory, 1985; Massey, 1984, 1996; Massey and Allen, 1985; Soja, 1985, 1989; Thrift, 1983, 1997). This kind of argument has been reciprocated in sociology in Giddens' integration of spatial concepts into social theory and in his call for a materialism that is not only historical but geographical (Giddens 1984; Urry, 1987, 1996). This raises the question of whether most social theory is flawed by its abstraction from space and needs to be thoroughly reworked (Soja, 1989).

One of the most striking manifestations of the discovery of the importance of space is in the peculiarly belated questioning of what the social sciences take to mean by 'societies'. With surprisingly little justification, it had generally been assumed that 'society' meant – or at least corresponded to – 'nation state'. In an increasingly interdependent world, this assumption has become ever more misleading (Urry, 1996). It is not only a matter of recognizing that different societies influence one another, but that their relationship to particular spaces has been increasingly disrupted. Thus, class is not an unproblematically national phenomenon – likewise gender and ethnicity: there are internationally determined social class, gender and ethnic relations *within* a nation state, such is the interdependence between local and global processes (Urry, 1996; Massey, 1996).

In this chapter, I want to discuss in what respects social science has to be spatially or geographically aware. To what extent is social theory undermined by its traditional disregard of space? What *kind* of difference does space make? To what extent does the need for historical specificity have to be supplemented by geographical specificity? On the face of it, the answers to these questions seem paradoxical, for while it is easy to find examples of practices in which space makes a crucial difference, it is not clear that existing social theory is greatly compromised by its abstraction from space. Ironically, those who have argued most strongly for a major revision of social theory along these lines have found it difficult to say much that is specific about space in their reworkings of social theory (for example, Soja, 1989; Harvey, 1989; Lefebvre, 1991). This, I shall argue, is not a deficiency on their part but an inevitable consequence of the nature of space. At the same time, the vagueness of the spatial content of this reworked social theory should not be taken as implying that it lacks importance.

My answers to these questions are informed by realist concepts of natural necessity, causal powers, stratification and emergence, which can assist enormously in the clarification of the difference that space makes. I shall begin by highlighting the tendency to abstract from space and the dangers therein. Next, I shall develop some tools for evaluating these dangers by discussing the nature of physical space and the different ways it is involved in social processes. Then follows a discussion of space in theory and empirical research, concentrating particularly on attempts to develop theories of the spatiality of capitalism and modernity and the dangers of 'spatial fetishism' or 'separatism.' The chapter ends with an evaluation of the need for geographical, as well as historical, specificity in social theory.

The Abstraction from Space

Social scientists are generally unaware of the extent to which they abstract from space. This is evident not only in the absence of references to space in the work of economists, sociologists, political scientists, anthropologists and so on, but in a common attitude towards what human geographers do. According to this view, geographers have a particular – and perhaps peculiar – interest in looking at the spatial dimension of phenomena, as if that were a mere by-product of the key social processes, a secondary dimension one can 'add on' if one is so inclined, but as inessential to social science. However it would be more correct to say that the spatial dimension is first removed by aspatial social science, for of course space is there in the first place: the concrete is always already spatial.

In some cases, the abstraction from space has serious consequences, in others, not. One of the most telling examples in the former category is the theory of perfect competition in economics – already widely attacked for its abstraction from historical time. Of course, as economists in particular are wont to point out in their defence, we proceed by the power of our abstractions, but such an argument serves to conceal a lack of concern about *how* one should abstract. Abstraction has to be sensitive to the structure of its objects if it is not to make a nonsense of their explanation. Economists generally treat the theory of competition in space as a minor accessory of little interest. Yet competition always takes place between actors and across markets that are spatially extended. When this is recognized, the aspatial perfect competition model is transformed into a model of central places in which sellers have spatial monopolies, thus inverting the lessons of the model. It is perfect competition that should be considered as a curiosity, not spatial competition theory.

At the same time as there are these dramatic examples of the difference that space makes, there are others where the abstraction from space does only minor damage. Consider research on patriarchy and technology in employment, such as that of Cockburn (1983, 1985); it is not clear that the failure to say much about the internal spatial organization of the workplace or its setting in a particular area or region detracts much from its value. An intermediate case of moderate damage resulting from abstracting from space is the theory of the circulation of capital, as in Volume 2 of Marx's *Capital*. Naturally the circulation of capital requires the spatial interlinking of the various activities involved, and their degree of proximity will affect the time economies so vital to capital accumulation. But while it may be useful to remember this, and to go on to consider that the achievement of time economies promotes spatial integration, and vice versa, such points do not undermine the theory in the way that the perfect competition model is undermined by its abstraction from space and time. The implication of these examples then is that the violence done by abstracting from space varies from fatal to minor. We could take such questioning further: for example, just how much of a problem is the fact that, say, Max Weber, Jurgen Habermas, Donna Haraway, Claus Offe, Ulrich Beck, Nancy Fraser, or any number of theorists have very little to say about space? How much we decide 'geography matters' should depend on answers to such questions, that is, on substantial arguments; the answers should not depend on disciplinary loyalties.[1]

The Nature of Space

To make sense of these puzzles we need to consider more carefully what is meant by 'space'.

At the outset, let me make it clear that I am addressing *physical* space, and that, while it may be useful to talk metaphorically of psychological space or social distance, this is not the same thing (Lefebvre, 1991, p. 3ff). By 'social space' I therefore mean the subset of physical space that is colonized, reproduced and transformed by human societies. As material beings, people and their relationships are not outside space but are themselves spatial: they have spatial extension. It is also possible and indeed important to note that our views of space (including those outside social space) are always socially mediated interpretations, and that we routinely change and construct spaces, but both the interpretations and constructions are *of* physical space. I will not say much about the existential or expressive aspects of space, about such matters as the experience of space, the attachment to place, etc. (see Pickles, 1986; Simonsen, 1991; Massey, 1996). This does not reflect any judgment upon their importance, just a wish to focus on problems of inadequate concepts of (social) physical space.

In everyday life, as in science before Einstein, space is treated as absolute, as an empty container defined by a coordinate system. But what is empty is nothing, and what is nothing cannot be (Blaut, 1963). According to the relative concept, on the other hand, space is constituted by matter. All matter has spatial extension, possibly a certain capacity for mobility, and sometimes a particular shape or geometry as a necessary condition of it being that kind of thing. What happens to things – whether they change or remain stable – depends on their relations to other (spatially extended) things or processes located around them. Space only exists through its constituents and there is no friction of distance in terms of some abstract, immaterial metric, only frictions of particular substances. Although our language can only denote it through three separate words, space-time-matter form a single whole; to talk of just one of these is to abstract – perhaps unknowingly – from the other two. Usually we refer to objects or processes without making their spatial and temporal dimensions explicit, thereby avoiding clumsy locutions. Likewise, inverting the abstraction and referring only to space or time – as in 'I haven't got time', or 'I don't have room' – can, in context, be quite harmless. But these seemingly innocuous features of our language invite misconceptions too. The difficulty of deciding whether someone is using the word 'space' in a way that implies the possibility of it existing independently of process (and hence implying an absolute concept of space) or merely as a short-hand for space-time-process, makes it particularly difficult for even the debate on space to be conducted. To uncover the problems we need to look more formally at physical space.

First, there are well-known contrasts between space and time: time has only a single dimension, while space has three; movements are reversible in space,[2] but time is irreversible; and while many things can exist at the same time, two things cannot exist in the same place at the same time (the property of physical exclusivity). Any social science which conceptualizes its objects in ways which contradict these properties – like neoclassical economics, for example – is taking serious risks.

Now consider the following letters:

ABC

A, B and C stand in a spatial relationship. Whatever A, B and C are, they constitute a spatial form. Without substances such as those denoted by A, B or C, there is no space. Yet we cannot say that this or any other spatial form has any material effects, or makes any difference until we know what kinds of things, with what causal powers or liabilities, A, B or C are. Thus (pre-1989), if we knew that B was the Berlin Wall and A and C the two Germanys, then the spatial relation of 'betweenness' in which B stood would have some material significance. Of course, there are many other spatial forms or relations besides that of betweenness, but whatever the form, and however complex it is, the same conclusions follow.

However it is also essential to appreciate that, although space only exists through its constituents, it is not reducible to them; ABC is not the same as:

B
A C

even though the constituents are identical.

So spatial form arises through the relations between (and within) the constituents of space. Whether causal powers are activated, and with what effects, depends upon their context or conditions, that is, upon the objects (and their causal powers) with which they are in contact, and this in turn depends upon spatial form. Hence, *pace* Peet (1998, p. 176), space certainly matters for critical realism. This is also why scientific experimentation involves such attention to the spatial configuration of its objects. Note that this does not imply, as Sheppard (1996) claims, that causal powers can only be activated or mediated by their immediate surroundings; action at a distance via information or other flows is also possible provided there are intervening media through which they can exert influence.

The above has implications for the way in which we should talk about space in social science. Some writers, such as Castells in his early work on urbanism, sprinkled their texts with the word 'space', creating the impression that they were saying a great deal about it, but in fact saying very little about actual spatial configurations (Castells, 1977). Without further specification, such references at best merely served as a reminder that cities had spatial extension. It may indeed be useful, given the tendency to forget space and treat society as if it existed on the head of a pin, to be reminded that social objects such as cities or households have spatial configurations, spatial extension, mobility, location and areal differentiation, but unless we say something *about* those aspects and their spatial configuration they amount to little other than a list of categories to be filled in by empirical research. This has been a recurrent hazard in writing about society and space, as is indicated by the continuing stream of articles on social theory which begin and end with token references to the importance of space but fail to say anything much about it in between. Space *is* certainly important, but to say what that importance consists in, we normally have to move to a more concrete kind of analysis where we identify particular kinds of objects, relations and processes constituting it in concrete spatial conjunctures.

We can now identify more clearly the dangers of abstraction from the unity of space-time-process. In abstracting substance or process from space and time, it is tempting to imagine that there are 'aspatial processes', thereby neglecting a necessary property of matter that it has spatial extension and physical exclusivity. Conversely, regarding the abstraction of space from process, there is the danger of attributing powers to space (whether in terms of geometry, distance, location or movement) regardless of the causal powers of the objects constituting it. This has been termed spatial fetishism or separatism. (There is clearly an equivalent possibility of temporal fetishism, which attributes causal powers to the passage of time, irrespective of the nature of the processes involved.)

Spatial fetishism has done considerable damage in social science. In development studies, the substitution of spatial terms like 'centre' and 'periphery' for conceptualizations which comprehend the unity of space-time-process is a case in point. Although the spatially peripheral is often functionally peripheral and the spatially central often functionally central, they don't have to be. Thus, peripheral branch plants of multinationals are not necessarily any less vital to the survival of those firms than ones in the centre, in the metropolitan countries. It has also been common to say that one area or country exploits another, but this can be mystifying in that it obscures the fact that it is particular classes, institutions or individuals in one area which exploit those in another area. (See Slater, 1989, for a fuller discussion of this problem in development studies.) Note that under the second conceptualization, it is still perfectly possible, and indeed desirable, to recognize that the particular spatial relationship in which the actors stand makes a difference to their interaction.

It may help to appreciate the problems of integrating space-time-substance if we go back to an important formulation developed by Robert Sack (1980). In his *Conceptions of Space in Social Thought*, he suggests that, normally, we first abstract substance (or process) from space and then 'recombine' them. But we often recombine them in a way which fails to match the processes of interest to their relevant spatial form, like taking a machine to bits and then putting it back together wrongly so that we cannot see how it should work. The causal structure of the concrete situation is therefore 'scrambled' and obscured. Important relations can be severed and others subsumed under extraneous material, as when class is subsumed under area. Thus dependency theory had the advantage of using an implicit space-substance recombination which recognized rather than severed relationships of dependency between countries, but at the same time, tended to conceal class relations *within* underdeveloped areas.

As we noted at the outset, even those social scientists who are indifferent to space tend to include it inadvertently by recombining their social phenomena of interest with space at the level of the nation state. Although the nation state is an important social institution in its own right (and one whose territoriality is particularly vital), it is rarely asked whether some other spatial resolution or recombination might be more germane for the processes of interest, whether supranational (in the case of economic development) or subnational (for example, for labour market analysis). Thus, welfare programmes directed at a particular subgroup of households are sometimes targetted at certain areas such as inner cities, even though the correspondence between the distribution of households for whom the expenditure is intended and the designated area is only very approximate. Even where other, less coarse, recombinations of space and substance are used, there are often still serious mismatches. Nor is it simply a case of finding a single appropriate level of resolution or 'spatial container', for social processes at different scales are frequently interdependent. As the globalization literature stresses, local and global processes are increasingly articulated in complex patterns that defy resolution into neatly segregated and nested sets of spaces. Thus, in studying a firm operating in a particular locality, one might have to take account of a hierarchy of spaces ranging from the plant itself, through the local labour market, the local and regional administrative bodies affecting the firm, the national context at which most regulations binding the firm hold, and the international context of a global market and supranational institutions, such as the World Trade Organisation. But there are also processes cutting across such hierarchies – relationships with particular suppliers, customers or competitors in other countries that shape what is going on in any particular place. The relevant space for studying a branch plant of an electronics firm in Scotland might therefore include Palo Alto (California), Penang (Malaysia), Tokyo and Barcelona (see for example, Morgan and Sayer, 1988).

While it is easy to criticize inaccurate space-substance recombinations in principle, it is often difficult to avoid a certain degree of 'spatial approximation' in practice. Consider the case of labour markets. The idea of a single national labour market is a highly misleading recombination of space and substance since it 'scrambles' demand-supply relations disastrously, and produces a statistical artefact which might have a descriptive use but little else. The ideal level of resolution for explaining events in labour markets would be that of spatially determinant individual workers and individual jobs or vacancies, for the unique spatial location of each will influence outcomes. But as it would rarely be practicable to eliminate aggregation and scrambling totally, we usually compromise and aggregate (or disaggregate down from the national level) into labour market areas. In other words, we make it possible to allow for just some of the difference that space makes. In these circumstances, all that can be expected of quantitative analyses is approximation. As increasing mobility, spatial interdependence and complexity churn up formerly relatively neatly segregated geographical spaces, so that particular places cannot be identified with single types of people or activity, the dangers of inaccurate space-substance recombinations increase. For example, as globalizing processes develop, identifying places with particular ethnic groups increasingly misrepresents the complexity of their constitutive relations. The recent popularity of metaphors of networks and flows in sociology and human geography is an attempt to avoid the misrepresentations of simplistic identifications between areas and social groups or activities and find a way of thinking about them that is both more relational and spatially complex (Thrift, 1997).

Space and Society

Having explicated the dialectics of physical space, we can now outline various senses in which space or geography matters in social science. To save unwieldy constructions, I shall henceforth use 'space' as a short-hand for '*spatial form of relevant objects*', and 'institutions' as a short-hand for '*social relations, structures, processes or objects*'.

Space and the Constitution of Social Phenomena

The spatio-temporal situation of people and resources affects the very nature or constitution of social phenomena. In turn, the effects of actions are influenced by the content and form of their external settings or contexts. The constitutive property of space can work in two ways, often in conjunction: in terms of material preconditions of actions, and in terms of their constitutive meanings.

A good example of the role of space in the material constitution of institutions is that of capital. As part of its conditions of existence, capital needs to bring together a labour force and the necessary plant and equipment. These are not ubiquitous and their presence in the right place is a condition of existence of capital. If they are at hand, the form of their spatial organization of the firm's business can have a major impact on the success of the firm. Thus, Fordism and later the just-in-time system of production are essentially highly rationalized ways of resolving space-time coordination problems. The existence of capital is also dependent on access to buyers who again are often located elsewhere: unless they can be reached, capital cannot be reproduced.[3]

Similarly, the reproduction of households requires that their members can regularly complete certain tasks, given the spatio-temporal form of relevant resources and constraints. As parents of young children are only too aware, this can be far from straightforward; often a certain local opportunity, such as a job vacancy, cannot be taken up because of space-time coupling constraints arising through interdependencies with other people (for example, who will pick up the children from school?) (Hägerstrand, 1985). Here the constitutive aspect of space works in terms of both material conditions and meanings. Thus, the separation of parents indicates a change in the meaning of their relationship.

In some cases, space-time coupling problems can come to threaten the repro-duction of certain institutions. One of the reasons why apartheid crumbled was that it had become increasingly difficult to maintain the spacing and timing of processes necessary for its functioning. Restricting the black population of South Africa to the 'homelands' lowered their costs of reproduction and hence main-tained a cheap labour force to support the white minority and urban industry and services, but the spatial separation between these spheres also created growing problems in the daily functioning of South Africa's cities.

Settings and Context-Dependence
We noted earlier that the effects of the operation of mechanisms are always mediated by the conditions in which they operate, hence the importance of experimentation in natural science for controlling the production of events. In the same way, space makes a difference in terms of settings or contexts, for while institutions have spatial extension and perhaps a particular shape and degree of mobility, they also are set in a spatial relation to other objects: social processes do not occur *tabula rasa* but always 'take place' within an inherited space con-stituted by different processes and objects, each of which have their own spatial extension, physical exclusivity and configuration. This is one of the consequences of the open character of social systems and most physical systems. Marx's famous dictum that people make their own history but not in circumstances of their own choosing should be understood to include inherited spatial settings. Insofar as these make a difference, theories of particular processes cannot be expected to anticipate much about the spatial form that they will assume. Conse-quently when an institution changes setting, its effects are usually modified. Alternatively, if it is to get the same effects in a new place, it has to change. For instance, industrial management methods, such as Fordism or Toyotism, origi-nated in response to particular settings, but tend to work differently when adopted in new places: hence the problems of exporting Japanese management methods.

More broadly, the issue of settings puts in question social theory's traditional abstraction from context, which allows it to produce accounts of 'normal' capi-talism, industrial society, patriarchy or whatever, on the basis of particular (usu-ally Western European/North American) variants of these. In looking at other cases, say Japanese capitalism, western theorists might initially be tempted to marginalize them as special cases, but the implication we should draw is that cases which are more familiar to western theorists are no less context-dependent. Thus, for example, we are led to ask just how much of what has been taken to be characteristic of capitalism per se is a consequence of the Western European/North American) context. Nevertheless, if we distinguish between 'capitalism' as a concrete social formation, and 'capital' as an abstraction identifying its key constitutive elements, we could argue that the latter is common to all capitalisms, so that while our account of concrete capitalism always has to be geohistorically located, the abstract account of capital does not.

One of the main lessons of attempts to theorize the spatiality has been the recognition of the 'spatial flexibility' of most actors and institutions, that is, their ability to maintain their integrity and operate in a variety of different settings. Reductionist accounts which suppose that one could 'read off' particular spatial forms from theories of substantive processes or institutions underestimate this flexibility. For instance, the New International Division of Labour thesis implies that its particular spatial forms are the only possible outcomes of contemporary capital accumulation (Fröbel et al., 1979). Yet, the spatiality of capitalism, or indeed of most social institutions, is enormously flexible and varied; in a sense they have a certain context-*in*dependence.

The strongest case for context-dependence can be made in relation to the way in which the spacing, timing or setting of actions is constitutive of their meaning; practices have a particular time and a place, as is indicated by the concept of front and back regions. As always, such spatial divisions are enabling as well as constraining, and agency depends upon actors having a practical command of such spacings; our posture and the position we take up within a room can signal our social position and relation to others, be it one of respect and deference or domination and condescension, be it one of opposition or solidarity (cf. Connerton, 1989). Space is also gendered. Occupying a particular space and time can be a way of claiming a gendered identity, as in the case of working class adolescent boys' claim to the freedom of the streets. And being in the 'wrong' place or time can therefore challenge gender roles themselves (the lone woman in the pub). Finally, there is an obvious symbolism of space in the positioning of buildings and the construction of our entire 'built enviroment'.

Hence the manipulation of space-time contexts is an important aspect of social behaviour because it makes a difference to the meaning of action; an action performed at the wrong time and place is liable to be misunderstood, not noticed or seen as threatening. In some cases, most obviously ritual and dance, spatio-temporal synchronization of actions are very tightly defined (see Bourdieu, 1977). However, the spatial specificity of actions should not be exaggerated. There are many types of action whose meaning is fairly stable across a range of different forms and contexts, and indeed communication itself involves sharing meaning across different contexts (Bhaskar, 1979). Language cannot be totally context-dependent, otherwise units of meaning couldn't be re-used and recombined in so many ways; even indexical terms like 'here' and 'now' can be applied and understood transcontextually.[4] Yet neither is language wholly independent of context, for we rarely find ourselves in situations where we can say anything we like and expect to be understood (Bloch, 1989, p. 39).

The role of space in the constitution of meaningful action involves a process of reciprocal confirmation between actors' concepts (usually as part of their practical, rather than their discursive consciousness) and the order built into their material practices and products, including the environment they inherit and construct. Thus, a person's place confirms their social position, which in turn justifies their place. Pre-eminent in theorizing this reciprocal process has been Pierre Bourdieu, whose analysis of the significance of the spacing and timing of action in Kabyle society in his *Outline of a Theory of Practice* has been widely cited. Consider a typical passage:

> All the divisions of the group are projected at every moment into the spatio-temporal organization which assigns each category its place and time: it is here that the fuzzy logic of practice works wonders in enabling the group to achieve as much social and logical integration as is compatible with the diversity imposed by the division of labour between the sexes, the ages, and the occupations. (Bourdieu, 1977, p. 163)

Brilliant though this study is, we should recognize the special nature of the object before attempting to emulate it – a society in which social integration figures very much more prominently relative to system integration than in our own. As Bourdieu himself notes in the final chapter of the book, once the economy of money transactions comes to take precedence over the economy of symbolic exchange, and system integration dominates social integration, the need for highly regulated timings and spacings of actions weakens, as the interdependencies between people in the division of labour become looser and more functional. Money allows us to choose with whom we exchange and provides a store of value across space and time. But while on the exchange-value side, synchronization in time and space becomes looser, on the use-value side, the production of material goods and services across an extraordinarily complex division of labour requires the resolution of time-space coupling problems on an unprecedented scale. Greater synchronization of activities is needed for the timing and spacing of flows of people and goods, which in turn require the development of standardized clock time (Simmel, 1965; Thompson, 1967; Thrift, 1990). Where synchronization exists primarily for reasons of enforcing unity and conformity among the Kabyle, it exists for instrumental reasons of economy and profit under capitalism. Amid the creative destruction of capitalism, there are many more mismatches between the spatial and temporal codes of practical logic and their settings than among the Kabyle. The modernist experience is one in which the objective results of our daily practice frequently do not fully match and confirm our practical logic or practical taxonomies; arguably, being 'out of place' is consequently not so unusual, or so significant, as in pre-modern societies. Therefore, while it is fascinating to follow the intimate and intricate synchronization and sequencing of actions and the reciprocal relationships between identities, social relations and space and time among the Kabyle, we cannot expect to do for capitalist society what Bourdieu has done for the Kabyle. It is also consequently not surprising that Bourdieu's work on contemporary French society is far less specific about space (Bourdieu, 1984, 1988).[5]

Two lessons regarding space can therefore be drawn from Bourdieu. Firstly, as he is at pains to show, although traditional societies are often rendered by anthropologists as texts inscribed within the spacing and timing of actions, the open-ended, contingent and unexamined character of actions in time reminds us that this rendering is a misleading form of objectification produced by an academic spectator's point of view – one which tends to treat such actions retrospectively as products of a text-like discursive consciousness. Regular spacings and timings should instead be seen as precarious achievements.

Secondly, the dangers of such a characterization are all the more glaring where modern societies are concerned for while spatial form can still be constitutive of the meaning of actions, the meanings for actors are even less inscribed into their geography.

We can now introduce a further distinction – between 'dependence on context' and 'dependence on spatial setting'. A high degree of context-dependence need not mean that practices are dependent on very limited and limiting spatial forms. In order to do my job, I need certain specific contextual conditions, but the spatial arrangement of those conditions is quite flexible. One of the most important features of human beings (and other animals) is our flexibility, the ability to do to do the same kinds of things in many different settings. Although we need certain resources (but can often find substitutes), the precise relative location of actor or institution to their settings can vary, sometimes quite widely, without making a big difference to the way they work. Often, therefore, while we need to take note of context-dependence it is sometimes quite safe to abstract from the precise spatial form of those contexts – which, of course, is what social scientists do much of the time. Even geographers do it, for though one can say, in principle, that the precise spatial form makes some difference, in practice, it is often difficult to say what that difference is. In some cases it may be trivial. However, this is clearly double-edged. On the one hand this flexibility implies that many variations in spatial form can be coped with easily, thus implying that the difference space makes is of minor importance. On the other hand, the very fact of this flexibility, this ability to adapt, acknowledges the difference that space makes – otherwise flexiblity would not be needed.

I now want briefly to comment on a number of common spatial features of societies, especially modern ones.

Space-Time Distanciation   If we consider the broad evolution of the spatial organization of societies historically, one of the most significant features is the stretching or 'time-space distanciation' of activities, enabled by the development of literacy, money, division of labour, telecommunications and so on (Giddens, 1984). This has by no means merely been a passive output of social change, rather it was often actively pursued, as in the case of imperialism, and the way it has allowed the extension of system integration relative to social integration has been a crucial and irreducible element in the development of societies. Thus, for the business historian Alfred Chandler, one of the most important causes and consequences of the rise of the large firm in the USA was its ability to stretch and synchronize activities across space (Chandler, 1977).

Note that although this kind of dramatic time-space distanciation might appear to reduce the power of agency, as structures become ever larger, agency gains a longer reach too, only with the result that often more of the consequences become hidden. The ever increasing distance between cause and effect in so many aspects of human activity increases the obstacles to the recognition of its social and eco-logical implications.

Time-space distanciation has been accompanied by what Harvey terms 'time-space compression' (Harvey, 1989). At the extreme, instantaneous transmission across space transforms processes formerly associated with nation and locality, incorporating them into global processes. As postmodernist theorists have spec-ulated, the resulting collages of images and information relating to things at different times and places which bombard individuals (at least those in rich coun-tries) could dissolve any sense of individual identity (Urry, 1996).

AREAL DIFFERENTIATION   Another major aspect of spatiality lies in the significance of areal differentiation, be it between nations, regions or in the microgeography of daily life. Here it is vital to question the tacit assumption that societies are simple unitary objects corresponding to nations. Precisely because, as Mann (1990, p. 4) reminds us, societies are much messier than our theories of them, because they consist of overlapping and articulated institutions existing at a num-ber of scales, areal differentiation must be treated as constitutive of societies. Yet concerns like regional differences are commonly regarded again as secondary. Several false grounds commonly underlie such thinking: the view that the parts are somehow less real than the whole; the dubious belief that the internal struc-ture of the whole is irrelevant to its behaviour; or the idea that the characteristics of the parts are merely deviations from the national norm, when in fact the national picture may merely be a statistical artefact, a product of an inappropriate recombination of space and substance. But as we saw earlier, this is not simply a question of choosing lower levels of resolution, for the relevance of neat, nested hierarchies of nations, regions and subregions has been radically undermined or disorganized by globalization processes.

There is a further problem in disregarding areal differentiation, for abstracting from space can also suppress the recognition of difference or 'otherness'. While one could, of course, recognize difference (for example, in ethnicity) in abstrac-tion from the spatial form it takes, such an abstraction might still suppress signi-ficant differences in the experience between places. There are always many things going on at once in different social spaces, and they usually differ consid-erably, often because of their positioning relative to other processes.[6] This multi-plicity of different (but interrelated) histories creates huge problems for any narrative of society, whether lay or social scientific, as we show in the next chapter. What often happens is that a single account is given of a whole social space, be it a household, a city, a region, a nation or the globe, in which certain local stories or external connections are suppressed, and in which the experience of a particular part is passed off as an adequate summary of the whole. Thus, accounts professing to be about British society, often amount to the restricted view from the south of England. Where other experiences are noted, they are identified as those of the 'Welsh', 'Scots', 'northerners', and so on, that is, as exceptions or deviations from the norm.[7] More telling still are those accounts of globalization which do not notice that they are primarily about a minority of rich countries, or to use a crude space-substance recombination, about the North, not the South. One of the most remarkable things about history – or rather geohistory – is that it is so uneven, that poverty and wealth, civility and barbarism can develop in such proximity. Given the ubiquity of spatial interactions, this uneven development is always combined or interdependent. Overlooking this contributes to myths of local or national cultural and ethnic purity. These points are of course convergent with the common postmodernist critique of the way in which totalizing narratives conceal their specific and situated character.

However, the emphasis on (spatial) difference has been controversial, even within human geography, for some have regarded it as indicative of a retreat from general theory. For example, this was one of the reactions to the emphasis on differentiation (between and within industries, classes and places) in Doreen Massey's influential *Spatial Divisions of Labour* (Massey, 1984,1996). I would suggest that the fears of the critics are derived from two misconceptions, which are also of wider significance. The first is the view that differentiation implies separation and independence, so that to emphasize it is to neglect the connections between different processes. But as Massey and others have been at pains to show, difference, and even uniqueness, usually derive precisely from interdependence, or 'combined and uneven development' (Massey, 1993). Thus, the uniqueness of Rome owed much to its relationship to its empire. The second error involves an unexamined attachment to a Humean view of theory as tied to the search for regularities among events, rather than to the (realist) search for necessity in the form of causal mechanisms, regardless of whether the mechanisms and the events they produce are unique or common.

MOBILITY   The relative mobility of actors and institutions is also an important spatial attribute, but often curiously overlooked. Although we cannot escape from time, we can, like refugees, avoid situations by moving. Differences in mobility are of great importance in affecting social processes; capitalist uneven development and its geography of industrial growth and decline is structured both by the enormous disparities in the mobilities of money capital, fixed capital and labour, and by their mutual dependence (Harvey, 1982).

Often changes in social practices involve significant changes in the patterns of movement of actors, but without making much difference to the material environment; for example, the patterns of movement associated with new management methods or role change within households largely fit in with the existing built environment rather than change it. It is therefore possible to have a new geography of individual movement or use of space without a new geography of the physical environment of constructed or natural spaces.

SPACE AND POWER   Control over space is a major condition of the exercise of power and domination. This generally involves the monopolization of particular spaces, as in the dependence of property capital on its control of land and buildings. Moreover, as Foucault demonstrates, the detailed partitioning of space and movement empowers and disempowers actors and creates preconditions of surveillance (Foucault, 1977; 1980). By the same token, being beyond the reach of such surveillance creates certain possibilities. As Anton Blok notes, the development of the mafia in Sicily owed much to the difficulties absentee landowners and the state had in enforcing their powers at a distance, for it allowed the mafiosi to insert themselves as an intermediary between them and the peasantry (Blok, 1974).

So far, we have separated out several aspects of space one by one, but in practice their effects usually operate in concert. Consider one of the most important kinds of lay geographical knowledge people, especially women, need to have, regarding the geography of fear and (male) violence. The subordination of women is greatly supported by the tacit curfews placed on women's movements at certain places and times by the threat of male violence (Valentine, 1989), indeed this is probably the most significant case in everyday life of domination exercised through the control of space. 'Reclaim the Night' movements (despite the use of a temporal rather than spatial slogan) challenge the way in which space is gendered, the way in which power operates through differences in mobility and through the control of movement and location. However, this example also tells us something about the spatial flexibility of actors and provides a warning against spatial, or architectural, determinism: it is common to see alterations to the physical environment being proposed as ways of reducing male violence in cities, though this is generally unsuccessful for the efficient cause of the problem is (spatially flexible) violent men, not the spatial form of the urban environment.

Some Origins of Misconceptions of Space

So far we have endorsed the view that spatial form is not a constraint upon pre-existing non-spatial social processes but is constitutive of those processes: there is no such thing as non-spatial processes. But it is also worth considering why it is so tempting to imagine otherwise, to posit 'aspatial processes' apart from spatial contexts and to consider space as absolute and independent from objects. (Social theory should explain, as well as criticize, false ideas). Firstly, the absolute concept gains credence from the fact that spatial form can remain the same for different objects; a cube is a cube whatever it is made of, thus it is tempting – though dubious – to suppose that such a form could exist independently of any content. Secondly, while objects, whether natural or social have spatial extension and perhaps a particular shape as part of their nature, they often stand in a contingent relation to many aspects of their context and hence can survive in varied locations. For the purpose of explaining the nature and powers of those objects – though not for the purpose of explaining what they actually do in practice – we can often abstract from the second kind of spatial aspect. Yet it is usually only this second kind that is noticed as 'geographical'. Hence the common belief in 'aspatial' phenomena and contingent geographical settings or consequences.

Theory, Empirics and Space

We are now in a position to define the spatial content appropriate to theory and empirical research.

Abstract theory is concerned with the structures, necessary conditions and powers of objects, rather than with what they contingently do in particular situations (Bhaskar, 1979; Sayer, 1992). In this regard, acknowledging the necessarily spatially extensive character of social objects doesn't say much about their spatial form. For example, as Mann insists, state theory must recognize that states control territory, but the shapes of the territories can be as different as those of Chile or Romania. (While the shape and internal geography of states do of course make some difference, it is always in terms of the causal powers of their constituents). This is very typical. The particular concrete spatial form of social objects which we may theorize, such as capital, ethnic minorities or social movements, and their location with respect to others, invariably depends upon many contingently related conditions. Similarly, regarding mobility, we may be able to say that something has a certain potential mobility but not what movements it actually makes. In realist terms, the enormous variety of possible spatial forms is again a corollary of the fact that social systems are open (see Bhaskar, 1975, 1979, 1989; Sayer, 1992), and of the spatial flexibility of actors mentioned earlier.

But the role of theory does not end here for it is also applied in empirical research where it provides conceptualizations of the contingent conditions as well as the central processes of interest. But it cannot anticipate much about the form of those spatial settings; it can only conceptualize them retrospectively. Consequently there is *some* justification for social theory's traditional abstraction from space.

On the other hand, concrete research, which attempts to understand conjunctures composed by many interacting but often contingently related phenomena, has to be attentive to spatial form, or else risk obscuring causality. Precisely because of the interdependence of space, time and process, concrete studies have to struggle with all three aspects. To neglect one is to mis-specify the other two (see Chapter 6). Thus, to explain the spatial dimension one has to recognize the specificity of the processes and their temporal ordering, otherwise spatial fetishism and reductionist explanation will be the result. Equally, even if researchers are not particularly interested in spatial aspects, concrete research has to recognize the space-time properties of its objects if it is not to misidentify causality. Therefore the finishing point would be the same. Much of the inconclusiveness and weakness of the kind of empirical research that hopes to find robust empirical regularities derives from its unaware abstraction from, and consequent 'scrambling' of, the difference that concrete spatial form makes to outcomes. In other words, concrete research has, in some degree, to combine its abstractions in a way that respects the time space dimensions and patterning of its objects. Nevertheless, practical difficulties in recombining space and substance may make some approximation and scrambling unavoidable, but then the spatial flexibility of actions may – remembering our earlier qualifications – make that approximation unimportant.

However, there is a way of increasing the specificity of inferences which can be made about spatial form and its implications on the basis of abstract theory, and that is by building into the theory an assumption about the form of the particular (contingent) spatial setting that happens to exist, so as to work out what would happen to a process of interest (Sayer, 1992; Sheppard, 1996). Thus, as we saw with the case of central place theory turning neoclassical economic theory on its head, locational modelling can produce interesting conclusions about the difference that space makes by starting from hypothetical assumptions, usually involving isotropic plains and the location of the processes of interest on them. For example, by such means, Sheppard and Barnes (1990) have produced a series of important challenges to aspatial economic theory.

In effect, these models hypothesize a closed system. In real, open social systems, the settings are not isotropic but make uneven differences. Moreover, things happen over time and take place successively. Thus, a housing market does not clear at a point in time over a whole area but evolves sequentially and is constrained by wherever and whenever vacancies and potential buyers crop up. One could build simulation models of such processes, though their outcomes would be likely to be origin- and path-dependent rather than converging to any equilibrium (Sayer, 1976). It is an interesting question how far open system outcomes differ from those of hypothetical closed systems, but as the example of central place theory's demonstration of the monopolistic tendencies of spatial competition shows, the heuristic value of such models may be considerable.

So, to summarize:

1 Theory seeks to identify the necessary spatial qualities and conditions of its objects, but these spatial qualities can often vary considerably for a given kind of object. The spatial content of theory is therefore characteristically vague, and necessarily so. Only by building in assumptions about the particular contingent form the situation of interest might take, can we expect to obtain more specific inferences about the difference that space makes.
2 Empirical research (theoretically informed) is required to discover the concrete forms that social objects contingently take. In all cases, the concrete forms will make some difference to outcomes, though in some cases the difference may be trivial.

Not surprisingly, earlier versions of this argument (such as Sayer, 1985) have not been popular within geography for it implies that its modifications of social theory are likely to be less sweeping than claimed by many (for example, Soja, 1989), and this at a time when human geography's status in the academic world was rising. But what social theory can legitimately say about space is not a matter of disciplinary imperialism and status but of argument, and in many cases the unpopularity of the position advanced here derives from various misunderstandings of what it involves:

(a) It does *not* say that space is irrelevant in abstract social theory, only that what one can say about it at this level is inevitably somewhat vague. Thus, concepts such as 'time-space compression' (Harvey, 1989) are important for understanding capitalism and the experience of modernity, but clearly they cannot give us a very specific idea of the actual spacing and timing of social processes therein.
(b) Contingent means 'neither necessary nor impossible'; it does not mean undetermined or uncaused. To say that two things are contingently related

is to say that they could exist independently of one another, not that they could exist independently of anything. And just because the co-existence of A and B in a particular (spatial) form is contingent, it does not follow that there is nothing necessary about how, once configured in this way they interact. (This latter possibility has been termed by Bob Jessop 'contingent necessity' (1990)).

(c)   The argument does *not* say that everything about space is contingent. A phrase like 'contingent spatial relations' doesn't logically entail that *all* spatial relations and forms are contingent. We must acknowledge, for example, that human beings necessarily have a certain spatial form and structure. But then the particular spatial forms of the situations in which they exist are incredibly varied and open and not likely to be anticipated by theory with any specificity, though of course their empirical observation will be theory-laden.[8]

(d)   Contingency is also not to be confused with importance! Contingent relations may be unimportant or important. Some may have some effects, some not. Thus, the contingent spatial relation between the reader and the computer on which this was written is of no importance, but that between North Sea oil and Britain is of considerable importance to its economy. The issue of importance is a separate one from the issue of how much a theory of social space can say about space. The fact that it can't be very specific does not mean that what it can – or can't – say is unimportant. Since the spatial relation between yourself and a bus is contingent, I can't produce a theory saying much about it. But if, through empirical research, I found that the bus had contingently run over you, that would be important, wouldn't it?[9]

One author who offers a more ambitious prospect for space in social theory is David Harvey:

> Geographical space is always the realm of the concrete and the particular. Is it possible to construct a theory of the concrete and the particular in the context of the universal and abstract determinations of Marx's theory of capital accumulation? This is the fundamental question to be resolved. (Harvey, 1985, p. 144)

Though Harvey is clearly hopeful of an affirmative response, the simple answer to Harvey's question is No – and in my view his own work supports such an answer. For example, in *The Condition of Postmodernity* (1989), he strives to define the spatiality of capitalism and its relation to modernism and postmodernism, yet he can't get beyond vague terms such as 'time-space compression', 'fragmentation', 'unevenness', 'incarceration', and so on. I am not saying that Harvey is at fault in this respect, for these terms are all that one could expect of an attempt to theorize spatiality at an abstract level, and Harvey's interpretations are consistently important, interesting and insightful. What I am criticizing is the view implied in the quotation that one could have a theory of concrete space which could anticipate its form with some degree of specificity. As we shall see, it is but a short step from this view to a new kind of spatial separatism.

The same goes for Edward Soja's work on spatiality. For example, in his *Postmodern Geographies* (1989), he builds upon the work of writers such as Lefebvre, Foucault and Poulantzas in attempting to characterize the spatiality of capitalism. Thus he quotes Poulantzas:

> Separation and division in order to unify; parcelling out in order to structure; atomization in order to encompass; segmentation in order to totalize; closure in order to homogenize; and individualization in order to obliterate differences and otherness. The roots of totalitarianism are inscribed in the spatial matrix concretized by the modern nation-state – a matrix that is already present in its relations of production and in the capitalist division of labour. (Poulantzas, cited in Soja, 1989, p. 338)

Notwithstanding the purple prose, there are some suggestive ideas here, but the attempt to say more than this becomes a somewhat desperate search for alternative spatial metaphors and for new ways of stringing these together. Again, no-one could get further, and be more specific, without shifting to a more concrete kind of analysis, which recognized the influence of processes and circumstances contingently related to the central relations and drives of capitalism or gender relations, or whatever the process of interest might be. Moreover, without shifting to such a level, the claims that are made remain particularly ambiguous and questionable. It may be true that capitalism both homogenizes space and differentiates and fragments it: either description seems acceptable. But unless one is told with more specificity which aspects of capitalism lead to homogenization or which to differentiation, such claims are of little use. The practical import of closure, distanciation, compression, fragmentation, and so on, cannot be judged without specifying the processes actually constituting and affected by them. For example, space-time compression or implosion is described by Harvey in largely negative terms, yet such compression is arguably progressive in terms of the preconditions of democracy and environmental responsibility. Again, to omit to say what is being 'compressed', 'fragmented' and so on, is to invite spatial fetishism.

This is not to deny that there is a point to the renewed interest in the spatiality of capitalism and modernity, but there are pitfalls in such exercises. Consider an important insight regarding time-space distanciation and narrative form. Many authors have argued that as the division of labour deepens and comes to integrate progressively more of the world's peoples into a world system, the extent to which processes in one place are interdependent with those in others increases, so that we are struck not by the 'linearity' of successive events but by the experience of many things happening at once, and the co-determination of processes across space. Traditional linear narrative is inevitably increasingly inadequate to the task of comprehending such a situation. Hence as Berger puts it, 'Prophecy now involves a geographical rather than historical projection; it is space, not time, that hides consequences from us...' (cited in Soja, 1989, p. 337). At one level one can accept this, for it is a particularly forceful way of making the point. But it is but a short step from this kind of statement, treated as a shorthand for space-time-process developments, to one in which space itself 'splits off' and is attributed powers of its own.

Such elliptical formulations also sound impressive and portentous – the distanced language of the Olympian view. But this kind of rhetoric actually says less than more ordinary and concrete descriptions. There is, of course, a sense in which space divides and conceals processes, but one can still say more about social divisions by reference to the likes of gender, class, race and ethnicity, taking into account whatever spatial forms and associations they have. Certainly, as we have seen in the case of gender, these means of differentiation involve particular spacings and timings of actions, and time-space distanciation can conceal the dominant from the subordinated, where once there was a face-to-face relationship; nevertheless, discussing the spatial aspects in abstraction from the substance/process element is risky. When 'space' is substituted for a substance term it may serve to remind those who aren't accustomed to thinking spatially that social processes are spatial, but it also discards critical information, by failing to specify the materials which give the spatial form a particular effect. Rather than be swayed by the Olympian language of an attempted theory of space, it is better to address concrete social relations in terms of their actual spatial form and setting and to assess what difference this makes.

It might suit the ambitions of the discipline of geography if everything were entirely dependent on spatial setting, for then there would never be any circumstances in which we could abstract from geography. But then this speculation is idle because cognition and language would then become impossible! Thus, the inferences that Marx drew from considering the labour processes in localities such as 19th-century Manchester would have no application elsewhere. In fact, his theory of the labour process is remarkably broad in its applicability to other spaces and times, though, of course, it has to be combined with other theories and material when applied concretely.

The major texts of Lefebvre, Harvey, Soja and Smith on space and society amply illustrate the impossibility of a spatial theory of the concrete. All of them are battling against the ontological limits to theorizing posed by spatial flexibility or contingency; Lefebvre's repeated references to the 'preliminary' character of his theorizations can be taken as an attempt to deny this point (Lefebvre, 1991). Given the ontological nature of the limits, their limited success in increasing the specificity of the spatial content of social theory in no way reflects on their own ability.

Theory, History and Geography

The problem of the relationship between theory and history has been recognized for a considerable time. There is first a common worry that excessive emphasis upon historical-specificity will deny theory any role in explanation. As already noted, this is a misconception based on a Humean view of theory, which mistakes its task as the encoding and explanation of regularity rather than necessity (Sayer, 1992). There is then the question of the extent to which theoretical claims have to be qualified as historically and geographically specific, or 'context-dependent'. This, in turn, depends on how far, or at what depth, social structures and processes are context-dependent. Are they only modified in minor ways by differences in context, or are they so deeply influenced that social theory cannot usefully abstract from any geohistorical context (see Chapter 6)?

Secondly, there is the question of whether the unity of space, time and process, and the close relation in social science between theory and empirical research, imply that human geography, history and social theory should become indistinguishable. I would argue that it does not, though they are currently insufficiently related. As we have seen already, in explaining concrete processes there does indeed need to be such a unity of geographical, historical and social research; the idea of explaining just the temporal or spatial aspects of society in abstraction from their content is absurd. Historians and geographers therefore cannot afford to be ignorant of social theory, and social scientists studying concrete situations need to be aware of their spatio-temporal character. I have already discussed in what sense social scientists in their role as theorists need to be aware of the historical and geographical limits of their objects. But it does not follow from this that social *theory* is indistinguishable from concrete (historical and geographical) research.

To demonstrate this, we need to clarify the role of theory in history and the sense in which events are 'determined' and hence explicable. The contingency or open-ended nature of action means that it is impossible to have a theory of history in any but the weakest sense. Although theory can identify tendencies, these are not probabilistic forecasts about patterns of events but claims about the inherent powers of objects. It is of course necessary to interpret history in terms of theory, but vital to recognize the asymmetry which Abrams highlights: viz. retrospectively, we can try to establish the conditions of existence of concrete conjunctures, but this does not mean that only *that* conjuncture could have come about, for the world is open; it is shaped but not pre-determined (Abrams, 1982; Bhaskar, 1975). Thus, there is no contradiction in saying retrospectively how I got here and what was necessary for me to get here, while acknowledging that beforehand it was contingent whether I would.[10] The open nature of social systems and the contingent nature of their reproduction means that the historical and geographical course of development is always an empirical question. This is why, despite their strong inter-relationships, we can still recognize the difference between social theory and concrete (properly geographical and historical) research: they do not do the same job.

David Harvey is unhappy about the possibility of distinguishing between the 'constitutive structures' and necessary powers of an object and the 'contingent conditions' in which it may be found (Harvey, 1987). The criticism is directed at both the general realist distinction between essences or causal powers of objects and the accidental properties or features of objects and their settings, and the contrast I have proposed between the spatial form of objects and the contingently related spatial settings in which they are found, for example, between your body and this book. This follows from his espousal of an ontology of universal internal relations, i.e. in which every object is internally related to every other one. Of course he cannot stick to such an ontology, for he is particularly concerned with abstracting out social institutions or relationships that can be reproduced at many different times and places. Similarly, Richard Peet claims 'It is impossible to separate things from the relations in which they exist' (Peet, 1998, p. 175). On the contrary, it is a condition of the possibility of cognition, language and naming, not to mention other human practices, that we can pick things out that can retain their integrity and their independence from many (not all!) other things with which they may be associated. The table at which I am sitting would be the same table if I moved it to another house, capital accumulation can take place in Malaysia as well as Manchester, and so on. Like anyone using ordinary language, Harvey and Peet cannot escape using nouns identifying objects which can retain their identity, sometimes in more than one shape, and in many different spatial settings: language itself always involves abstraction or individuation and it does so successfully much of the time. To be sure, as we saw in Chapter 4, there are objects which lack essences and which are so affected by contexts that there is indeed a difficulty in specifying what they are in abstraction from context, but there are plenty of social objects which are not like this.[11]

Conclusion

While we always exist within particular settings with their own spatial forms, we can often move between many different settings while retaining our identity and integrity. This property we share with animals and many inanimate objects. Language and memory (among other things) differentiate us from animals and provide further scope for practical forms of abstraction from space, allowing us to transcend the immediacy of sensory experience (Giddens, 1981 and 1984). Conversely, the abstraction from the here and now is a necessary condition of the existence of language, reflection *and – to a large extent – theorizing*. At the same time, in practical activity, and in concrete research, we invariably have to take some account of spatial form if we are to be successful. There is consequently a central paradox in theorizing about space and time; and one which the recent 'discovery' of space has overlooked: it involves bringing back to our attention that which theorizing (and, more fundamentally, language) *must* (largely) abstract from. Not surprisingly, theorizing about space itself largely requires an abstraction from particular spatial configurations; certain things may have to be spatially connected or proximate, but this leaves open a wide variety of spatial forms in which such conditions may be met.

So does geography matter? Yes and no! In some respects space or geography are absolutely vital, in others – illustrated by the ability of things and people to remain much the same in different settings – it makes only small differences. In cases in which geography does matter, if we are to say much about *how* it matters, then either we have to move towards a more concrete analysis, which looks at particular cases and specifies the form of those relations that are contingent, or else conduct the kind of theoretical research, which achieves some spatial specificity by assuming a hypothetical space as a starting point, like the isotropic plains of spatial analysis, so that the contingent aspects are controlled.

I must confess that I have been disappointed by the fact that while the formulation defended here (presented first in Sayer, 1992 and 1985) has provoked many brief mentions in the literature, most of them have misrepresented the argument and omitted to provide an argued reply[12] (for example, Smith, 1990, Johnston, 1993, Harvey, 1996); I have come across only two replies which set out a reasoned case (Sheppard, 1996; Peet, 1998). Although I argued that space is a necessary dimension of all material phenomena, social ones included, in that they have spatial extension and spatial exclusivity and sometimes a limited range of shapes, many ignored this and seized on the accompanying claim that physical space is also characterized by many contingent relations, that is, spatial relations between things which don't *have* to stand in such configurations to be the kinds of things that they are, and whose form cannot therefore be anticipated theoretically. Perhaps those unhappy with this should counter it through demonstration – by saying something specific about the spatial forms of the social processes which interest them in advance of empirical inquiries into particular concrete instances of them. Earlier, I gave the example of how noting the necessary spatiality or territorial form of nation states didn't tell us much about their spatial form. Those who object to the contingency side of the argument presented here need to answer this. I would therefore like to renew my challenge to critics to do just that.

Notes

1 Of course, disciplinary imperialism is a tiresome distorting feature of work in other social sciences too.

2 Strictly speaking, while we can return to the same location we were in before, things there will not be exactly the same, for the same reason as one can never step into the same river twice. Thanks to Doreen Massey (personal communication) for discussions.

3 Marx told the story of the English aristocrat who took a shipload of people to Australia imagining that he could set up a community there in which they would work for him. But of course, such was the amount of unenclosed land that he could not gain a monopoly over it and thereby make his intended workers dependent on him for access to means of production. They therefore became independent producers. Workers, means of production and a would-be-capitalist existed, but their spatial form meant that capitalist social relations could not be established.

4 I think Pred is guilty of exaggerating context-dependence in his interesting essay on language and the locally spoken word (Pred, 1989).

5 Though it is possible Bourdieu is guilty of some degree of underestimation of spatial differentiation in *Distinction* and *Homo Academicus*.

6 Again, thanks to Doreen Massey for discussions.

7 That those from the south do not call themselves 'southerners' illustrates the fact that, unlike northerners, they are accustomed to taking themselves, and not others, as their point of reference.

8 Smith (1987) and Harvey (1987) in their criticisms of realism appear to assume that what theory can't antipate it can't explain, when of course post-hoc explanations also draw upon theory.

9 We could of course make conditional claims about contingent necessity here, and theorize that should a bus contingently run over a person, it will necessarily have dire consequences for them.

10 As Bhaskar notes, although in terms of content, the concrete is richer than the abstract, the latter is richer than the former in terms of possibility.

11 Harvey, Peet and also Neil Smith (1987) and Kevin Archer (1987) seem troubled by the fact that realism does not give them the answers to substantive questions about society.

6

Geohistorical Explanation and Problems of Narrative

In the 1980s, radical geographers and sociologists interested in space moved from developing abstract theory to empirical studies of particular geographical spaces, studies which were concrete in that they tried to synthesize numerous processes that came together in those areas. At the same time there was a shift towards middle-range theory, typically dealing with the varied institutional forms taken by capitalist processes. Both shifts were partly a reaction against reductionist applications of abstract theory which explained away concrete events by reducing them to the former's terms (Sayer, 1981a, 1985). More simply there was a feeling that having developed the abstract theoretical equipment it was now time to apply it. The changes were also arguably indirectly associated with a political shift away from Marxism, which is one of the reasons why they proved to be controversial (Harvey, 1987; Smith, 1987). The British locality studies associated with the Changing Urban and Regional Systems programme were the best-known examples of these tendencies, but there were also experiments with a 'new' regional geography (for example, Cooke, 1986; Lancaster Regionalism Group, 1985; Gregory, 1982; Pred, 1986). These were self-consciously theoretically informed empirical studies and ones which proved to be theoretically informative too. For many years, they provided a focus for a considerable volume of theoretical and methodological debate (for example, Gilbert, 1988; Gregory, 1978, 1987, 1988; Pudup, 1988; Smith, 1987; Thrift, 1983; Massey, 1991; Sayer, 1991; Peet, 1998). Views differed not only how such studies should be done, but on whether they were worth doing at all.

In the 1960s, there had been a debate in geography between idiographic and nomothetic approaches, that is, between explanations or descriptions which treated their objects as unique and ones which treated them as law-governed and susceptible to generalization. This was central to the battle between the atheoretical empiricism of the old regional geography and the new positivism of spatial analysis, and, at the time, the former was clearly routed. However, it was a pre-realist debate, in which both sides assumed that theory was essentially about generalization and the search for regularity and that the unique was not susceptible to theoretical explanation. When the issue of how to explain regional conjunctures re-surfaced in the 1980s, it proved difficult to escape the old terms of debate. Accordingly, many assumed that the preoccupation of the new locality and regional studies with differentiation and the particular could only mean an abandonment of theory, since they associated theory with generality and the search for regularities. However, critical realists argued that theory was concerned, firstly, with conceptualization, and hence was applicable to both unique and widely replicated events, and, secondly, with the identification of necessity, regardless of whether it was instanciated repeatedly or just once. The realist dissociation of causality from regularity also meant that the new concern with differentiation did not signal any abandonment of interest in causal explanation, but rather its pursuit in a form appropriate for the study of open systems.

The attempt to make empirical studies theoretically informed has brought into question the relationship between analysis and narrative, and between law-seeking or nomological approaches and contextualizing approaches, while the problem of writing texts which construct geohistorical syntheses has raised the issue of the composition of narratives. The latter issues have until recently been ignored by anglophone philosophy of social science. In its preoccupation with settling its accounts with natural science, this philosophy has been blind to the challenges posed by the overlapping problems of the social sciences and the humanities. The philosophers of social science write as if there were no problems of narrative, as if texts were nothing more than the sum of their individual sentences, considered one by one, and as if the act of interpretation merely needed to be defended against behaviourism, not studied in its own right.

In this chapter, I want to discuss some of these questions so as to clarify the challenges of geohistorical explanation. There are three major themes: first, an assessment of the reasons for the discovery of locality and the calls for a new regional geography; second, a summary of realist views on how the old idiographic-nomothetic debate has been transcended; and third, a discussion of the methodological issues associated with the problems and rival claims of narrative and analysis as applied to geohistorical syntheses. Around these topics a number of minor themes revolve – the relationship between theory and empirical research, generality and particularity, and political economy and ethnography, and the persistence of positivist views of scientific knowledge – even among its opponents. The chapter ends with some comments on an alternative type of geohistorical analysis developed by Edward Soja.

Regions and Localities in Question

The movement of geographers in the 1960s and 1970s into the social sciences to learn about the processes producing spatial forms eventually brought about a new realization of the extent to which those processes were not only historically specific but geographically specific too, and that 'geography matters' (for example, Gregory, 1981; Massey, 1984; Massey and Allen, 1985). At first, this took the form of studies of how 'general' processes and structures are modified in particular contexts, but more recently it has been recognized that the general structures do not float above particular contexts but are always reproduced within them. This, coupled with the diversity of conclusions from empirical studies of different countries, regions, and localities, in turn raised the possibility that what we had formerly considered to be general structures were themselves geographically specific, context-dependent phenomena that had mistakenly been treated as universal. For example, comparative studies of western and Japanese capitalism frequently provoke the ethnocentric conclusion that the latter, though not the former, is heavily influenced by its national culture. But perhaps many of the features of capitalism we take to be 'normal' are just a western variant, equally influenced by context. Such problems raise the fundamental question of *how far, or at what depth, are social structures and processes context-dependent?* Are they only modified in minor ways by differences in context, or are they so deeply influenced that social theory cannot usefully abstract from any geohistorical context? Between these two extremes, of course, lie many possibilities.

Locality studies, the 'new *regional* geography' and the new spatially conscious sociology differ from traditional regional geography: they do not privilege a particular scale of analysis equivalent to the traditional geographic region; any scale of study from the global down to spatial divisions within buildings would apparently qualify, provided it involves geohistorical empirical research[1] (compare Jonas, 1986). They also differ in their philosophies, methodologies, and politics, and, as already noted, in their attitude to social theory. For example, Thrift (1983) makes an excellent case for situating action and practical consciousness in their space-time settings, particularly localities, and recognizing these as constitutive rather than as passive. It is not just that localities differ from one another; even where they do not they are still required in the explanation of action and practical consciousness.

The concept of locality is one whose time came in the mid-1980s, even if there was later growing uncertainty about locality studies and some strong reaction (Smith, 1987, 1990). The conjuncture in which such studies arose was characterized by growing spatial polarization, exemplified in Britain by the rise of concern over the 'north-south divide' and the increasing heterogeneity of the country's political geography, by the discovery of space and place in social theory, and by a more general 'empirical turn'. Yet I would argue that there were unspoken reasons behind the last of these: in particular, there was the conjunction of the Left's domination of social theory with the political sea change of the 1980s. Although radical theory had become accustomed to a discrepancy between its conclusions regarding peoples' 'objective' political interests and actual peoples' political behaviour (for example, the conservative trade unionists), a gulf between the two opened up at the beginning of the 1980s. One response was to turn to empirical research in order to find out what on Earth was going on. What were real people, as opposed to the ciphers of social theory, doing and thinking?

In order to improve our understanding of people's consciousness the characteristic move has been to shift from simple, aspatial material determinism to locality studies which situate people in the space-time settings of everyday life and hence grasp their circumstances concretely instead of abstractly. Thus, to understand 'class de-alignment' in political behaviour, or to explain why women's initiatives have been prominent in some Labour-controlled areas and absent in others, it is necessary to look at localities concretely (Halford, 1987; Savage et al., 1987; see also Agnew, 1987a). A sophisticated example of this locally dis-aggregated and specified materialism from the work of the Lancaster Regional-ism Group has been presented by Warde (1988). Warde demonstrates that paradoxes such as the coincidence of the decline of the Right and the growth of the Labour Party in Lancaster with the *decline* of blue-collar manufacturing employment, become intelligible once the issues are looked at with sufficient specificity and in context. (This need not mean purely locally, for of course many of the processes have outside influences.)

Yet, despite its sophistication, such research stumbles into what is perhaps the major problem of social science. For, although this 'concretization' is a marked improvement, it still does not face up to the problem of the relative autonomy of consciousness, to the fact that people can interpret the same situation differently. Not all differences in consciousness can be traced unambiguously to differences in material circumstances, perhaps not even at the level of individuals. In other words, it is still not clear that we have broken entirely with the habit of combin-ing sophisticated theories of our own knowledge as academics, with a crude behaviourist reflection theory about the consciousness of others. Is it not strange that we feel insulted when someone explains the way we think purely by refer-ence to our material circumstances and yet we have no qualms about doing the same to the people we study? According to Warde 'There is near universal con-demnation of both economic determinism and its opposite, political spontaneism, but no accepted way to unpack the proposition that "politics is relatively autonomous"' (Warde, 1988, p. 77). I would argue that, since consciousness is also formed out of pre-existing cognitive and cultural materials, a more ethno-graphic approach is needed. Although this is to a certain extent recognized in some research (for example, Harris, 1986), most locality studies do not go beyond the 'restructuring' variant of the political economy tradition, even if they have made important advances within it. And, even where locality studies do seem quite successful in rendering political and other behaviour intelligible, political economy without ethnography leaves the reasons for that intelligibility implicit: the behaviour seems intelligible only to the extent that it resonates, not because we have articulated the constitutive structure of understanding or feeling.

At this point, interestingly, we meet some other academic explorers coming from the opposite direction – anthropologists calling for a unification of ethno-graphy with political economy. Marcus and Fischer (1986) mention neither local-ities nor regions nor place, but they are well aware of the need to integrate studies of relations of presence and absence, unacknowledged as well as acknowledged conditions of action, local and global phenomena, and so on.

Such an integration is, of course, easier said than done, not least because of the lack of clear theoretical structures in dealing with the more interpretative con-cerns of ethnography (for example, there is no equivalent in cultural studies of the spatial division of labour approach for providing a model for relating the local to the global). But before we assent to the necessity of joint political economic-ethnographic locality studies, it is worth questioning why place and region should have to be brought into this integration of ethnography and political economy. As the main setting for the constitution of daily life and the formation of consciousness and identity? Perhaps. But meaning is also in some ways context-independent, indeed the point of communication is to render experience in different contexts mutually intelligible.

Some of the most widely cited examples of studies which do integrate ethnographic and political economy dimensions do not give much emphasis to place or locality; for example, this is true of Willis's study of why working-class boys get lousy jobs (1977). This was a study set in 'Hammertown' in the West Midlands, but the author does not attach much significance to the locality and its conclusions have been widely assumed to be applicable to all working-class schoolboys. Yet Day's study of working-class schoolboys in a different locality – 'Piertown' on the south coast of England – suggests otherwise (Day, 1987). But before we leap to score points by drawing attention to these oversights of how place or geography matters, it is worth remembering the dangers of discipli-nary imperialism interfering with matters of intellectual judgment. If the abstrac-tion from localities or regions does seriously weaken the analysis, then the onus is on geographers not merely to complain, simply in principle, that it is indiffer-ent to space and place, but to say, in concrete terms, exactly what difference it makes. It may still be the case that we can make general claims about certain rela-tionships in abstraction from their local context, provided that we specify them a little more. For example, we might find that there is not one but three types of response of working-class boys or girls to schooling, and that these can be related to the incidence of three socio-economic characteristics which have common effects wherever they are located. Whether this is likely, depends upon just how context dependent action is, and upon just how different the contexts of action are. Although this is one of the key issues in philosophical debates about the nature of social science, empirical studies of localities or regions can help to determine the significance of the problem. Ethnography has always pulled towards contextualizing explanations or interpretations, political economy towards law-like, context-independent explanations. What is methodologically challenging about geohistorical syntheses is precisely that they have to attempt to hold the two in tension. As we shall see, although there is more than an echo here of the old idiographic-nomothetic debate, there are now ways of moving beyond it.

Beyond the Idiographic-Nomothetic Debate

The old debate about regional geography was, of course, closely associated with that between idiographic and nomothetic approaches. The basic constituents of the idiographic-nomothetic debate were shared by both sides and involved a set of dualisms which have now been thoroughly taken apart and reconstructed: they include science/art, objective/subjective, generality/uniqueness, theory/empiricism, and so on. However, it is surprising how many researchers, includ-ing those hostile either to traditional idiographic or to nomothetic spatial analytic approaches, have allowed themselves to fall back into those old assumptions (for example, Harvey, 1987; Smith, 1987).

Realist philosophy has provided many of the tools for the deconstruction (Bhaskar, 1979; Sayer, 1992). Although I think realism falls short of resolving the problems of geohistorical narrative and interpretation which are the prime subject of this chapter, it prepares the ground for that discussion, particularly in getting us past the related idiographic versus nomothetic, and theory versus history, debates. It does so firstly because it breaks with an assumption common to both sides of the old idiographic-nomothetic debate – the Humean association of laws and causation with regularities among events. Enduring, precise regularities need only occur in closed systems not available to social sciences. Instead, realism roots theory and explanation in the discovery of necessity. Thus history does not elude theory because of any lack of regularities in what it studies. Theory can grasp unique as well as repeated events, by demonstrating necessity in the world. Theory is no longer associated with generality in the sense of repeated series of events but with determining the nature of things or structures, discovering which characteristics are necessary consequences of their being those kinds of objects. Generality, in the sense of extent of occurrence, thus depends upon how common instances of the object are, and upon the circumstances or conditions in which objects exist, these determining whether the causal powers and liabilities of objects are activated, and with what effect. For theory to improve its grasp of these properties requires continual refinements of the way in which objects are conceptualized: thus, the hallmark of theory is not the formalization of regularities in empirical events but conceptual analysis. Finally, empirical analysis is never theory-neutral: the only sense in which it can ever be empiricist is in failing to be aware of this fact.

All of the above applies to natural and social science, but the overlap between theory and empirical research has to be greater in social science and history. I can explain this best via Abrams's arguments about the integration of history and sociology (1982). We can endorse Abrams's view that sociology has to be historical and that history has to be aware of social theory regarding its objects, and similar arguments can be made regarding social science and geography (for example, Giddens, 1984). And we have already made the point that empirical research should be consciously theoretically informed, though we have still to deal with the question of how empirical research might inform theory. Yet it remains the case that social theorizing is not – and probably will never be – the same as doing empirical geographical-historical research.

In what ways are these kinds of research different and in what ways are they related? I have introduced the argument elsewhere (1985), but it turns on recognizing both what Bhaskar terms 'the geohistorical earthing' of social activity *and* the general principle of 'spatial and temporal indifference' (1986, p. 212ff). Abstract research, being concerned with the character, powers, and preconditions of social structures, has to take account of the fact that they are neither aspatial nor 'a-chronic', and that their time-space distanciation makes a difference to the way they work (though exactly what kind of difference will generally depend on empirical specification of the form of that time-space distanciation). If the structures are widely distributed, such as those of capital accumulation, then this implies that, although they have some spatial and temporal preconditions, these can be met in a wide variety of spatial and temporal contexts. Alternatively, we could say that they carry their geohistorical conditions with them. In virtue of this, they have the same kind of spatial and temporal indifference as that which allows most scientific experiments to be conducted anywhere in the world without this making any difference to the results. Durable, pervasive structures (which are therefore to a certain extent context-independent), once empirically discovered, can therefore be theorized independently of further empirical research. Yet, even where more durable structures are involved, social theory can rarely be applied to actual situations without supplementary empirical information (theory-laden of course), because action is invariably co-determined by other structures and conditions (Sayer, 1992). By contrast, structures which are less durable (for example, cultural forms) are too influenced by geohistorical contexts for their explanation to be divorced from those settings. *Contextualizing and law-seeking approaches should therefore be seen not as competing, but as extremes of a continuum ranging across different kinds of object.*

In the middle of this continuum lie cases where a structure is in the process of becoming, or of transformation, or in which it takes innumerable forms, the differences between these forms being more than cosmetic; the institution of marriage is a good example of both possibilities. In such cases, concrete and abstract social research need to be in far closer dialogue than is ever necessary for their natural science equivalents of pure and applied research. An engineer is not likely to find the laws of physics changing in her attempt to apply them, and she therefore does not need also to be a theoretical physicist. But a student of, say, historical geography or sociology is quite likely to be faced with change in social structures themselves, and is obliged to do some social theorizing about their changing nature and powers. Consequently, we should expect empirical research in social science not only to be theoretically informed but *theoretically informative or creative.*

All knowledge of structures is derived empirically (informed by earlier theory). In social science, the empirical research is restricted to open systems, unlike much of natural science, which has access to or can create closed systems. Empirical social research is never simply the documenting of the contingent, contrary to a common misunderstanding of realism. It also permits the checking and refinement of knowledge about necessity in the social world and can make new discoveries of necessity or internal relations. However, as I argued earlier, the latter need not be particularly general in the sense of regular or widespread, but then realism, unlike positivism, does not confuse necessity with generality in the sense of regularity. The best example I can give of the way in which empirical research is theoretically creative comes from feminist studies of trade unionism. Studies such as Cynthia Cockburn's of strongly unionized male workers show how their solidarity is not simply – or even largely – a matter of class but of gender solidarity, for their ability to defend their class or occupational position derives as much from their solidarity as men with common interests in dominating women. This puts a wholly different light upon the history of radical trade unionism. So, although trade unions as such and patriarchy need not be internally related, particular concrete forms of trade unionism have come to be patriarchal at a deep level; indeed, in the case of some of the aspects of a trade union action which Cockburn discusses, it is virtually impossible to disentangle the class-based from the gender-based (1983). A more geographical example might concern the extent to which protest in a particular region derives from some general class basis, where the industry in question just happens to be concentrated in that region, or whether it derives from locally specific non-class bases, such as regional identity.

Although realist philosophy can illuminate such issues, some common misconceptions have arisen regarding its use.[2] These are related to the problems discussed already about the nature of theory, and so on, but I now want to deal with some common problems in theorizing what might be termed the 'metaphysics of the local and the general'. (See, in particular, debates about the 'empirical turn' and realism, Smith, 1987; Harvey, 1987.) The widespread but unexamined use of suspect oppositions, such as 'general causal processes and local contingencies', or 'general theory and local empirical studies' – and worse, their attribution to realism! – has created considerable confusion. In such cases we see a pervasive tendency to align and conflate different dualisms, such as necessity-contingency with global-local, and to elide their differences, thereby generating a series of confusions (analysed more fully in Sayer, 1991). One such problem involves a type of epistemic fallacy (Bhaskar, 1979) in the shape of a confusion of the movement from abstract to concrete *in thought* with chronological sequences or geographical movements in reality. Thus realism most certainly does not license a view in which capital forms first in the abstract simply as capital, as a 'general process' somehow disengaged from any context, local or whatever, and then collides with concrete, local, contingently related circumstances. Capital is always constituted from the start in particular places, in open systems. Abstraction identifies the necessary conditions of existence of phenomena, but that is different from showing how actual instances of them come into being.

Second, the abstract is not the same as the general in the sense of supralocal, nor is the concrete or the specific synonymous with the local. The supralocal – for example, the nation-state or the multinational company – is no less concrete than the local state or company. And one can make abstractions from certain aspects of phenomena regardless of whether they are unique or widely replicated.

Third, to say that there is a contingent relationship between certain social phenomena which span many localities and phenomena unique to particular localities is not to imply that the local is nothing but a mass of contingencies, or by contrast that the general in the sense of the supralocal is the sole province of necessity. The problem with these curious assumptions is again that the epistemic (the abstract-concrete movement) is 'ontologized'. But it also involves a simple misunderstanding of necessity and contingency: just because the coexistence of A and B in a particular form is contingent, it does not follow that there is nothing necessary about how, once configured in this way, they interact. On the contrary their interactions follow necessarily from their constitutions and relative dispositions.[3]

Thus, 'local' and 'contingent' in the phrase 'local, contingent factors' are not to be construed as synonyms. There is no reason to believe that internal, necessary relations are any less common at this geographical scale than at any other. In consequence, although the move from the abstract to the concrete in thought involves the posing of empirical questions about contingencies, empirical research also includes the discovery and examination of internal relations, and hence can be theory-informing.

Last, we might note how frequently arguments about generality and specificity, about theory and empirical research, and about general and local processes, are undermined not only by a facile alignment of these three dualisms, as if they identified related oppositions, but by an unaware slippage between two different meanings of 'general' – first, as widely replicated instances of identical events or phenomena, and second, as large, supralocal, but singular objects. For example, in relation to a particular university in a certain locality, central government might be described as involving 'general processes' in the second sense, as opposed to local processes, and yet not be 'general' in the first sense.

I will return again to the way in which concrete research can inform theory at various points later in the paper, but first I would like to draw attention to a major omission in Bhaskar's treatment of these relationships. It stems from the fact that his comments on hermeneutics are limited to making qualified concessions to it in principle. The problem is that the interpretation of meanings and actions in society does not yield to the same kind of logic as causal and structural analysis (Sayer, 1992). Interpretations of meanings involve not a concrete-abstract-concrete movement, but movements within hermeneutic circles, and it is difficult to see in what sense they can be approached in a theoretically structured way, even if, as Thrift (1983) suggests, the movements within the circles are determined and determinate through following specific channels of communication and social interaction. To be sure, we can use 'theoretical concepts' in the sense of concepts different from but illuminative of 'actors' concepts' (for example, gender or authority), but they do not seem to function in relation to actors' constructs the same way they do in relation to material structures and processes.

In this regard, Geertz's rather dim view of the role of 'megaconcepts' is understandable as his experience is related to interpretive anthropology: 'Theoretical formulations hover so low over the interpretations they govern that they don't make much sense or hold much interest apart from them' (1973, p. 25). Consequently he concludes that successive ethnographies do not contribute to some general theory but are just 'another country heard from' (p. 22). Will the same apply to geohistorical syntheses, each successive monograph being just another book on the shelf, dealing with phenomena which are so context-dependent that scarcely any of their conclusions are applicable outside them? Perhaps not. As Geertz argues, '[in ethnography] progress is marked less by a perfection of consensus than by a refinement of debate. What gets better is the precision with which we vex each other' (1973, p. 29). Ideally, each study broadens or otherwise challenges the range of schema with which we make sense of the world. In fact, Geertz's gloss also involves something very close to a realist conception of theorizing – the refinement of our concepts through the reconstruction of their patterns of associations (Sayer, 1992). And since the understandings of others have to be situated in the context of their practice, the successive studies would go beyond the reconstruction of 'webs of significance' to the analysis of structures of interdependent material practices. (Despite Geertz's insistence on the way in which the symbolic is embedded in the practical, I think he shares with many ethnographers a tendency to deal with it rather 'thinly'.) But in any case it still leaves the general problems of what we can expect of theory in this context and how we can evaluate different ethnographic interpretations.

As far as I am aware, discussions on this vital latter question in anthropology do not push far beyond debating relativism, the problem of translation, and problematizing the position of the interpreter (for example, Clifford and Marcus, 1986; Marcus and Fischer, 1986; and similarly in literature, Eagleton, 1983). Yet, however aware we are of these problems, it still leaves the problem of what is a good interpretation. Matters might be eased if greater attention were paid to the interpenetration of causal explanation and interpretive understanding; even those who see the two as reconcilable have little to offer regarding the evaluation of the latter (for example, Bhaskar, 1986 – perhaps because it is not a problem in the same way for natural science). It is here, above all, that the dialogue between the philosophy and methodology of the social sciences and the humanities is most needed.

A further deficiency of the philosophical literature, especially in the analytical tradition, is its exclusive focus on the microstructure of explanation, as if the problems of doing social science could be understood through exemplars such as 'why the column of mercury rose' or (equally notoriously), 'why the man shut the window'. It therefore ignores the possibility that we might understand each sentence but still miss the point of the story. In other words, it assumes that all difficulties are reducible to problems of microscopic explanation, and that the content of knowledge is indifferent to its form. This, coupled with its lack of concern for the social conditions and forms of production and communication of knowledge, explains its disinterest in what might be called problems of narrative. Although these might indeed be minor for microsociological studies (such as those which interest Giddens, 1984 or Harré, 1979), they are chronic in macrosocial science, and nowhere more so than in major works of geohistorical synthesis.

Problems of Narrative

Given the outrageous elasticity of recent uses of the term 'narrative', it is necessary to clarify the senses to be used here. I am not going to use 'narratives' as a synonym for specific theories, knowledges, or discourses. By problems of narrative I mean, first, problems of writing in general, of constructing texts (narrative in the broad sense), and, second, problems with narrative as a way of giving an account of social life in terms of a story of successive events (narrative in the narrow sense). In the latter sense, though not the former, it functions as an antonym for a specialized usage of the term 'analysis'. The broad-narrow distinction is admittedly a fuzzy one, not least because the second type is characterized by an acceptance of, rather than by a qualified resistance to, the linearity of narrative in the broad sense. Nevertheless, I think the distinction can help to avoid confusion.

We should also beware of confusing narratives, of any kind, with what they are about (even in cases where they are about other narratives); this is an 'epistemic fallacy' which has plagued hermeneutics (Bhaskar, 1979). Regional change is not a narrative, although narratives exist within it. 'Academic' narratives (of either kind) therefore stand in the kind of relationship to their objects shown in Figure 6.1.

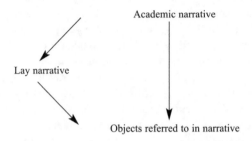

Figure 6.1 Relationship between narratives and objects

Both in broad and in narrow senses of the word, problems of narrative are crucial in relation to geohistorical synthesis: the complexity of such research makes the construction of texts particularly difficult; and in conducting such research we need to be aware of the relative merits and disadvantages of narrative and analysis.

Narrative (in the Narrow Sense) Versus Analysis

In history, the narrative versus analysis debate (for example, Dray, 1966; Hempel, 1962) was the contemporary of the idiographic-nomothetic debate in geography. Historians used to discuss the problem by reference to the explanation of the causes of World War I, geographers by reference to the explanation of the development of New York harbour. In both disciplines, the debates involved what was basically a positivist conception of science. Although I shall recall the resulting contrasting methods, my main interest is in the post-positivist debate.

The power of narrative derives from the way in which the depiction of events chronologically, in a story, gives the appearance of a causal chain or logic and the sense of movement towards a conclusion. Analysis – defined in realist rather than positivist terms – is concerned with abstracting common, widely replicated structures and mechanisms which endure throughout a number of different concrete histories. The power of analysis derives from its ability to explain much by little, but a necessary condition of this power is that the structures are indeed general and pivotal. This latter qualification distinguishes a realist interpretation of analysis from that of positivist nomothetic approaches, which assumed either that all phenomena are instances of regularities and hence are general in some sense, or that ontological matters did not constrain method. On the realist view, analysis deals with the necessary conditions and powers of its chosen structures, abstracting from the particular historical contingencies which brought those conditions into being. Analysis can take the form of theorizing the nature of such structures in abstraction from concrete situations, or, alternatively, it may be applied empirically to the explanation of concrete circumstances. In this second case, which primarily concerns us here, the attempt to explain the concrete (that is, many-sided) by reference to just a small number of its constitutive elements involves certain hazards, which will always need careful assessment. Thus, when we try to explain the development of, say, an industrial agglomeration, we risk identification errors or reductionism, if effects which are attributed to our chosen structures and mechanisms are actually the result of other processes. For example, effects actually arising from Government intervention may be attributed to the agglomeration itself. Second, we risk functionalist errors, if, in abstracting from the origins of the conditions necessary for the central processes, we assume that whatever is functional for them was created in order to fulfil that function. Third, and related to this, it risks the errors of structuralism if it fails to acknowledge the contingency of the reproduction of social structures. However, these three problems are only hazards, not unavoidable problems of analysis.

In our society, narrative is the taken-for-granted, natural form of discourse in everyday accounts of the world, through which events 'seem to tell themselves' (White, 1987, p. x). We rarely question whether the world really presents 'itself to perception in the form of well-made stories with central subjects, proper beginnings, middles, and ends, and a coherence that permits us to see "the end" in every beginning' (p. 24). By contrast, the legitimacy of analysis, and the irrelevance of narrative, are taken for granted in the natural sciences (with the possible exception of evolutionary biology). Since atoms and the like do not have histories (or geographies) but change only in fixed ways we do not expect physical scientists to tell stories about their objects of interest. Not surprisingly, social scientists tend to disagree over whether narrative or analysis is appropriate in their field. Those in the analysis camp worry about what Abrams terms 'the dereliction of method that results from excessive sensitivity to detail', whereas those in the narrative camp worry about 'the dereliction of scholarship that results from excessive attachment to theoretical generalization' (1982, p. 162).

Narratives suffer from a tendency to underspecify causality in the processes they describe. This is, firstly, because narrative, unlike analysis, is not *primarily* concerned with explaining the nature, conditions and implications of social structures. Secondly, its preoccupation with telling a story of a sequence of events tends to gloss over the difference between mere temporal succession and causality; as a result, they present only implicit, underexamined, aetiologies.

Ricoeur, an advocate of narrative from the perspective of hermeneutics, effectively admits this problem when he says that 'explanations have no other function than to help the reader follow further' (1982, p. 278). This seems to concede that storytelling pulls us along, makes us follow, but not necessarily thanks to the ability of its explanation to grasp what happens. Rather, as Abrams puts it, the principles of explanation underpinning the research are buried 'beneath the rhetoric of a story' (1982, p. 196). Discussing an example of the use of narrative in history, he comments:

> My own impression is that the function of narrative in this enterprise is to carry – in a highly persuasive way not accessible to intellectual scrutiny – those bits of the

argument the author does not choose to make available for direct critical examination on the part of his readers. (Abrams, 1982, p. 307)

It should be noted in passing that the fact that Ricoeur seems oblivious to the problem reflects the tendency of hermeneuticists to assume that society is *only* like a text, requiring *nothing more* than interpretation of its meanings. Yet although this interpretative understanding is indispensable, it is not sufficient to explain material change: causal explanation is still required.

A further problem of narrative is its tendency to neglect synchronic relations (the configurational dimension) at the expense of temporal successions (the episodic dimension).[4] Ricoeur objects to this judgment:

> [T]he activity of narrating does not consist simply in adding episodes to one another; it also constructs meaningful totalities out of scattered events ... The act of narrating, as well as the corresponding art of following a story, therefore require that we are able *to extract a configuration* from a succession. (Ricoeur, 1982, p. 278)

Thus, every narrative includes a competition between its 'episodic dimension' and its 'configurational dimension' (p. 279). But, given the linearity of narrative in the broad sense, it is inevitably more difficult to represent the configurational dimension than the episodic (Darby, 1962). Geography's concern with the spatial naturally gives it a stronger disposition towards the configurational, yet such was the theoretical bankruptcy of traditional regional geography that it still managed to underestimate the configurational. Thus, the besetting sin of traditional regional geographies was that they rarely gave more than a glimpse of their regions' incorporation into the wider structures of global capitalism: the global economy was little more than a passive, structureless backcloth. Underlying this neglect of synchronic structures were two reciprocal fallacies which persisted long into the quantitative revolution: that the uniqueness of places implies that they are independent of one another, and, conversely, that the discovery of regularity among events implies their interdependence. The concepts of variety and interdependence (Massey and Allen, 1985) or combined and uneven development have enabled us to escape from these fallacies (compare Gregory, 1988).

These criticisms of narrative are not intended to imply that explanations of concrete situations through analysis are *necessarily* better. Let us consider an example: the explanation of the rise of Silicon Valley. A narrative would take us through a series of events, leading in quasi-teleological fashion to its conclusion: the chance location of Stanford University, with its strong electrical engineering interests and the presence of Frederick Terman, who made great efforts to encourage the local development of commercial applications of university electronics research; the arrival of William Shockley, the inventor of the transistor, who chose to live in Palo Alto so as to be near his ageing mother; the proliferation of new firms spinning off from existing ones, and the emergence of a localized pool of top scientific and managerial skills, and so on. On the other hand, analysis would abstract from the 'historical accidents' and apply concepts like 'agglomeration economies' and 'vertical disintegration' (Scott and Angel, 1987). Yet it could equally confuse the accidental with the necessary, and indeed its attempt to explain much by little might make it prone to such identification errors. Thus, the proximity of firms to one another might be attributed to the need to minimize transaction costs, when, in fact, proximity may have come about for other reasons, even though it did indeed have the effect of minimizing them. In actual fact this criticism does not apply to Scott and Angel who are well aware of the problem, but it illustrates how, when applied to concrete examples, the explanations offered through analysis are only as good as the implicit local histories which they generate. In other words, it is quite impossible for an explanatory account to be good on the historical narrative but poor on the synchronic analysis, or vice versa: if an analysis of a specific case leads us to misspecify local history, then the synchronic structures and mechanisms must have been wrongly inferred, and, if an historical, explanatory narrative misconstrues the explanation of the local sequence of events, its implicit analysis of the configurational dimension must be wrong.[5]

As I noted earlier, there are still echoes of the idiographic-nomothetic debate in many post-positivist discussions of these kinds of issues. In view of this, it may help to summarize the equivalents of narrative and analysis according to empiricism/positivism, (1) and (2) below, and realism, (3) and (4):

(1)   *Atheoretical narratives.* By atheoretical, I mean the use of concepts and formulations in an unexamined way – one which is unaware of necessity in the social world and hence unaware of synchronic structures. Characteristically these present a narrative history either of a unique series of events or of supposedly typical series. At their worst, such narratives may be parochial, ignoring connections to changes elsewhere – for example, in the Silicon Valley case, ignoring the dependence of the microelectronics industry on defence spending and the advanced nature of the US electronics market.

(2)   The dual of (1) *is analysis in the positivist nomothetic mould.* This shares with (1) an event ontology and a blindness to necessity, but differs in that it treats events as replicable and expects to find enduring regularities which can be codified in generalizations or even laws. To this end, in Massey's fitting phrase, history is 'normalized' for, and structure is ignored. Hence in our high-tech agglomeration case, common factors are sought, typically by correlation analysis. If structures and hence the interdependence of unlike places are ignored, myths are perpetuated about the replicability of parts of those structures independently of the other parts. Witness the mania for Silicon Valley clones. A dilute version of (2) is the shopping-list-of-factors approach, which again regards its objects as simple events. This fails to show just how the factors combine, is weak at assessing their relative importance, and ignores the origins of the factors, despite the fact that they are often partly the product of the very thing they are supposed to explain (for example, Stanford University's electronics prowess).[6]

(1) and (2) are weak in terms of their treatment of both history and structure; it is absolutely not the case that they are strong on one and weak on the other. However, in recent years, in reaction to critiques of these kinds of work, other resolutions of the problem have arisen:

(3) *Structural analysis* recognizes that structures involve relationships of variety and interdependence, but tends to be interested in those which are widely replicated and more context-independent. It seeks *general* explanatory theories to account for the spatial shifts over time and is more concerned with the conditions of existence of particular structures than their specific contingent origins. (Thus the question would not be 'How did Silicon Valley develop?' – but 'What are the necessary conditions for the development of industrial agglomerations of a certain kind?'). Its basic objects of interest are not events (simple or complex) but structures and hence the key relationships which it studies are substantial rather than formal, like those of positivist nomothetic research (compare Sayer, 1992, Chapter 3). Whether this falls foul of the hazards of reductionism, functionalism, and structuralism depends not only on the awareness of the researchers of these problems but upon the question being asked, on how much simplification we are prepared to tolerate, and on the nature of the object. In some cases the kinds of approximation made may not be misleading. Despite the emphasis on structures, the proponents of this kind of analysis tend to be far more historically aware than researchers in tendency (2).

(4) *Realist concrete study.* This is an attempt to construct theoretically informed (and informative) narratives which make their aetiologies explicit and give appropriate weight to the synchronic or configurational and the episodic. (As we shall see shortly this creates extreme problems of narrative in the broad sense.) At root, it rests upon a conception, following Marx, of the concrete as a unity of multiple determinations. It therefore sees geohistorical explanation in terms of attempts to apply and synthesize – in a critical rather than eclectic way – a range of social theories, each one relating to different aspects of the concrete. Some of the processes studied will be highly context-dependent, others will not; there should be not presumption in favour of either, or in favour of the kinds of explanation which suit these, that is nomological or contextualizing; deciding on the balance must be an *a posteriori* matter reflecting the nature of the situation under study and the questions asked about it.

There is a great deal of argument and wavering between (3) and (4). Attempts at realist concrete studies tend to attract accusations of being 'atheoretical' and 'empiricist' (for example, Harvey, 1987). The senses in which these terms are used appear to be the old ones: they seem to involve concern about a retreat from theory and generality into uniqueness, as if the unique were inaccessible to theory. Although there is a more than an echo of the discredited categorical grid of the old idiographic-nomothetic debate in such charges, they are illuminating and do raise some genuine hazards.

The first concerns uniqueness. The problem here is that even though we break the fallacious association of the unique with the independent and recognize 'variety and interdependence', many of the interdependencies tend themselves to be *unique* rather than generalizable to other cases. This reminds us that theory is associated with the explanation of necessity, rather than mere regularity or generality. For example, the integrated circuit industry that grew in Silicon Valley was greatly supported by the US space programme, with its need to miniaturize electronics, and this was no less important than was the Ministry of International Trade and Industry's support for the Japanese industry. Although these two government-industry relationships are instances of variety and inter-dependence, the form of interdependence is not one we would expect to be replic-able. So escaping from a parochial focus only leads us to the general in a particular sense as 'supralocal': it does not necessarily open the door to generalizations about empirical regularities in patterns of events, though, as we have already argued, enduring, precise regularities cannot be expected in social science.

For realists, the solution to this problem lies in the distinction between structures and events, the concept of open systems, the recognition that the repro-duction of social structures is a contingent product of human action and that compared to natural structures, social structures are only relatively enduring. So, although variety and interdependence exist in fairly durable and widespread forms in some social structures, others are more restricted and transient. And this in turn reminds us of our earlier discussion of contextualizing versus nomologi-cal explanations, of the context dependence-independence continuum, and of why the relationship between active theorizing (as well as acceptance and use of existing theory) and empirical research overlap in social science.

A second aspect of the criticisms of realist concrete study is the alleged retreat from 'theory'. This raises again the irony of the extraordinarily unexamined char-acter of this term (Sayer, 1992). The charge of empiricism might derive from an unacknowledged supposition that theory-neutral research is even possible. As I have argued elsewhere (1992), taking this impossibility seriously requires us to adopt a less exclusive concept of theory as 'examined conceptualizations' which make claims about the nature of objects, particularly their structures and powers. Lay-knowledge or practical consciousness are only atheoretical in the sense that their conceptualizations and claims are relatively unexamined. Since lay-knowledge is both part of our object, and a rival account of it, our response to it must not be to dismiss it, but rather to examine it. There are no philosophically defensible grounds for using the term 'theory' as many (often otherwise sophis-ticated) social scientists do – where the only distinguishing feature of 'theoreti-cal' terms is their unfamiliar or esoteric character in relation to lay vocabularies. Despite its unexamined character, lay-knowledge has the advantage of being formed in a richer variety of contexts than academic knowledge, based as the latter is on abstraction and disciplines.[7] In any case, the double hermeneutic of social science requires us to understand and negotiate with 'actors' accounts', not dismiss them in order to maintain the purity of what we like to call theory. At worst, some social scientists seem unable to recognize theory except when its names are paraded up and down the page at the expense of other descriptions. The third aspect of the charge of a retreat into empiricism centres on the implications of the *concrete* character of the realist approaches, with their focus on the syn-thesis of multiple determinations. Now many tendentious metaphors and analo-gies have been used in defence of particular standpoints on theory: thus positivists used to talk persuasively of the prime role of theory in 'reducing the burden of fact', and it is still common to characterize theoretical concepts as those which 'explain much by little'. Such phrases play on the appeal of simplicity and economy, but at the risk of making us forget that the simplest, most elegant explanation may not be the most practically adequate and that there are also likely to be costs in deliberately depleting our vocabularies. Geertz's (equally tendentious) phrase 'thin description' nicely indicates the problem (1973).

Consider another tendentious analogy making the antipositivist or anti-instrumentalist point: social scientists are like artists or musicians; their skill derives not from being able only to use a limited number of techniques, media, structures, genres, and so on (three chords and simple rhythms) – the equivalent of reductionism in social science – but from knowing a vast range of such forms and from being able to combine them in a way which respects their compatibilities and incompatibilities – the equivalent of coherent, nonsyncretic synthesis in concrete research. On this view theories are not few in number, monolithic and distinct (as so many social scientists and philosophers assume without a hint of scepticism), but multiple and overlapping. If we couple this with our earlier point about lay-knowledge, then we begin to value not the density of uses of terms graced with the label 'theoretical' which are supposed to explain much by little. Instead we admire the highly developed and multiple sensitivities of the author, the richness and subtlety of the observation, the awareness of contextuality, and the command of language *period*, rather than of a supposedly 'theoretical' language. Further, if we add to this a recognition of the significance of the ways in which narratives (in the broad sense) are constructed for their ability to capture and communicate processes, then we are likely to evaluate the texts that come out of concrete research in a very different light. Raymond Williams is a good example of an author not only able to use 'megaconcepts' but also extraordinarily gifted in exploiting the cognitive power of everyday, plain words by using them in novel ways to yield insights unavailable to those with more restricted, if also more esoteric, vocabularies. This should not alarm the self-appointed guardians of theory. Concepts are not the same as the technical terms which name them and their power can often be enhanced by expressing them through other terms. So the sparsity of ostentatiously 'theoretical' language (in the sense of academic technical terms) does not necessarily make work atheoretical: on the contrary, it may enhance abstract theory by making us examine what is normally taken for granted.[8]

I repeat that these arguments about the role of theory all use tendentious analogies. Although the economizing view of theory is appropriate for abstraction, the second view is more appropriate for concrete research. But again, the latter approach is more easily said than done, and this is where the critics are on target. In practice, the attempt to combine many theoretical insights can easily become unmanageable, and the tendency to slide into ad hoc uses of unexamined concepts – a tendency present in most empirical research precisely because of the immediacy of lay-knowledge and the need to engage with it – becomes stronger than usual. I am therefore only too aware of the dangers of allowing the pluralistic view of the role of theory in concrete research to act as a cover for the re-emergence of the kind of pleas for an opaque and unaccountable 'craft' which gained notoriety in the old idiographic-nomothetic debate. We must obviously never return to the days when research students were told not to worry their little heads with theory but to go away and immerse themselves in the sources. The need to hold theoretical reflection and the refinement of abstractions in tension with empirical study remains, but takes new forms. For these reasons, the current debate between realist narrative and analysis is likely to continue.

Narrative (in the Broad Sense): Influences upon Texts and Research

Whichever side we take in the contemporary debate about narrative versus analysis, we are still left with the problem of narrative in the broad sense, that is, the problem of the composition of texts.[9] I would suggest that this can best be introduced in relation to a number of different structuring elements of research and texts. Some of these can be stated briefly:

(1)　The perceived structure of the object influences content, patterns of emphasis and form;

(2)　The conceptual structures and existential priorities of theories (note the plural) influence perception;

(3)　There is the influence of the interests of the researcher;

(4)　And, not entirely facetiously, another important structuring influence upon texts is the need to 'get-the-damn-thing-finished': texts are always the results of struggles over the use of time.

Other influences require more elaboration:

(5)　There is a tactical, hermeneutic structuring principle. Though academics are often strangely unreflective about this, we write for others, in order to communicate. Even if writing is seen merely as recording or storing information, it is inevitably influenced by the author's expectations about the preunderstandings of the audience. This is the hermeneutic dimension. More particularly, not only writing but research itself is influenced by its location within ongoing debates and against rival academic and political groupings. So we not only write about things but for, with, and against others (compare Eagleton, 1983, p. 84–5). In this sense, the researcher's motives are not individual but relational. In virtue of this hermeneutic and tactical dimension, astute authors may begin, not with the most fundamental part of the structure or argument they want to present, but with the part which they expect their audience will most easily accept or with a preemption of likely initial objections. There need not be anything devious about this; it may simply be the best way of making the content accessible. At the same time, such considerations may distort the text; indeed, this is why critics so often come to resemble their enemies.

(6)　Although all of these aspects influence the structure of texts, it would be a mistake to see texts as merely the outcome of these influences, for this would ignore precisely the problem of narrative in the broad sense. It is not only that narrative structures (including ways in which analyses are narrated) have a degree of autonomy and have a largely hidden influence upon how we 're-present' knowledge and how it is read. It is also that more or less implicit assumptions about the forthcoming structure of the text influence the content of the research itself.

> Literary processes – metaphor, figuration, narrative – affect the ways cultural phenomena are registered, from the first jotted 'observations' to the completed book, to the ways these configurations 'make sense' in a determined reading. (Clifford and Marcus, 1986, p. 4)[10]

Moreover, most forms of communication (with the partial exception of pictures or diagrams), whether written or spoken, have a linear, sequential form which inevitably favours the expression of the episodic over the configurational. Despite the fact that experience commonly registers many things happening at once, the re-presentation of that experience has difficulty in reflecting this. Grasping the whole is more difficult than grasping what happens next in the story.

There are of course many narrative devices for dealing with synchronicity ('meanwhile back at the ranch ...'), including use of the concept of structure itself. We can remind ourselves and our readers not to be misled into thinking that a break in the narrative (in the narrow sense) or in the analysis signals an equivalent breaking of the relationships to which they refer. But then there may equally be relationships we do not even notice because of prior decisions on composition.

(7)   A further problem of all verbal communication is the unavoidably rhetorical and elliptical character of any description or explanation. Thus, in my own case, writing about the growth of Britain's M4 corridor, it was tempting to write stuff like: '[T]here then followed a period of burgeoning development as agglomeration economies multiplied.' Here the theoretical aura of the term 'agglomeration economies' and the rhetorical power of 'burgeoning' might help to carry the reader along, perhaps not noticing that I had not unpacked the development process and demonstrated its constituent relationships. At worst one can easily slip into using a single word – 'development' – to explain what has to be explained! The content of our accounts cannot be divorced from their form. Even apparently minor matters such as the choice of tense can have rhetorical effects; in ethnographic accounts of actions the present tense tends to be a universalizing and objectifying idiom, the past tense a particularizing idiom which gives the impression of contingency (Rosaldo, 1987). Once again the philosophy of social science offers little help even in recognizing, let alone resolving, such problems (but see Nelson et al., 1987). On the other hand, the recognition of such problems in literary criticism is neutralized by its pervasive epistemological idealism which inhibits assessment of the ability of discourse to refer to real processes (Eagleton, 1983).

Some of the above structuring influences on texts may seem unexceptional when spelt out, but it is extraordinary how many methodologists have only considered the first two as important. Yet these influences overlap and interfere with one another: for example, the priorities of the research community and current political issues may divert us from recognizing certain structures of the object.

Some authors (for example, Olsson, 1991; McLuhan, 1967) have considered narrative form to be a tyranny and have looked for an alternative. Although the limitations of narrative are as much the reader's problem as the author's, writers who break too far away from received, understood narrative forms are likely either to be dismissed as obscure or not understood. It would be easy to dismiss the achievements of conventional narrative forms and replace them with anarchic textual forms which hid poor reasoning and explanation and which merely confused the reader or limited the readership to a tiny number of cognoscenti. However 'conventional' narrative forms may be, it does not follow that merely avoiding them will break down more barriers than they create. Art and music have the freedom to break out of restrictive narrative conventions because they need not be representational, but in social science, and some of the humanities, we have less freedom. Whether we prefer analysis or narrative (in the narrow sense), the word attempts to refer as adequately as possible, or as we used to say in less epistemologically aware times, 'truthfully'. Like any linguistic structure, narrative (in the broad sense) both illuminates and occludes. In acknowledging the latter we need to remember the former. The fact of 'learning-by-writing' confirms this: we do not first learn and then write it up, confronting the problems of narrative as we do. Rather we learn through writing, discovering and sometimes resolving problems precisely because we feel obliged to conform to conventional narrative forms. So, although there may be some grounds for Gregory's dismay at existing narrative forms in geography, we need to beware of a certain modishness which creates more problems than it solves (Gregory, 1987).

There are some authors who find they can write without experiencing problems of narrative in the broad sense, but it is arguable that these are not so much gifted writers as writers who fail to appreciate the interconnectedness of their subject matter, and hence the problems of straightening it out into a linear flow. Two recent books on high-technology industry and regional development boldly tackle their subject by dealing with questions of 'what, how, where and why' – *in that order* (Hall et al., 1987; Markusen et al., 1986). Although in terms of style of English they are well-written, the ability of the narrative to grasp connections tends to confirm the second, negative judgment, particularly in dealing with the insertion of local developments within wider structures. The 'logical' and business-like simplicity of such a straightforward narrative form may appeal, but the usefulness of this kind of 'logic' depends upon how it corresponds to the relationships it seeks to represent.

Work of geohistorical synthesis will surely not be able to use such simple forms. It will always insist on recombining the what, the how, the where, and the why. Acutely conscious of the combination of structure and agency, of relations of presence and absence, of the articulation of the local, the national, and the global, it will presumably have to develop new kinds of text or narrative, combining studies of processes previously thought separate. Thus, Agnew's *The United States in the World Economy* (1987b) is simultaneously a geography of the regions of the USA. Lash and Urry's discourse on *The End of Organized*

Capitalism (1987) which again has a novel combination of interests, spanning economic history, political and cultural theory, industrial restructuring, class theory, all situated in spatial context – whether local, regional, national, or global – is equally justified. Such developments may further alarm those who fear interdisciplinary studies, and certainly the manuscripts will perplex publishers. But equally they will not be able to break far away from clearly structured narrative forms, if their authors want a readership. The competition between the separate structures of the object as perceived (structuring principle (1) above) and of conventional narrative forms will still result in compromise rather than victory over the 'tyranny' of the latter. The attractions of discussing the similar *en bloc* will vie for position with the attractions of discussing the interconnections of the different. The attractions of pulling out the theoretical insights from the fine texture of a geohistorical synthesis and discussing them separately will remain (for example, see Gregory, 1982). So too will the attractions of organizing such texts around different spatial levels, even though it risks concealing their interconnections.[11]

The structure of texts is again a subject which has been illuminated by recent developments in anthropology. (From the point of view of an outsider, the attentiveness of anthropologists to the structure of their texts, rather than ideas within them, seems strange, but perhaps salutary.) Besides addressing the need for linking ethnography and political economy, Marcus and Fischer consider the implications for the kinds of text which this implies:

> What we have in mind is a text that takes as its subject not a concentrated group of people in a community, affected in one way or another by political-economic forces, but 'the system' itself – the political-economic processes – spanning different locales, or even different continents. Ethnographically, these processes are registered in the activities of dispersed groups or individuals whose actions have mutual, often unintended, consequences for each other, as they are connected by markets and other major institutions that make the world system. (1986, p. 91)

There is a danger here of confusing geohistorical synthesis with wanting to study everything – even syntheses still have to be selective (compare Allen, 1987). In distant conception, though surely not in execution, such a project might seem compelling, but it is worth reminding ourselves of the sometimes fatal attractions of novel research ideas: why do we want this, even if we accept the doubtful notion that it is feasible? Is it just out of some abstract wish for ever greater connection? At any rate, it would be slightly less difficult(!) to do a single-locale study which constructed the 'text around the strategic selection of a locale, while backgrounding the system, but without obscuring the fact it is integrally constitutive of life within the bounded subject matter' (Marcus and Fischer, 1986, p. 93).

This resembles a kind of historical study favoured by Abrams which picks as its focus a probably quite atypical but nevertheless strategically situated micro-situation, one which lies at the intersection of the key structures in contention or transformation, and uses that vantage point to illuminate a much wider canvas (Abrams, 1982, p. 199).

Marcus and Fischer draw parallels here with Williams's discussion of the 'increasing difficulty in realist fiction of representing whole worlds and complex social structures within the limited narrative frame of plot and set of characters ... the complexities and scale of late capitalism in the twentieth century seem to offer a much more formidable task for the politically and historically sensitive realist' (Marcus and Fischer, 1986, p. 77). Williams suggests 'combinatory texts, which link intimate, ethnographic-like detail concerning language and manners, with portraits of larger, impersonal systems that abstractly affect local communities, on one hand. and are an internalized component of characters' ... lives on the other' (Marcus and Fischer, 1986, pp. 77–8). Fiction can, of course, create imaginary individuals and localities in which an unusually large number of the structures of the wider society intersect and are exposed, but though illuminating and provocative that is not an option open to social science.

Another novel kind of concrete geographical study is needed of the way in which 'the local becomes general' (Storper, 1987); how social innovations initially formed in unique circumstances are imitated and adapted more widely. Although Lamarkian evolutionary analogies are tempting, such investigations would only be novel insofar as they avoided the naturalistic tendencies of spatial analytic diffusion theory. It is therefore essential that the spread and adaptation of social innovations are examined within processes of structuration, not as processes of contagion (Gregory, 1985). For example, studies of the generalization and adaptation of types of labour process organization, such as Taylorism, Fordism, or 'just-in-time' can show how what are usually taken as universal stages in the development of capitalism not only originate in specific geographical and historical circumstances – sometimes ones which are in a significant sense unique – but continue to develop in ways which bear the imprints of their geohistorical contexts (Cusumano, 1985; Littler, 1982; Sayer, 1986; Urry, 1986).

Conclusion

The above proposals are meant to be suggestive rather than exhaustive. By way of conclusion, I want to mention a more radically novel approach exemplified by Soja's recent essay on Los Angeles (1986). Neither narrative nor causal analysis, it focuses upon ironies of juxtaposition, that is, paradoxes which – if the phrase does not sound too grand – clarify the human predicament, or at least a few facets of it. Hence the astonishing combination of the massive involvement of the city in militarism and the entertainment industry – 'holocaust attached to halcyon' (p. 257) or Hollywood – a fitting home indeed for 'Star Wars' research. Soja makes frequent use of wordplay such as this, but the puns are far too accurate to be dismissed as frivolous. Of course, as the author warns, these juxtapositions, and indeed many of the more familiar covariances and patterns of urban areas, are coincidences rather than intentional products. Though the essay tells one little or nothing about the history of the region, about how the mechanisms of its development work, or indeed how it is seen by its denizens, it is nevertheless at least as interesting as any of those things.

Moreover, although subtitled 'Some fragments of a critical human geography', it is quite different from what is normally expected of critical theory. It asks us to reflect upon ironies, contradictions, and absurdities in order to make us see its object in a new way, hinting perhaps at a hidden order of bizarre (unintended) rationality behind the appearances. Although the more traditional approaches are certainly not dispensable, Soja's postmodernist approach helps us see their limitations. In common with a good causal regional analysis it shows how the national and the global are reflected in the local. But there the resemblance ends. Causal analysis carves up the world so as to capture chains of mechanisms, and refuses to attach significance to coincidence or paradox, even though they are not beyond human control, and even though we ought to be *surprised* that such coincidences or juxtapositions are *allowed* to occur. In other words, to be good causal analysts we need to explain things in relation to their 'causal contexts', abstracting from unrelated phenomena operating in different causal contexts. A purely causal analysis of the industrial base of Los Angeles would instantly make us forget its ironies by resolving them into separate causal groups. What we would overlook is precisely the fact that the society in question does split into these contexts of determination rather than other ones; we would miss the significance of the fact that the division of areas of action is made *this* way, in practice. Thus, for example, in industrial studies, the fact that conditions of employment are largely determined regardless of the domestic circumstances of workers, and the fact that production is largely undertaken irrespective of ecological consequences, are unquestioned in most explanatory analyses and narratives. Our methodological protocols lead us to take these things as given, in order to reflect their causal structures more clearly. Paradox is seen only as an irrelevance to be dissolved by causal explanation, not reflected upon and resolved through practice. Yet as Soja puts it, 'premeditation may be impossible to ascribe but postmeditation ... is in order' (1986, p. 259). The fact that we cannot find causes – whether material or intentional – does not reduce the need for critical reflection: if anything the contrary. The result of this kind of oversight is that the claims of realist and other explanatory kinds of methodology to belong to *critical* social science are blunted.

The following comment by Sim on Lyotard's antiphilosophy might equally apply to Soja's postmodernist essay:

> It is one of the virtues of such a text that its many paradoxes and silences provoke ideologically-loaded responses. and the responses so released reveal the shape of the reacting discourse's own theoretical pretensions with considerable clarity. (Sim, 1988, p. 35)[12]

Similarly the limitations of an interpretive view are exposed: an ethnographic study would probably be too tied to the self-understanding of its subjects (hovering low over the ground, as Geertz puts it) to capture the insights of Soja's aerial view. For these reasons, conventional approaches fail to probe deeply into what Thrift terms 'unknowing' in popular consciousness (1983).

At one level, the disregard of such a text for conventional explanatory canons seems shocking; indeed, it would be if it were intended to *replace*, rather than supplement, conventional (including realist) explanation and understanding. But there is also something shocking about a social science or geography that is blind to the great paradoxes of our society, and many of these concern the way in which things are juxtaposed in space-time.

Notes

1 For Giddens, whose work has had a huge influence upon the new regional geography, 'regions' include first and foremost microsociological settings, such as the shopfloor (Giddens, 1984).

2 The arguments of this section are more fully developed in Sayer (1991).

3 Bob Jessop terms this 'contingent necessity' (Jessop, 1990).

4 I have borrowed the terms 'episodic' and 'configurational' from Ricoeur (1982).

5 Alternatively, 'Historical narration without analysis is trivial, historical analysis without narration is incomplete' (Gay, quoted in White, 1987, p. 4).

6 Bourdieu makes many telling criticisms of this methodology at various points in his *Distinction* (1984).

7 In response to positivist covering-law explanations, Louch writes: 'We have, in fact, a rather rich knowledge of human nature which can only be assimilated to the generality pattern of explanation by invoking artificial and ungainly hypotheses about which we are much less secure than we are about the particular cases the generalizations are invoked to guarantee' (Louch, 1966, pp. 3–4).

8 If this alarms some readers as an apparent justification of empiricism, let them check, whether their concept of theory is compatible with a recognition of the impossibility of empiricism in the sense of theory-neutral research.

9 We can grant that even analyses have, in a sense, to be narrated and are learned within narratives. Even though analyses are not the same as the narratives in which they are known, their persuasiveness owes much to the power of these narratives and their exemplars (I am indebted to Chris Hall for this point). Compare Barnes's illuminating interpretation of Kuhn (Barnes, 1982).

10 Though the pressures of contemporary academic production are hardly conducive to such reflectiveness. Welcome though these anthropologists' sensitivity is in these matters, what is also noticeable about their work is the conspicuous absence of philosophy of social science.

11 Thus in writing a book about uneven development in the electronics industry (Morgan and Sayer, 1988), I found it impossible to avoid organizing it into successive global, national and regional sections.

12 Sim describes postmodernism as a 'philosophy of risk' and 'analytical' philosophy as a 'philosophy of caution', the former proliferating claims without concern for their grounding, the latter restricting claims to what can be grounded (Sim, 1988).

PART IV

CRITICAL REALISM: FROM CRITIQUE TO NORMATIVE THEORY

Introduction

Why *critical* realism? The prefix identifies Bhaskar's realist theory of social science with the project of critical social science (CSS), that is, a social science that is critical of the practices which are its objects of study. Bhaskar argues that where social research identifies misconceptions and avoidable suffering in the practices it studies, its explanations simultaneously amount to criticisms implying the removal of the misconceptions or suffering and whatever causes them (Bhaskar, 1979). If this is right, then social science can have an emancipatory potential. This argument is of course controversial, not least – in philosophical circles – because of its implication that we can deduce *ought* from *is*. In Chapter 7, I develop a different but sympathetic critique of the project of CSS and Bhaskar's reconstruction of it, arguing that many kinds of explanatory critique require the defence of normative or critical standpoints, and that these are not necessarily derivable from explanations of situations. Moreover, CSS has arguably often relied upon unexamined and problematic critical standpoints and hence been hampered by the absence of normative reasoning. Yet like many other advocates of CSS, critical realist authors have been silent about the latter.

It is probably 'no accident', as they say, that this dissatisfaction with the implicit normative standpoints of CSS should have arisen at a time when the Left has lost its earlier self-confidence, as a consequence of both the rise of the Right and the challenges posed by new kinds of radical thought and practice such as feminism, post-colonialism and green politics. Consider, for example, the 'impasse' of radical development theory and its increasing self doubts about both the pragmatics of development (usually arising from recognizing the need for concessions to non-socialist forms of social organization) and the moral-political implications of the very idea of development (arising from post-colonial thought) (Corbridge, 1993a and b; Nussbaum and Glover, 1995). This situation seems to have caused divergent responses – on the one hand, in some postmodernist quarters, a suspicion and rejection of normative thinking as implicitly authoritarian, and on the other a revival of interest in normative theory regarding politics and ethics. The first response of 'ethical disidentification' ironically fits comfortably with liberalism and its suspicion of normativity, and like liberalism, it can easily serve to protect injustices from criticism, since it is reluctant to assume any normative standpoint from which to criticize them. My sympathies lie firmly with the second response.

Chapter 8, based on a paper written with Michael Storper (Sayer and Storper, 1997), follows up the argument about the problems of attempting to develop a CSS without a normative framework or standpoint, by calling for a renewed concern with ethics and moral-political values, so that we can more effectively think though what is implied by different goals and conceptions of the good. There is a remarkable imbalance between our ability to think about the social world positively or scientifically, as something to be understood and explained, and our ability to think about it normatively, or even to think how it might be. The attempted expulsion of values from science and science from values (by reducing them to arational, emotive expressions) has not succeeded in producing a value-free science, but it has left normative thinking to wither in many parts of social science. The greater the extent to which normative discourse is marginalized, the weaker our ability to do it, and in turn, the greater the disincentive to others to take it up subsequently. This has happened despite the fact that thinking about what might or should be can also illuminate what is, by forcing us to ask searching questions about the conditions of existence of the familiar, and to conduct thought-experiments (Sayer, 1995).

Given the resistance to normative thinking in social science, we deal with a wide range of objections ranging from the view that the 'intrusion' of values 'contaminates' and undermines science through to postmodernist refusals of normativity. However, part of the reason for the gulf between positive and normative thinking in social science has to with the abstractness of most literature in moral and political philosophy, and its remoteness from the concrete problems and moral dilemmas of everyday life. In view of this, morality cannot be reduced to a set of principles abstracted from concrete situations but involves responses to those situations by situated actors with histories and geographies. If we are to close the gap we need to consider ethical issues more concretely and here we find that in many cases, such, as those of apartheid and its aftermath, the spatial dimension may be crucial. Moreover, even abstract moral reasoning has implicit geographical imaginaries, particularly regarding the shape of moral communities and the location of those excluded from them. (Incidentally, Chapter 8's discussions of normative theory in relation to space illustrates the claims made in Chapter 5 about the inevitable vagueness of theorizing about space, though as we also noted there, vague does not mean unimportant.) In short, the message of the following two chapters is that if critical realism – or indeed any approach to social science – is to have emancipatory potential it cannot avoid engaging with normative thinking about the social world.

7

Critical Realism and the Limits to Critical Social Science

Critical social scientists argue that explanations of social practices must be critical precisely in order to be explanatory, and that the necessity of critique gives social science a potentially emancipatory character. In practice, critiques of social phenomena are enormously contentious because it is difficult to establish agreement about what constitute problems, solutions or improvements, and whether the latter are feasible. The quest for emancipation therefore involves addressing normative questions and the feasibility of alternatives. Yet these considerations are unevenly represented in the practice of critical social science (hereafter CSS).[1] They are most prominent in newer CSSs such as feminism and green political theory, where discussions on topics such as the politics of difference or animal rights argue about the nature of problems and progressive alternatives. By contrast, until recently they were rarely seen in the older Marxist-influenced CSS, reflecting the traditional Marxist antipathy to moral discourse 'blueprints'.[2]

The new CSSs reflect the shift in politics away from the old certainties of class and distribution, where normative goals were largely taken for granted and the main concern was with attacking established power, to a politics in which debates about desirable alternatives are much more to the fore. There are now clear signs of a reawakening of interest among social scientists in ethics and political philosophy. For example, in development studies, critical social scientists who were previously sure of their value standpoints now realize they are problematic (Corbridge, 1993a and b; Toye, 1987).

However, as they stand, the philosophical reconstructions of CSS are seriously out of kilter with these developments, and are implicitly closer to the older CSS in their neglect of the normative side (Fay, 1975, 1987, 1996; Bhaskar, 1986, 1991; Collier, 1994a; Edgley, 1985). Critical realism in particular gives a complacent account of CSS in which *ought* follows straightforwardly from *is*, apparently bypassing difficult normative issues which elsewhere are the subject of interminable debate. For a philosophy concerned with emancipation, its lack of discussion of normative issues is astonishing.

While I accept much of the rationale for CSS and identify with its aims, I wish to argue here that there are important flaws in these reconstructions, which explain the limited success of those CSSs which neglect normative questions and the often contentious and inconclusive nature of those which do confront them. I aim to show that there are substantial limits to the applicability of the models of CSS, particularly critical realist reconstructions, and that accordingly their claims need to be moderated.

The chapter begins with a sketch of how CSS has been philosophically reconstructed and justified. Through a series of examples, I then discuss the need to examine the standpoints from which critiques are made and the desirability and feasibility of the alternatives they imply. I then assess the implications of uncertainties about standpoints and needs and what these in turn imply about the limits of CSS and its conception of emancipation.

Reconstructions of Critical Social Science

We may of course criticize social practices because they are an affront to our values, but the rationale of CSS, according to the philosophical reconstructions, starts from explanations rather than value positions, although of course we usually already have such positions. An account of patriarchal behaviour which failed to evaluate actors' assumptions regarding men's and women's abilities would fail as an explanation of what happens. Such critical evaluation would of course in no way deny that the suspect beliefs were held. Criticism of social practice in this kind of case is not an option which involves stepping outside social science, but is necessary for social scientific explanation itself. Criticism becomes critique when we not only show that certain beliefs are false but explain why they are held, and what produces them. Critique is therefore intrinsic to social science. More simply, and from another angle, there is no point in social science if it does not at least offer the possibility of some kind of social improvement, even if it doesn't go beyond enlightenment and reduction of illusion, to material change.

In philosophical reconstructions (for example, Bhaskar, 1989; Collier, 1994a; Fay, 1975, 1987), CSS is often identified as having four stages:

(i) identifying problems – unmet needs, suffering, false beliefs;
(ii) identifying the source or cause of those unmet needs, false beliefs, etc., such as a particular form of domination;
(iii) passing to a negative judgement of those sources of illusion and oppression;
(iv) favouring (*ceteris paribus*) actions which remove those sources.

In some cases the false beliefs (i) help to perpetuate the circumstances which generate them (ii).

There are two main variants of the model – the cognitive explanatory critique, which starts from the identification of false beliefs, and the needs-based explanatory critique, which starts from the identification of suffering, or frustrated needs (Collier, 1994a). Bhaskar argues that the transitions from (ii) to (iii) to (iv) are necessary, thus breaking 'Hume's Law' – that *ought* cannot be derived from *is* (see also Edgley, 1985). If a belief is known to be false, then, other things being equal, it makes no sense to deny that people ought not to believe it. Even if, in the case of the needs-based critique, we take the view that it does not logically follow that because a person is starving they ought to have food, it at least does not *make sense, ceteris paribus*, to deny that they ought to have it (Collier, 1994a). The *ceteris paribus* clause in (iv) is intended to cover situations where there is a conflicting and overriding need which makes it unwise to remove the initial problem and its sources.

Bhaskar and others argue that this approach offers the promise of an *emancipatory* social science, providing at least a necessary condition for the emancipation of its 'target groups' by enabling them to see how to replace 'unwanted determinations' by 'wanted and needed determinations'. It is recognized, of course, that enlightening people (or facilitating their own self-enlightenment) as to the source of the illusions and other unwanted determinations responsible for their plight is not a *sufficient* condition for their emancipation from them, and may indeed increase dissonance and despair: for emancipation, the mechanisms actually generating the problems must also be removed or blocked.

In a discussion of a related issue – values in social science – Charles Taylor has criticized emotivist and subjectivist conceptions of values as expressions lying beyond the scope of reason, and has argued that values are 'secreted' by theories and explanations of social action (Taylor, 1967). Thus, the explanation of profit in neoclassical economics in terms of the marginal efficiency of capital secretes the value judgement that it is a fair return to capitalists. The explanation of profit offered by Marxism secretes the judgement that it is an undeserved appropriation of workers' surplus labour by capital. We should choose the values secreted by the superior explanation. Values can therefore be assessed rationally[3] via an evaluation of relevant explanations. This argument compliments Bhaskar's point that the important question regarding values is not whether social science is value-free but whether values are science-free.

Attractive though these ideas may seem, they make CSS look all too straightforward and strangely at odds with the experience of practical instances. It is not always clear which among rival explanations is superior, or what the relevant explanations responsible for secreting particular values are, and as we shall see, there are some cases, concerning culturally specific needs and obligations to others, where normative judgements appear to be prior to and secrete explanations rather than vice versa. More simply we are often deeply uncertain as to what would constitute improvement or emancipation, and hence unclear as to what determinations we should want and need.

Most of the arguments in philosophy relating to CSS concern the controversial naturalist move from *is* to *ought*. While I accept that the move is legitimate where the *ought* term is unspecific, that is, where it means merely 'the false belief, or type of suffering ought to be removed', it is far more questionable where it means 'x ought to be changed in a certain way'. Clearly CSS would have little to offer if it was limited to the former unspecific directive; its claim to be potentially emancipatory would be decidedly feeble. An emancipatory social science worth the name would need to have a more specific and directive critical content, identifying what exactly was wrong and what specifically needed to be done to improve matters. But here we run into difficulties, firstly, regarding how we identify problems at the start (i), and secondly, concerning the issues concealed by the apparently innocuous *ceteris paribus* clause in (iv).[4] As we shall see, these two problems feed into each other and create uncertainties at the critical stage (iii). Both derive from a lack of examination of the standpoints from which critiques are made.

Critical Standpoints

To identify unmet needs and decide that certain beliefs are false is to make judgments of good and bad, and of what ought and ought not to be, and hence to engage with normative questions. CSS therefore implies a connection between positive (explanatory/descriptive) social science and normative discourses such as those of moral and political philosophy. But in much of the literature on CSS, this normative dimension is hardly acknowledged (for example, Bhaskar, 1986, 1991; Collier, 1994a; Fay, 1975, 1987; Edgley, 1985). In the case of the best known CSS, Marxism, it is often denied and suppressed. The historical reasons for this are well known and widely criticized (Buchanan, 1982; Lukes, 1985), but the problems are perpetuated rather than countered in the philosophical reconstructions. However, it is noticeable that the younger CSSs of feminism and green theory have a far stronger focus on normative issues and have a closer relationship between their positive/explanatory literature and explicitly critical/normative debate (for example, Bock and James, 1992; Gilligan, 1982; Benton, 1993; Collier, 1994b; Dobson, 1990; Martell, 1994; Young, 1990a). Without an examination of normative questions, the standpoints from which social phenomena are evaluated in CSS are left to intuition.

Any criticism presupposes the possibility of a better way of life; to expose something as illusory or contradictory is to imply the possibility and desirability of a life without those illusions and contradictions. This much has been established by critical theorists such as Habermas and Apel. Yet the notion that critique implies a quest for the good is a highly abstract one. Up to a point, particular critiques do imply something a little more specific than the standpoint of a better life. The critique of capitalism's anarchic, uneven development implies a critical standpoint or contrast space of an imagined society with a rationally ordered, even process of development. The critique of class implies the desirability of a classless society. But this does not take us very far unless it identifies the determinants of class so that they might be eliminated. Naturally, society would be better if its illusions, injustices, conflicts and contradictions were reduced, but we need to know how this could be achieved. The desirability of a life without contradictions or illusions does not make it feasible. If we develop an explanatory critique of something but can see no feasible or desirable alternative, then the force of the critique is weakened, to say the least. Thus, the critique of capitalism's anarchic and uneven development would lose much of its force if all advanced economies were necessarily anarchic and uneven in their development.[5] All this is not to argue that the absence of plausible superior alternatives should render radical political economy silent in the face of the ills of capitalism or whatever. The lack of such alternatives might blunt the political force of its critiques, but it would still be important to have a CSS which identified the causes of social ills, even though, for the time being, we could not see a way of eliminating the causes without generating greater problems.

There are two kinds of feasibility which might be considered:

1 whether a certain desired end state or goal can be realized, for example, how people can be politically mobilized to make it happen; and
2 whether, assuming enough people are willing to try to make it happen, the goal or end state is feasible in itself, for example, could one have an advanced economy without money?

While many might think it idle to ignore 1, it is surprising how little attention is given to 2, especially in socialist politics, as if the journey mattered more than the destination and large-scale political mobilization could precede a reasonably well-worked out conception of a feasible alternative.

As Steele (1992) points out, arguments about the merits of utopianism frequently get confused by two different concepts of utopia. If utopias are treated as being infeasible by definition then that prejudges any questions about their merits; merely to mention the word 'utopia' is then to slam the door on rational assessment. If, on the other hand, we leave it open as to whether utopias can be feasible, we avoid excluding possibilities and enable a more rational assessment to be made. Considering utopias is therefore compatible with 'science' since it is consistent with asking counterfactual questions, conducting thought experiments and scrutinizing critical standpoints. Indeed, as Steele puts it, political thought would be more scientific if it were more utopian (Steele, 1992, pp. 374–5).

This is not the same as asking for blueprints for it merely involves attempting to think through the likely tendencies or mechanisms of different forms of social organization: for example, can highly complex economies be subject to detailed ex ante control by participatory democracy? Would a change in property relations tend to eliminate externalities? Could markets be regulated so as to avoid regressive effects? Although we obviously cannot predict the future we can make some judgments about what is or is not feasible and desirable. In the terms of critical realism this is not a request for 'actualist' predictions of what will happen at the level of concrete events. Such a request is unanswerable because the open nature of social systems means that both the activation of mechanisms and their effects are not pre-determined but depend on contingent conditions. What can reasonably be requested is that we explore as far as is possible what the causal powers and liabilities of alternative forms of social organization are likely to be. For example: what would be possible and impossible for an economy of worker-owned enterprises? In what respects would their behaviour be likely to differ from capitalist enterprises? Answering these questions does not necessarily involve major leaps into the unknown since possible analogues and prototypes – both successful and unsuccessful – are usually available, in this case, in the record of socialist experiments. Even if actual examples of similar practices are not available, conducting thought experiments and asking counterfactual questions is at least better than leaving alternatives unexamined (Sayer, 1995).

Critical standpoints and alternatives don't have to drop from the skies or be vacuous. They can come from what Wellmer terms a 'draft meaning' – a particular area of existing progressive practice, which provides a model which we would like to generalize (Wellmer, 1972). Thus the equal treatment of people as voters might be taken as a draft meaning for the extension of democracy to industry, or the norms of mutual respect and equality of the public sphere might be extended to the private sphere. Useful though the concept of draft meanings is, the main problem is that it is tempting to assume that just because a particular practice or institution is progressive, it must be generalizable to other situations, when in fact it may not be; it may be a 'niche' phenomenon rather than an embryonic version of something potentially large. Thus, regarding the extension of democratic control, it is necessary to consider whether the costs of participation are likely to outweigh the benefits. We therefore have to assess the possibility that the generalization or extension of a currently restricted, progressive phenomenon may be either infeasible or inappropriate. In this context, Michael Walzer's critique of the extension of principles appropriate to one social sphere to others where they are inappropriate is salutary (Walzer, 1983).

So, when considering any concrete example of a critical theory, it is important to ask what the standpoint is from which its criticisms are made, and we are likely to want a more specific answer than 'the standpoint of a better life'. We need to know enough about the critical standpoint and the implied alternative to be able to decide first whether the critique is justifiable. Since knowledge is 'situated' and often bears the mark of its author's social position, this includes taking these questions into account: does it privilege the position of a particular group (for example, male workers, advanced countries)? Does it imply a society without difference? If it implies greater equality, on whose terms is equality to be defined? Secondly, it involves assessing whether the alternative is feasible and desirable. We have to ask whether remedying one set of problems would generate others (it usually does), and whether these would be worse than the original problems. As Billig et al. put it, social life is frequently 'dilemmatic', eluding attempts to identify and resolve problems in the straightforward manner assumed in many reconstructions of CSS (Billig et al., 1988, see also Toye, 1987). These tend to assume not only that the nature of the good and the bad is unambiguous, but that mechanisms producing good and bad effects are always separable.

These possibilities are rarely considered in the old CSS of Marxism, the usual implicit assumption being that all bad things go together in capitalism and all good things under socialism/communism. Yet it is possible that some of the 'contradictions' involve dilemmas which can't be eliminated along with capitalism. Evaluations in terms of desirability therefore need to be cross-checked with evaluations of feasibility, and optimistic assumptions of inevitable improvement suspended.[6] Often – again, particularly in Marxism – the problem is that while certain mechanisms responsible for problems can be removed or blocked, the mechanisms which are supposed to replace them are unspecified. For example, as Buchanan notes, Marx and later Marxists 'simply assume not only that a highly productive alternative to market coordination is feasible, but that a high level of productivity and a system for efficiently distributing what is produced can be achieved by a system of democratic decision-making' (1985, p. 29).

In the terminology of critical realism, we could describe the dilemmatic character of social life in terms of either structures which have both desirable and undesirable mechanisms, or mechanisms which tend to produce both desirable and undesirable effects. For example, to oversimplify, markets render people both free to choose and free to lose, by allowing individuals to choose among competing sellers and by increasing inequalities and insecurity. More generally, given the profound ambivalence of many of the leading social theorists of the last two centuries about modernity, it should be no surprise that the good and the bad are not always separable.

One dimension of modernity underlying this ambivalence of social theorists relates to the tensions between anarchy, rationalization and liberty in societies with an advanced division of labour. The 'anarchic' character of development under capitalism generates inequalities, insecurity and numerous irrationalities. Inevitably, responses involving strategies of rationalization seem attractive, but these tend to limit individual liberty, and lead to the Weberian 'iron cage' scenario. On the other hand, defending liberty in terms of freedom from interference encourages anarchic and inegalitarian tendencies. In advanced industrial economies, attempts to escape this triangle of problems through democratization can have only limited success, not so much because democratization leads to further rationalization, but because the division of knowledge restricts the extent to which the latter can succeed in reducing the anarchic qualities of development. The relationships between anarchy and rationalization, liberty and equality, are more complex than this of course, and disputes about them form a major part of the diet of political theory and philosophy (Sayer, 1995). The point of drawing attention to them is a) to juxtapose them to the simplistic view of social problems assumed in many accounts of CSS, and b) to suggest the relevance of some well known areas of normative discourse to the latter.

One of the reasons for the underestimation of the dilemmatic quality of social life in the philosophical reconstructions of CSS is simply that, for the sake of clarity, they take single mechanisms one at a time. Yet concrete CSS has usually to deal with several interacting mechanisms simultaneously. The reconstructions are obviously likely to underestimate problems of the justification for a change in one mechanism being overridden by the danger of losing compensating benefits.[7] It is not enough, for example, to argue that if the capital-labour relation can be shown to be unjust, it therefore follows that capitalism must be overthrown (for example, see Carling's case against capitalism, (for example, 1992, pp. 145–6). Capitalism in the inclusive sense consists of more than the capital-labour relation, and the ignored features may produce effects which offset the ills of exploitation within the relations of production. It also has to be demonstrated that there is a superior alternative. All too often critical theorists ignore these points and judge and condemn whole (concrete) systems on the basis of a selective, abstract analysis of just one of their parts and invoke an unspecified, imaginary society as automatically superior. To be useful, evaluations or critiques need to involve 'intersystemic comparisons', in which the systems are evaluated in equal depth, involving comparisons of balance sheets of strengths and weaknesses instead of isolated points of condemnation (for example, see Buchanan, 1985; Putterman, 1990).

At one level, these kinds of problems could be said to be pre-empted by the *ceteris paribus* clause in the final stage, stage (iv) of the model of explanatory critiques. This is a highly economical device for describing such problems, and one which may be uninteresting from a philosophical point of view. Yet from a practical point of view it is crucial, and the implications go beyond the final stage of the model. In some cases the complications represented by factors covered by the *ceteris paribus* clause are liable to prompt us to revise our initial judgements of what constitutes a problem – stage (i) in the model of explanatory critiques – and how we should respond to those conditions – stage (iii). This is likely where the factors over-riding the initial arguments for change involve mechanisms which are ubiquitous, and which produce beneficial as well as bad effects, and hence where they are not easily removed without causing further, more serious problems. It is therefore not merely the 'output' – stage (iv) – of the model which is affected here, but its prior, internal stages.

Uncertain Standpoints and Contested Needs

While there is unwarranted confidence in certain critical realist quarters regarding answers to questions of values and needs, in the actual practice of CSS we find uncertainty and frequent *inconsistencies* in the implicit or explicit critiques made of social practices, and fundamental disagreements where alternatives are considered. Is the problem of industrial decline one of ineffective competitive behaviour, or a consequence of the very existence of a competitive framework? The rise of green critiques of growth are particularly important in upsetting traditional, radical assumptions in favour of industrialization. Do we say of a backward region or country that there's a lack of growth? Or do we say that growth is the problem? One of the hallmarks of the structuralist influence on radical thought was that it taught theorists to see problems as deriving not from the way particular players played the game, but from the very structure of the game itself. Valuable though this distinction is, there now seems to be less confidence about it, perhaps because, even though the problem might lie with the structure or game, we don't have a convincing alternative game, so we revert to seeking better strategies within the existing one. Thus, for example, in radical studies of industry, there has been an apparent shift from Marxist critiques of capitalism, implicitly in favour of socialism, to critiques of Fordism, implicitly or explicitly – and with many qualifications – in favour of 'post-Fordism' and particular varieties of capitalism, for example, social democratic rather than neoliberal, (Amin, 1994). Such shifts and inconsistencies indicate the difficulty of choosing critical standpoints where there is insufficient understanding of, and confidence in, alternatives.

This is not to suppose that a stronger focus on normative issues – as found in green CSS – necessarily makes matters clearer; witness the fundamental disagreements regarding the rights of non-human species in green politics and theory, where the problems extend to initial identifications of false beliefs and frustrated needs. Consider also the debate around work such of that of Nancy Chodorow and Carol Gilligan which bears upon qualities associated with femininity, mothering and caring (Chodorow, 1978; Gilligan, 1982). Such literature involves both an empirical, positive dimension regarding what is the case, and whether it is so necessarily or contingently, and a normative discussion challenging dominant evaluations of these matters. Yet the authors' own evaluations have been widely criticized. On the one hand, positively valuing the practices and attitudes associated with caring appears to oppose dominant values associated with masculinity. On the other hand there is a danger of supporting rather than challenging patriarchal hegemony and its essentialist characterizations of women, as such valuations could be construed as celebrating what are arguably actually effects of women's subordination, which patriarchy might be only too happy to endorse. Moreover, the very terms of such arguments can be contested, as in the debate over Gilligan's 'ethic of care' (for example, Benhabib, 1992). This illustrates the enormous difficulty of deciding on the nature of the good: what are the false beliefs and frustrated needs here?[8] On issues such as this, perhaps the best that CSS can do is raise consciousness or 'enhance reflexivity' so that the debate becomes internal to its object.

The rationale of CSS provided by critical realism is that although descriptions of social phenomena are likely to be already 'valuey', as Andrew Collier puts it, in that we are rarely completely indifferent about them, we can decide what are problems and what would be solutions via a naturalist route, moving from explanations to critiques and proposals of solutions (Collier, 1994a). This is most convincing in the case of 'cognitive' explanatory critiques, where we identify mistaken beliefs – for example, concerning race – which influence action. Some instances of needs-based critiques, involving transcultural or naturalistic needs, such as our example concerning the implications of knowing that someone is starving, are also relatively straightforward.

Matters are not so simple when we move to needs which are culturally specific and hence not reducible to biological properties or indeed to any universal social properties. It is one thing to argue that just because all natural needs are socially interpreted and mediated they are not thereby purely 'socially constructed'; but some needs are so specific to particular contingent kinds of society (for example, the need of a religious group to attend church) that they may indeed be regarded as entirely socially constructed.[9] While we can still accept that there are some universal human needs, as Nussbaum (1992) and Doyal and Gough argue (1991), others are local and contested. To proceed with such matters, CSS would have to engage with normative issues such as those of pluralism and tolerance – standard fare of moral and political philosophy. But then, how extraordinary that advocates of CSS could imagine that they could bypass such issues!

Of course, it is possible to define universal needs sufficiently abstractly and openly to allow more culturally specific needs to be defended under their ambit. For example, if a general need for sociability were posited, this could allow for a vast range of more specific needs through whose satisfaction it might be met. This helps to show why much CSS can only come up with the vaguest of solutions to the problems it addresses; it has to be vague in order to leave a space for pluralism and to avoid neglecting cultural difference. The alternative is to put forward locally specific, contextually sensitive claims (Nussbaum, 1992); a danger here is of assuming a *parochial* context, which ignores relevant connections of the target group to others who may be unfairly disadvantaged by the solutions. Moreover, it is not merely a question of measuring circumstances against relevant local conceptions of culturally specific needs, for these are likely to be in question too. In such cases, we/they have to consider what kind of society and individual we/they want to become.

At one point in *Scientific Realism and Human Emancipation* Roy Bhaskar notes in passing that a thoroughly reworked ethics is needed to compliment critical realist social science (1986, p. 187).[10] That reworking would certainly and immediately reject emotivist or subjectivist treatments of values and defend some kind of ethical naturalism. But as these last arguments indicate it would also have to go beyond ethical naturalism to consider a communicative or discourse ethics in which needs would have to be the subject of democratic determination in something approaching an ideal speech situation (Habermas, 1984, 1990; Benhabib, 1992).[11] It would presumably be desirable for participants in such a discourse to be aware of relevant explanatory critiques made by CSS; this would help to counter the common criticism of discourse ethics as being merely procedural and formal[12] and hence oriented to providing consensus and legitimation rather than truth or moral validity.[13] However, as we have seen, they can only apply to a limited domain. Beyond this domain, where issues such as culturally specific needs have to be decided, discourse ethics, by specifying the conditions for a democratic and 'open-ended moral conversation' (Benhabib, 1992), offers the least bad way of proceeding.

Uncertainties regarding critical standpoints are also likely to be serious where CSS is concerned with problems deriving from the nature and distribution of social obligations or responsibilities. Yet these are not considered in the reconstructions. The dominant conception of emancipation in CSS is one of escape from domination, through removal of unwanted and unneeded constraints or determinations. Bhaskar does talk of a move from unwanted and unneeded determinations to wanted and needed sources of determination. Thus for a starving person, food is obviously a wanted and needed determination. In the case of overcoming illiteracy, the needed determinations are the commitment of time and resources to education. This feature of the critical realist model is an advance on some libertarian kinds of 'radical' social science, which imply a search for maximum individual liberty through minimizing restrictions on individual choice, or worse, presuppose what Andrew Collier terms an 'out-of-gear' conception of freedom as freedom from necessity (1994a, p. 97). Against the latter, critical realism acknowledges that freedom requires recognition of necessity and that to have some purchase on the world it must have some causal influence upon us.

However, critical realist reconstructions of CSS fail to recognize that in many cases, deciding what are wanted and needed determinations requires consideration of the nature and distribution of responsibilities in society.[14] Indeed often the problems facing societies or particular groups may be better couched in terms of unmet responsibilities than unwanted determinations. Often the problem is not that some people or groups have too little freedom, but that they have too much freedom from responsibilities. Recently fashionable concern with 'empowerment' suffers from the same problem – it implies having fewer constraints and more resources and is silent on responsibilities, and sometimes on the disempowering effects on others (though these may of course be justifiable). It is, of course, always easier to talk of rights than responsibilities. To reply that obligations are the flip side of rights and therefore already implied in the discussion of rights can easily serve as an evasion of the question of just what the obligations should be. What our responsibilities are, for example towards distant strangers and future generations, and whether some should be delegated through divisions of labour – are central to any assessment of possibilities for social improvement (Ignatieff, 1984). The fact that some of these sorts of question are being addressed by green CSS (for example, O'Neill, 1993) shows how the philosophical reconstructions lag behind current practice.

To illustrate the difficulty regarding wanted determinations which involve responsibilities, consider problems relating to responsibility for childcare. In explaining these do we say:

1 The problems are caused by a lack of state provision of nurseries and after-school clubs, and so on?
2 The problems are caused by the lack of involvement of *men* in childcare?
3 The problems are caused by the failure of parents to make adequate provision and sacrifices for bringing up their children (in other words, why should you subsidize my child's upbringing)?

Note how closely the definitions and explanations of the problems are bound up with normative judgments about what ought to happen, and where responsibility ought to lie. Not surprisingly, the very selection and definition of a problem implies a value standpoint and is highly contestable. Of course, any self-respecting critical social scientist would want to check empirical evidence regarding the situation – for example, how much state provision actually exists. However, no matter how complete the evidence, it would still leave open the normative question of responsibility. Again, answers cannot be derived from explanatory critiques but require an open-ended moral debate.

Conclusion

The claims of CSS regarding its emancipatory potential need to be moderated by recognizing the limits of its method. The main problems lie in justifying the standpoints of its critiques and of finding alternative social forms which generate fewer problems than those they replace, and hence lead to net improvement.

The dominant message of critical realism's reconstruction of CSS is that explanation enables us to decide how to judge the situation under investigation, hence indicating what critical standpoint we should take. In this way, the difficulty and contestability of normative judgements are downplayed.[15] This model is relatively compelling where cognitive explanatory critiques are involved, or needs-based critiques concerning universal human needs. It is less convincing where the alternatives on whose development emancipation depends are themselves problematic in terms of their desirability and feasibility, and often the main problem is not removing a cause of suffering but finding an alternative which is less bad. Furthermore, where we are dealing with more contested matters such as culturally specific needs, or responsibilities, as in our childcare example, it seems that prior values determine explanations, so that the latter largely follow from the former.

The extraordinary degree of interconnection or integration of modern societies is such that piecemeal changes have multiple unintended and sometimes damaging consequences. Is it so surprising that little can be achieved towards emancipation without the articulation of a feasible, politically and ethically desirable alternative? Again, the childcare example illustrates the problem; it is not a question of merely removing obstacles to the realization of a certain group's freedom but of deciding what kind of society we want and what would be desirable and feasible in terms of an allocation of responsibilities that would benefit all groups, though the very nature of some of the groups – for example, parents – may need to be fundamentally altered. It would also inevitably have major implications for other spheres of life – the terms of employment, taxation and the welfare state in particular. In this way an initial concern with what appears to be a limited problem affecting a discrete target group addressable by explanatory critique leads us into a much larger, open-ended series of normative issues.

As societies become more interdependent and multi-cultural, a wide range of needs which are culturally specific come to have implications for members of other cultures with different values and who may find those needs false or abhorrent. The more diverse this world, the more difficult it is to find a consensus or at least an accommodating framework. Both liberalism and Marxism implicitly expected difference in terms of religious and other affective communal attachments and identities to wither with the rise of modernity, through the growth of either individualism or the class-conscious proletariat. Actual social developments and recent concerns with difference in social and political theory underline just how mistaken this was. On the other hand, the more integrated and interdependent the world becomes, the more such a unifying normative framework is required.

A moderate definition of postmodernity which does not involve a contradictory attempt to abandon modernism altogether could be that it is modernity coming to terms with its own limitations (Bauman, 1992). As yet, critical realism and the older CSSs appear not to have come to terms with these limitations. It should by now be glaringly obvious both that social change is inherently contradictory and dilemmatic and that while those contradictions and dilemmas continually mutate there is no sign of any reduction in their number or severity. This should not induce defeatism or an outright rejection of CSS's project, just a greater regard for the need to consider critical standpoints, and more generally to engage with normative questions of social organization and behaviour.

Notes

1 CSS refers to critical empirical studies of substantive objects, such as feminist and Marxist research, as distinct from *critical theory*, associated with the Frankfurt School and Habermas and others which is pitched at the level of meta-theory.

2 Now, particularly through the rise of analytical Marxism (for example, Bardhan and Roemer, 1992; Roemer, 1994; Wright, 1994), radical political economy is showing signs of a normative turn, although there is still an imbalance between the sophistication of its explanations and the underdevelopment of the alternatives it offers. In some of the new CSSs, positive analysis is arguably being neglected, and discussion of desirable alternatives is running ahead of assessments of feasibility. I leave without comment the tendency of 'ethical disidentification' and relativization/subjectivization of values in postmodernism (Connor, in Squires, 1993).

3 One might want to exempt aesthetic values from this claim, but this does not affect the argument of the paper.

4 See Fay, 1987, for an excellent (sympathetic) critique of other aspects of CSS.

5 However, one could still criticize advanced economies – not just capitalist ones – from the very different standpoint of 'deep ecology', calling for a return to small-scale, more primitive economies (Dobson, 1990).

6 Fay at least recognizes that CSS might lead to a change which removed one source of suffering but do so 'by producing another sort of society with a new and worse form of suffering… It…would make no sense for a critical social scientist to condemn a social arrangement and call for its alteration, while at the same time admitting that the alternative arrangements which would emerge will be worse than the original' (Fay, 1987, p. 30). However, he does not follow this up with an acknowledgement of the necessity of normative analysis.

7 In another context (concerning the case of justifying irradiating food by reference to experiments in closed systems), Collier himself notes the dangers of moving straight from abstract to concrete (Collier, 1994b) and he notes that the partial emancipation of people in Eastern Europe in the 1989–90 revolutions has left many worse off.

8 The situation may sometimes, as in this case, be eased by the possibility of it being left to personal preference whether to take certain life courses or follow certain codes of behaviour.

9 However, even social constructions or conventions only work if they keep within the bounds of natural necessity. They have their own causal powers and liabilities; for example, to say something intelligible you have to speak mostly within the limits provided by the resources and rules of a language your audience understands. However this does not help us decide on their desirability.

10 In his latest book, *Plato, Etc.* (1994), Bhaskar does take up questions of ethics and other matters of value, defending a moral realism and ethical naturalism. He also notes in *Plato* that emancipation is always constrained, and he mentions that feasibility is a limit on the logic of dialectical universalizability (p. 151). Otherwise, as far as I can see, his discussions do not remedy the problems identified here. However, I have to note that like many other readers, including other enthusiasts for critical realism, I was largely defeated by *Plato, Etc.*'s Niagara of neologisms, most of them inadequately explained, even in the glossary. The description of the dialectic of freedom in *Plato, Etc.* is extraordinary for ignoring the warnings which were included in his earlier works about moving from philosophical to substantive claims; it leaps from the transcendental deductions of critical realist philosophy, to indications of the shape of a 'eudaimonistic' society, ignoring substantive social and political economic theory on modernity and the intractable practical dilemmas which it identifies. The resulting impression is one of pulling global salvation out of the critical realist hat.

11 In *Plato, Etc.*, Bhaskar also notes in passing that a rapprochement with Habermas's ethics is possible and he acknowledges communitarian points about the diversity and relativity of moral belief.

12 Habermas himself notes that theories such as his own cannot make substantive contributions regarding particular ethical problems (Habermas, 1990, p. 211). Rather his aim is to encourage a participatory public-life democratic politics instead of providing particular norms, which he would see as pre-empting citizens' rights to democratic politics (Benhabib, 1992, p. 81).

13 Equally, like any science, CSS, assumes that evaluation of its claims will take place in conditions approaching an ideal speech situation.

14 In *Plato, Etc.*, questions of responsibilities are only momentarily alluded to under the heading of 'civic duties' including 'providing care and sustenance' (1994, p. 157).

15 Note that Bhaskar rejects (as 'scientism') the view that theory can create values where none had existed before, but what I am addressing here is the alteration of pre-existing values in the light of theory.

8

Ethics Unbound: For a Normative Turn in Social Theory[1]

In the last 20 years many researchers have come to accept that social science must be critical of the practices it studies, whether their topics be mainly economic, political or cultural. Any social science claiming to be critical must have a standpoint from which its critique is made, whether it is directed at popular illusions which support inequality and relations of domination or at the causes of avoidable suffering and frustration of needs. But it is strange that this critical social science largely neglects to acknowledge and justify these standpoints. For example, a rich understanding of the ways in which power is embedded in social space has developed; although it is generally accepted that power is not wholly negative, the writing in this area is undeniably critical in tone, and yet little attention is given to normative implications, to how things ought to be different.

Critical theorists such as Habermas and Apel have shown that all criticism presupposes the possibility of a better life. Yet critical social scientists have been coy about talking about values. They frequently use negative terms such as 'racist', or positive terms such as 'democracy', which carry a strong evaluative message, but there is often a refusal to present the arguments for the evaluations. Indeed even to ask for such justications is likely to be taken as shocking and threatening – as implying the acceptability of the thing being opposed – rather than just a request for clarity about what exactly we oppose or favour, and why and with what implications.

If values – regarding rights, ethics and more generally the nature of the good – are seen as purely subjective, emotive, a-rational responses, and hence beyond justification through argument, then the critiques which they inform might be dismissed on the same grounds. If they are not to be dismissed in this manner, values need to be subjected to scrutiny and justified as carefully as would any explanation. Without such scrutiny, critical social scientists could be accused of basing their critiques on values which are no more than the product of unmonitored peer pressure: 'We're against such-and-such because people like us generally are'.

One of the great ironies of post-war social science is that while Marxists and related radicals criticized liberal positive social theory as reactionary and apologetic, liberalism had a longstanding and far more developed normative side, as indicated by its sophisticated discussions of the relations between liberty and equality (for example, Rawls, 1971; Gray, 1986; Kymlicka, 1990; Nozick, 1974; Plant, 1991) building on the earlier work of writers such as Locke, Smith and Mill. By contrast the normative basis of Marxist-influenced radicalism was under-examined and flimsy. Outside the disciplines of politics and philosophy, most social scientists had little or no acquaintance with normative theory.

In recent years this omission in critical social science has begun to be remedied and there has been a (re-)awakening of interest in normative theory (for example, Squires, 1993; Harvey, 1992; Benhabib, 1992; Benton, 1993; Smith, 1994; Osborne, 1991; Phillips, 1991; Poole, 1991; Fraser, 1995). In the newer feminist and green or environmentalist critical social sciences, there is less of a gulf between the normative and the positive, with theorists on either side acknowledging each other (for example, Barrett and Phillips, 1992; Dryzek, 1987; Dobson, 1990). Debates have ranged from the alleged universality of the conclusions of western political philosophy to writings regarding specific substantive issues such as development, gender and urbanism.

Such changes are of course connected to wider social change. The rise of political movements around feminism, anti-racism and post-colonialism, ecologism and sexuality, the increasingly multi-cultural character of many societies, the break-up or diversification of families, and the growth of reflexivity – all these brought to the fore a range of ethical and political concerns that went far beyond the simple class or distributional agenda of the old Left and the rights-based agenda of liberalism (Fraser, 1995; Taylor, 1992). They also challenged the very terms within which normative political philosophy and theory had operated (the public/private divide, the assumption of discrete societies and unitary subjects, the neglect of nature, and occidentalism). This, coupled with the challenge of the resurgence of the Right, the collapse of traditional class politics, and the end of the Soviet empire, led to a loss of confidence in the old, taken-for-granted standpoints of critical social science and a period of growing uncertainty about its normative implications. While one response of postmodernists has been a wholesale rejection of ethical issues, others have become more concerned with developing normative theory.[2] On the Left, the years of complacency regarding alternatives and ethical positions are coming to an end. It is not surprising that times of major social change prompt far more ethical debate than periods of relative stability.

In what follows we want, first, to enlarge upon the reasons for taking up normative issues and answer likely objections to this; second, to discuss the problems of the implicit socio-spatial assumptions in normative theories such as ethics and the difference that space makes in such matters; and third, to discuss human sameness and difference.

Refusals of Normative Questions

Notwithstanding the signs of a resurgence of normative theory there is still a surprisingly strong resistance to it. This takes a variety of forms, some long-established, others recent, many of them revealing problems of the practice of critical social theory.

1 An old source is the belief in the possibility and desirability of value-free social science. On this view, values are seen as a form of contamination in science and as logically independent of the matters of fact which concern science.[3] Although often conjoined, these two perceptions are oddly incompatible, for if values were logically independent – neither having implications for, nor being entailed by, questions of what exists – then it is hard to see why they should be seen as threatening to science.

The response of critical social science to the value-freedom position is that matters are different where we are studying society, for social phenomena are influenced by beliefs, some of which may be false, and the falsity of the beliefs makes a difference to what happens (Edgley, 1985; Bhaskar, 1986, 1991). Therefore, explanations are inadequate unless they note the falsity as well as the existence of those beliefs. Thus the reproduction of gender relations depends heavily on popular but false beliefs about the naturalness of gender differences, and both the existence and the falsity of these beliefs must therefore figure prominently in social scientific explanations. Without noting that these beliefs are indeed false – and hence thereby adopting a critical stance towards both the beliefs and the practices which support and are supported by them – we simply could not understand what was going on. Furthermore, it is argued that social science cannot help but identify instances of avoidable suffering; while doing so might not logically entail criticism of these instances and their causes, it makes no sense to resist the critical implication that the suffering should be avoided (Collier, 1994a).

2 A very different kind of resistance comes from Marxism, following Marx's (in)famous dismissal of moral questions. This was never a consistent argument for if we cannot justifiably argue that capitalism is wrong there are absolutely no grounds for presenting critiques of it and fighting it. Of course, despite Marx's impatience with moral questions, even his most analytical works are written in strongly condemnatory terms and continually detail the reproduction of avoidable suffering by capitalism (Buchanan, 1982; Lukes, 1985).

3 Another kind of resistance 'sociologizes' normative questions out of existence. It does this not only by insisting – rightly – that particular norms and values are embedded in particular social forms and must be analysed with these in mind, but by concluding – illogically – that this makes normative discourse redundant. Even though a norm may be specific to a certain context, it is still important to consider what is good or bad about it: the norms of male domestic violence are of course specific to the home but that does not mean that they can escape normative evaluation. Marxism provides another variant of the attempt to evade questions of values by contextualizing them. Marx and Engels dismissed ethics on the grounds that while purporting to be universal it derives from and legitimizes the special interests of the ruling class.[4] In this way, various forms of domination specific to particular societies have been

naturalized and legitimized. This is almost certainly true, but a bad and hypocritical use of ethical arguments need not drive out good ones.

A further variant has been popularized by postmodernism, arguing that defences of particular moral positions universalize and hence conceal the situated character of their origins. Most commonly, white male western theorists treat as universal propositions those which are actually specific to their own limited positions, and in so doing suppress those of their others. This is a major problem with regard to normative questions and one which needs to be taken seriously. However, the criticism needs to be argued for specific cases rather than used as an *a priori* basis for ignoring such theory. Not all normative universalizing is incapable of self-criticism or unaware of others, indeed it may derive precisely from such self-criticism and consideration of others. The issue is not simply one of situatedness versus universalization; there is also the question of legitimate versus illegitimate universalization. Moreover, the charge of illegitimate universalization does not remove the need for normative principles:

> What scares the opponents of utopia, like Lyotard for example, is that in the name of such future utopia the present in its multiple ambiguity, plurality and contradiction will be reduced to a flat grand narrative.... Yet we cannot deal with these political concerns [undemocratic, authoritarian practices] by rejecting the ethical impulse of utopia but only by articulating the normative principles of democratic action and organization in the present. Will the postmodernists join us in the task or will they be content with singing the swan-song of normative thinking in general? (Benhabib, 1992, p. 229)

Here again postmodernists frequently take a contradictory position. The concern with situatedness and diversity is coupled to a utopia of sorts – that of 'radical democracy'. This utopia of full, non-hierarchical expression of postmodern complexity is rarely questioned, either in philosophical or practical terms. If, as appears to be the case, it is just a fashionable term for a radical deepening of procedural democracy (through the giving of active, rather than passive voice to marginalized groups), then why should it not be scrutinized in the same way we do for other political philosophies?

4 Another sociological argument which is sometimes used against normative theory is that behaviour is overwhelmingly habitual rather than guided by rational assessment according to normative principles. This is almost certainly correct in relation to a great deal of everyday behaviour. However, there are plenty of common situations – for example, teaching a class of schoolchildren – which require continual though not necessarily major moral judgments, and others – like family breakup or assessing whether to support a war – which are less routine but pose considerable moral dilemmas.[5]

Arguably, social science has radically underestimated the everyday practice of evaluation, interpretation and justification by actors in seemingly ordinary situations (Boltanski and Thévenot, 1991). Almost all situations of everyday interaction involve uncertainty, which is 'resolved' for the actor by routines and conventions. But there is a continual evaluation of each situation according to the implicit notions of the appropriate, fair and just which are contained in every set of routines and conventions (Storper and Salais, 1996; Etzioni, 1988). These conventions, routines, containers for the fair and the just, display very considerable social and spatial variation. They are highly situated, but essential to all action. Actors are unlikely to think about such issues systematically and in general terms, in the manner of ethical theory, and there are many practices which they may strongly believe to be right or wrong without being able to articulate fully the reasons for such beliefs, although theorists might have done so. But this is not the same as merely acting according to habit. Thus, though they often become matters of habit, norms still figure in behaviour and hence help to explain it.

5 Particularly with the rise of postmodernism, rejections of normative discourse on relativist grounds have grown popular. Here the argument is that values and norms are not merely situated or embedded in particular contexts but that the justifications for them are purely internal to the discourses associated with them and are therefore immune to evaluation from outside, on the grounds that this will always be from an incommensurable standpoint. Like all relativism, it licenses dogmatism while appearing to let a hundred flowers bloom, for it allows each to disqualify the criticism of others by claiming that there are no common grounds for argument. Indeed, it has recently been argued that postmodernism is itself strongly universalizing while refusing to admit it. The very emphasis on a plurality of identities and, most especially, on the choice of identity, is an outgrowth of western, and specifically Anglo-American (much less so Latin) liberal individualism, and the philosophical claims made in its favour would elevate it to a superior universal principle of social life (Taylor, 1989, 1992).

There are no ultimate foundations for normative theory any more than there are any in epistemology. But just as this does not make positive (descriptive/ explanatory) discourse impossible or prevent it from informing successful practice, so normative discourse is not necessarily arbitrary, ineffectual or misguided. If different values are in contention with one another, then that assumes some common referent or principle over which they contend rather than total incommensurability. As has often been remarked, while the allegedly arbitrary character of values and needs might be entertained in the seminar room, they take an imperative character in crises, such as famines, that makes the former doubts look affected.

Relativism is the flip-side of the problem shared by ethnocentrism and androcentrism. As Gellner (1970) put it, cultural relativists are 'liberals at home and conservatives abroad', or as we might put it now, they are fallibilist about their own knowledge and foundationalist about the knowledge of others. It is only wrong to be critical of our others on two conditons: if we refuse to listen to criticism of ourselves by our others, and if our criticism of others is not based on a sincere and sustained attempt to understand them in their own terms. The problem with ethnocentrism, androcentrism, and so on, is not that they are critical of their objects (that is, their others), but that their criticism is not based on understanding of their others, but upon misunderstandings generated by an inappropriate framework which is ignorant of the other. Criticism of others need not be made from such standpoints. Relativism licenses reactionary idealizations of community in which questions of morality are reduced merely to 'what we do round here' (Kymlicka, 1990), and internal as well as external criticism and protest are dismissed as irrelevant.

6   A still more radical rejection of normative questions comes from Nietzschean post-structuralism, which 'reduce[s] normative problems of justice and morality in complex societies to simple patterns of interest and power camouflaging' (Benhabib, 1992, p. 195).[6] While such a view is critical in the limited sense that it questions customary assumptions about values, it is, if followed consistently, completely uncritical, for it has no grounds for finding fault with any social phenomena whatsoever. As Amy Gutmann points out, it is contradictory to argue that the content of all intellectual positions derives purely from a will-to-power, and to criticize them for doing just this, not least because it must undermine the critic's own arguments too. The reduction of all intellectual disagreements completely to conflicts of group interests is simply anti-intellectual and it is not clear why those who believe in the reduction bother to make a case at all when there are more direct routes to political power available (Gutmann, 1992). Such a radical reduction is not sustainable: those who sneer at values and morality get as upset as anyone else when someone treats them improperly. Moral discourse is indeed sometimes little more than a camouflage or legitimation of power, often hypocritical; but again, a bad use of such discourse need not drive out a good use.

Further, as we saw in Chapter 4, another feature of post-structuralism – anti-essentialism – appears to liberate those whose oppression has been legitimized by being represented as naturally grounded, but if it also denies that people have any particular properties, as human beings and as organic bodies, then it loses all critical purchase on any oppressive exercise of power (Soper, 1995a and b), for it appears that there is nothing that can be harmed. While the doctrine of ethical naturalism – that the nature of the good can be derived from our nature as human, social beings – does not adequately deal with the conventional or 'socially constructed' character of values and the striking diversity of cultural norms, a total rejection of it undermines any criticism of oppression because it cannot say *what* oppression is bad *for*, or what it does damage *to*.

A further structuralist and post-structuralist characteristic, the 'death of the subject' – the reduction of the subject to a position in discourse – is not only incoherent (since it denies what the act of asserting it presupposes), but utterly incompatible with critical social science since it kills off any normative vision of politics and ethics (Soper, 1991; Benhabib, 1992).[7] The subject need not be unitary, transparent to itself and perfectly centred to be a moral actor. Moral action is precisely about grappling with the diverse demands of different social relations.

7   A common populist rejection of normative theory argues that we already know who or what we are for and against. This is reminiscent of the empiricist refusal of theory – 'we don't need theory, we can just observe' – and just

as problematic. Workers may not need Marx to know they are exploited and women may not need feminism to know that they are subordinated, but we are likely to need theory to know how and why these things come about. In a complex society with competing value systems it is foolish to ignore normative theory's sustained and systematic reflections. Similarly the refusal of normative justifications on the grounds that 'it's all a matter of politics' tends to be cited as if it were conclusive when it merely begs the question of the morality or goodness of the means and ends of the political struggles.

We do not underestimate the difficulty and dangers of normative theory. The dilemmas of defining the good, and of course the bad, as regards qualities and practices which take place within and derive from relations of domination are particularly fraught. This is illustrated by the debates around Gilligan and Chodorow whose work bears upon the qualities of femininity, mothering and caring (Chodorow, 1978; Gilligan, 1982). As we saw in the last chapter, on the one hand, these qualities might be celebrated because they appear to embody qualities which stand in opposition to dominant male values and practices; on the other hand, it can be argued that these are actually consequences of women's subordination which patriarchy would be only too happy to endorse.

There are indeed dangers in engaging in normative theory, not only of empty moralizing, but of assuming that whatever is agreed to be good, will therefore come into being. We need to question whether normative goals are *feasible*, that is, not only in terms of whether we can get from A to B but whether B would be feasible anyway. Normative thinking is frequently associated with 'utopianism'. Too often 'utopia' is used to mean not merely an imagined better future state but a clearly infeasible one at that. Just as it is absurd to reduce morality to power play, so it is naive to imagine the former displaces the latter. It is important that normative theory avoids what Weber saw as:

> [T]hat soft-headed attitude, so agreeable from the human point of view, but nevertheless so unutterably narrowing in its effects, which thinks it possible to replace political with 'ethical' ideas, and to innocently identify these with optimistic expectations of felicity. (Weber, cited in Bellamy, 1992, p. 216)

But we should not dismiss a different kind of utopianism that attempts to think about the feasibility of desirable alternatives in terms of how the recommended social processes would work, asking counterfactual questions, conducting thought experiments and scrutinising critical standpoints. As we argued in the previous chapter, these are certainly not questions which a viable critical social science can avoid.

Ethics and Implicit Social Geographies

> Modernity is changing the locus of belonging: our language of attachments limps suspiciously behind, doubting that our needs could ever find larger attachments. (Ignatieff, 1984, p. 139)

If we are to think normatively about good and bad forms of social order we also have to think positively (that is, descriptively, explanatorily) about what forms of social organization actually exist and, as far as we can see, could feasibly exist at some other time. Unless the normative ideas are related to recognizable or at least imaginable kinds of social organization and individual, they are liable to become utopian in the bad sense – imagined felicitous communities populated by ciphers and largely irrelevant to existing and possible alternative societies. Yet normative political and ethical theory tends to be sociologically and spatially naive in a variety of ways. Particularly common is an overly simple conception of individuals, often as atomistic, unitary and pre-social, as having needs and wants prior to entering social relations.[8] Moreover, the individuals' characteristics often tend to be specific – men, adults, westerners, white heterosexuals – rather than universal.

One of the principal utopias invoked by communitarians and postmodernists, is 'community', with little specification of what form it might take. For the former, it is usually traditional (families) or territorial (neighbourhoods); for the latter, an identity-based group. Evading such partly normative, partly positive questions inadvertently perpetuates the honorific status of 'community' in popular ideology as a warm and secure alternative to the anomie of modern society. Slides between descriptive and normative uses of 'community' tend to conceal the divisions of the former behind the harmony and consensus of the latter.

For normative purposes we may want to define community in abstract terms as involving shared beliefs and common identities, but we need to know what would count as an instance of it. There are serious questions here. Is the presence of divisions of labour or gender and class differences consistent or inconsistent with 'community'? Is a 'community' any group that decides to be such, including, for example, neo-nazis and paedophiles? There are obviously legitimate and illegitimate definitions of collective identity. Community then, is not merely an intersubjective (hence liberal) decision to be made willy-nilly. It has to involve at least two things: *real*, that is, pragmatic bonds between people that can stand up to external tests, and do not fall away at the merest challenge. Communities cannot be self-indulgent identity wishes. Communities can define themselves over and against their others, and purely in terms of their own interests. This is problematic not only because the inclusion implied by the definition of a community also involves an exclusion of others, and may function as a licence for suppressing internal dissent, but because it has nothing to offer wider humanity. Hegel raised this problem in lamenting the particularistic and defensive nature of German national identity. It could be argued that communities should mobilize participants in such a way that they are compatible with other communities, and more than this, they should have something positive to offer wider humanity. On this latter view, communities are not defined in purely defensive terms – through mere 'boundary wish' – but must propose something which is universal, out of their situated particularities. If this seems superorogatory, it needs to remembered that communities are not discrete but are invariably embedded in wider social systems, participating in wider divisions of labour and exchange, sharing infrastructure, often language and a host of wider economic and cultural phenomena.

Discussions about ethics also typically assume 'a society' as the reference group of the behaviour in question. This usually appears to be homogeneous or else only has differences at the level of individuals, or is implied to be equivalent to a nation. But of course modern societies increasingly diverge from this model as processes of globalization remap social relations, giving rise to unprecedentedly complex senses of place and belonging, or 'webs of attachments' as Ignatieff calls them (see also Massey, 1993). However matters are improving and in recent years, work on justice and ethics such as Iris Marion Young's shows a determination to do better than 'limp along' behind these increasingly complex micro- and macro-social geographies (Young, 1990a). Recognition of this complexity is welcome and it is important that it not be swept under the rug, though it often leads back to a confused sort of relativism.

In addition to these belatedly addressed questions about the forms of social organization being implied in normative theory we are now seeing an awakening of concern with the relationship between people and nature (for example, Whatmore, 1997; Benton, 1993; O'Neill, 1994; Soper, 1995b), including our internal nature as embodied beings. Together, these developments represent a new setting for ethical discussions, in which nature and culture are both present, and both close-in and distant concerns are reflected.[9]

This is important because ethical principles are not indifferent to forms of social organization; what is appropriate to one form is not to another. We would not expect parents to treat their children in the same way as liberals treat strangers, merely respecting their rights to be left alone and assuming them to be responsible for their own survival. While ethics have traditionally and in androcentric fashion been overwhelmingly concerned with relations with 'generalized others' in public life, as in the case of relations between strangers, an 'ethic of care' is arguably appropriate with regard to those 'concrete others' whose biographies and characters we know and with whom we are involved in intense, enduring, multi-dimensional relations (Gilligan, 1982; Benhabib, 1992; Poole, 1991).[10] Yet there remains the problem of this becoming a licence for privileging those we know. The 'modernist principle' of universalism with respect to certain kinds of rights and privileges was precisely intended to break up the system of clans, as in 'for my friend everything, for everyone else, nothing' (see also Tronto, 1987; Young 1990a; Smith, 1994). In the absence of a common context, perhaps the modernist concept of rules and social duties is essential, though it is clear that its development needs substantial modification. It is also clear that postmodernist relativism undermines calls for a extension of an ethic of care to our others, for relativism denies the existence of any universal grounds for caring about them; relativists need only worry about themselves.

In addition, as Walzer has shown through his concept of 'spheres of justice', different principles are appropriate for different forms of social organization, such as markets, states, voluntary organizations, friendships, and so on, and major problems arise where the principles appropriate to one form of organization, for example, for accumulating wealth in markets come to dominate and distort the principles appropriate to another form, for example, for providing education (Walzer, 1983).[11] Thus, good reasons for excluding someone from sharing a house with us do not necessarily serve as good reasons for excluding them from an institution such as our university, or from our neighbourhood or country.

If ethical principles have to relate to particular kinds of social organization then there is a sense in which they must also have histories and geographies. Indeed, geographers have shown that social organization involves not only social interdependencies, but spatial ones as well, including relations of proximity and ordered inter-place relations of exchange at a distance. Often the implementation of a normative principle implies some kind of spatial organization, as in Locke's principle of individuals being allowed property in land and resources so long as they leave 'enough and as good' for others. Whether we focus on individuals, families, institutions, neighbourhoods, communities, states, international organizations, humanity as a whole or humanity in nature – or, as some authors recommend, relations or networks linking and constituting all of these – there are always 'geographical imaginaries' involved, even though they are necessarily vague and rarely made explicit. Actual geographies of these forms of social organization have always been complex, involving patterns of mixing and exclusion, boundaries and hierarchies that reflect economic, cultural, political and technological influences. It is doubtful that there was ever an original state in which many of these relationships had a geographical form which was tidily segregated and simply organized and the forces of modernity continue to stretch and churn them up. Where this spatial complexity involves unwanted ties and spatial intermixing, social/spatial separatism might seem attractive. But this kind of spatial fix based on a longing for simpler social geographies is far from innocent: the bantustan policy of the old South Africa, and 'ethnic cleansing' in former Yugoslavia and Rwanda testify to the fact that such 'purified' geographies can usually only be constructed at appalling human cost.

The embedding of actions and their consequences in space produces territories which are a palimpsest of past rights and wrongs which continue to affect the lives of subsequent generations. Issues such as restitution of property in Eastern Europe or land reform after apartheid pose problems of justice which more abstract discussions that ignore spatial settings and temporal change fail to address (Smith, 1994). From the abstract perspective, a wrong, such as theft, is a wrong whenever or wherever it occurs, and the stolen goods or land should be returned, however long after the crime. (As Kymlicka notes, if the seizure of property is *not* a crime, then there's nothing to stop anyone seizing it back, and if it *is a* crime, then it *ought* to be seized back! (Kymlicka, 1990)). But in a geohistorical world, there are ethical as well as practical problems in righting the past wrongs (Waldron, 1992). There is not only the improbability of the idea of returning a modern society to a state of distribution which held many generations previously, or the realpolitik of challenging the current incumbents' power; there is also the ethical problem of making current generations who innocently inherited or bought the property pay for their ancestors' crimes. If redistributive policies are to be ethically principled rather than based on revenge, then correcting past wrongs has to make concessions to the rights of the present generations, even including those who, more or less inadvertently, may have benefitted from those wrongs.[12]

We can connect this appreciation of the material and spatially embedded character of social relations and hence of matters of justice and morality to one of the key criticisms of liberalism's negative conception of liberty. The standard

Left criticism has always been that the liberal conception of freedom was merely formal and negative; the lack of formal or legal restrictions on certain kinds of behaviour, which people may value as necessary to flourish, doesn't mean that they are necessarily in any meaningful sense free to do them. We are formally free to have a home, but if we cannot get the means to do so, and can only afford to sleep in shop doorways, this freedom is a sham: we need a positive kind of freedom which allows people certain basic resources – cognitive and discursive as well as material – to be able to begin to pursue our goals. Though there are dangers in pushing this alternative concept of liberty too far, our point is that this argument against merely formal kinds of liberty both reinforces and is reinforced by an appreciation of the materiality of the circumstances of justice, morality and liberty. However abstracted from daily life discussions of ethics, rights and the good may seem, they must all ultimately involve what people, living in specific material contexts, do *with* and *to* others, and what others can do with and to them. Yet sensitivity to context is not, as we have tried to argue, by any means equivalent to a plea for particularism or relativism: these are distinct issues, and it is possible to conceive of situated universalism as a form of normative theory.

One form of implicit socio-spatial naivety in ethical discussions involves the assumption that relations with our 'others' are always external, such that they are separated from us by a clear socio-spatial boundary. As soon as it is recognized that different societies no longer live separate lives, or that the others are part of the society which sits in judgment on them, then the binaries of us and them and their implied geographies begin to break down. Immigrant ethnic minorities are not only involved in host society relations from the moment of their entry, but take on increasingly hybrid identities with successive generations, and since identity is strongly relational the same goes for the members of the ethnic majorities. Gays and lesbians are traditionally invisible as such, yet they are in practical terms highly integrated into the worlds around them, while also occupying hidden social and spatial niches in the society. The problems involved are not merely imagined ones – false conceptions, but are real products of actual forms of social organization and the conflicting norms associated with them. How should a predominantly secular majority relate to minorities which demand a religious basis to social organization but which are multiply implicated in the wider secular society through work and exchange, schooling, taxation and use of public resources? How should liberal societies relate to anti-liberal groups within them? Can an 'ethic of care' be applied to relations with distant others about whom we know very little? Many of these questions have long been asked in philosophy but in order to provide helpful answers we need a better appreciation of the complexities or network forms of the social geographies involved. At the same time, the mere fact of spatial and social complexity does not lead automatically to a currently fashionable norm of multi-culturalism, but it does permit the posing of normative questions in a clearer and more practical form.

Weber's point about the idle kind of utopianism is strengthened all the more when we acknowledge the extraordinary durability of the spatial, material forms in which inequalities and injustices are embedded. The bantustan system in South Africa no longer exists in name, discursively, but the lives of most black South

Africans are of course still trapped within its objective products, its objective spatial containers. It is easy to note in the abstract, as is now becoming common, the point that individuals are embodied (isn't it amazing that we need to remind ourselves of that?) and socially embedded, but we sometimes suspect that those points can be accepted without fully remembering that people are also – in varying degrees – physically, geographically constrained and limited to particular spaces, with their homes and social ties, and unable to escape to better ones.

In recent years sociology and human geography have come to a much richer appreciation than hitherto of the way in which power works in and through material spatial forms, not only constraining but constituting identities. This being the case, it should be clear that precisely because there are micro- and macro-geographies of power, normative proposals must be highly sensitive to these flows and sedimented forms, and not fall prey to a facile kind of utopianism, whether with respect to power in general or its relationship to the organization of space in particular.

Traditionally, writers on ethics have frequently failed either to acknowledge the social context of the actions under discussion or their own particular social position with respect to them. Their search for universal principles is obviously compromised by the unacknowledged particularity of their position. For example, with the benefit of hindsight we can see the effects of this particularity, or situatedness, quite clearly in Aristotle or Adam Smith, in their discussion of the 'virtues' and 'moral sentiments', in terms of their androcentric standpoints, their valuing of military achievement, and so on. However, we take the view that though it is undoubtedly compromised thereby, traditional (and indeed contemporary) ethics can not be dismissed merely by invoking cultural or social relativity and the postmodernist critique of universals. As David Smith notes (Smith, 1997), even someone as deeply suspicious of universalism as Iris Marion Young applauds certain themes in traditional ethics and principles of justice. Whether principles purporting to be universal are actually only locally appropriate is not something which can be decided *a priori* but has to be argued case by case, thesis by thesis. Cultures are indeed strikingly different, but there are also many similarities and historical continuities, which is why we still find theses of value in the classical and modern literature or, if we ignore it, unknowingly reinvent them.

The Politics of Identity and Recognition

Our insistence on the material and spatial embedding of social relations in no way implies that discursive relations can be ignored, for communicating and representing are of course actions in themselves. It is increasingly being realized that our rights and obligations to others go beyond what we can expect in terms of being allowed to do and possess, to matters of identity and recognition. As Charles Taylor argues, since identities are formed dialogically in social contexts, they require recognition from others, not denial or misrecognition, and hence withholding recognition can be a form of oppression (1992, p. 36; see also Fraser, 1999). Since we all need identities and cultures, then the universal demand for recognition works out in terms of demands for recognition of the specificity of particular identities. From this claim, however, it is not self-evident *what* these identities are to be: they might take the form of Anglo-American identity politics, but they might equally assume more corporatist forms, as in much of continental Europe, or more traditional forms as in the Muslim world. This opens up many thorny issues.

In its minimalist sense, recognition of others might simply be equivalent to liberal indifference to the self-regarding acts of others: 'you-go-your-way-I'll-go-mine' (provided we don't harm each other). But recognition of identity involves much more than this, not least an element of respect. There are two stages to this (Taylor et al., 1992)[13]. In the first, there is a presumption that every-one deserves equal dignity, simply as fellow human beings, who deserve thereby to be listened to. The hermeneutic encounter involved in this listening will be all the more difficult and lengthy the more the respective frames of meaning differ, but the result should be a transformed way of seeing the other. In addition, where we and our others are strongly interdependent – as in a markedly multi-cultural society – we also have to acknowledge them as members of it and as therefore having claims on – and responsibilities towards – us. In the second stage, respect is accorded *conditionally*, following a process of *judgment*, and of course that might mean we deny them respect or recognition in the sense of acceptance. Unlike ethnocentric judgments, such decisions would have some claim to being based on understanding rather than ignorance. I might initially to have to suspend my impulse judgments regarding the beliefs and actions of Serbs or Northern Ireland Orange Order members, and try to achieve a hermeneutic fusion of hori-zons. But that does not mean I must thereafter grant them recognition in the sense of unconditional, uncritical acceptance. The demand that all cultures be evaluated as equally good amounts to a rejection of all standards for evaluation, contradic-torily undermining judgments of equal worth as much as those of inferiority (Wolf, 1992, p. 78). As Taylor et al. interestingly observes, such unconditional acceptance on demand would in any case be worthless in terms of respect: 'The giving of such a judgment on demand is an act of breathtaking condescension. No-one can really mean it as a genuine act of respect … such an act involves con-tempt for the [other's] intelligence … [and] demeans' (1992, p. 70). And as he adds, neo-Nietzschean attempts to turn the whole issue into one of power and counterpower have nothing to do with respect or recognition but merely involve arbitrarily taking sides.

Complicating all of these questions of understanding and judgment is the problem of deciding what identity is being understood or judged. Hybridity is developing to such an extent that it is difficult to know how to be sensitive towards multiply different identities, and difficult to know what to call ourselves and our others, indeed the very opposition of self and other overlooks the in-between character of increasing numbers of people (Bhabha, 1994). What should a white, 'anglo', British person assume about a third-generation, 'Asian-origin' British person, and vice versa? Most of those labels are questionable, and under certain circumstances possibly insulting (why should only some groups be classified by their generation, or by their 'race'?) Yet, individuals may at some times play roles which do have clear outside identities – representing white male entrepreneurs, or representing the interests of gays – and at other times shift into other roles, or into their private multiple and overlapping identities. An I-know-where-you're-coming-from attitude towards our others is not only patronizing but usually plain wrong. Why should we assume that someone has the same identity we imagine – rightly or wrongly – their 'community' to have? Why should we assume that a person belonging to a certain group – be it one of gender, sexuality, ethnicity or whatever – should always want to be recognized (that is, categorized and treated) as someone bearing that identity? Insofar as the groups are internally diverse and constituted by networks of relations, it is perhaps better if more difficult to put aside the group classifications, especially the binary ones, and try to work out how to act in relation to hybrid identities. Respectful relations with others has become far more intricate and fraught than any insider-outsider, us-and-them formulations can ever grasp, and this is in part a consequence of the fact that our social geographies are overlapping and interdependent too.

Sameness and Difference

One of the most striking features of recent political discourse and practice has been the remarkable rise of concern with 'difference', which is for many postmodernists replacing the longstanding dominance of equality. While acceptance of a certain kind of equality was generally asserted in political philosophy, there were always problems regarding what this involved. Who was included and excluded in considerations of equality and citizenship? (Slater, 1997). At what level, or in what respects, were people to be regarded as equal, and of course, how far should equality be pursued in practice, and on whose terms? From the point of view of those excluded or whose equality was purely nominal, such theory appears fraudulent in practice, though there is still the question of whether remedying the exclusions would make the theory more consistent or show it to be untenable.

Though liberalism and Marxism are fundamentally opposed in their respective individualism and collectivism, they both shared a modernist expectation or wishful thinking that differences, such as those of ethnicity, were pre-modern residues that would gradually wither away with the development of modernity. For the liberals, this would leave individuals, who might be infinitely varied but who would not define themselves as belonging to particular groups or cultures having authority over them as individuals. For Marxists, class interest overrode all others, and when the interest of the working class in transcending class had been realized under communism, the way would be clear for a harmonization of the general interest with the individual interest. Liberalism marginalized forms of domination other than that of individuals by the state and Marxism marginalized non-class differences. They affect and hope for a kind of neutrality or consensus, and both in their different ways are sociologically naive regarding the continued reproduction of difference under modernity.[14]

There are different kinds of difference – biological, geographical, imposed, inherited and chosen – and they therefore cannot be treated in the same way; thus ethnic difference is not equivalent to gender difference. Some demand recognition and respect, even celebration; some are oppressive – to many of the insiders as well as outsiders. Many require deconstruction, or a 'revisioning' involving challenges to the very terms and relations on which difference is presently constituted, as Cornell has argued regarding gender (Cornell, 1993). Not surprisingly, where existing relations of difference are challenged, there is often uncertainty about what alternative identities and patterns of difference should develop. The politics of difference today vacillates between recognition of existing differences as a goal in and of itself, and a strategy for changing them into less oppressive, stigmatized or unequal forms. It remains unclear how the latter can be brought about, and how a balance can be struck between the emphasis of difference as 'positive' versus tolerance via an emphasis on the fundamental sameness of people.

Relations between difference and equality remain fraught. Defenders of difference worry that universal equal treatment will undermine difference, and mean equality on the terms of the dominant group (for example, treating men as the norm). Defenders of equality fear that acknowledging difference will licence inequality (Phillips, 1987) and fragmentation, although a relational concept of difference avoids the latter, and concepts of networks and hybridity take us beyond simple notions of individuals and groups being constituted by a single axis of difference. Those who object to inferences about human needs based on the assumption of human sameness and who emphasize difference do not escape the normative challenge; they are still left with the choice between a relativist, agnostic response regarding normative questions and saying what should happen in relation to difference. Thus a critique, from the standpoint of difference, of ethical arguments invoking human commonalities, challenges the assumption of universal commonalities, but does not undermine the case for ethics.

Concern with difference and the critique of the special interests so often hidden behind universal claims are bound to make attractive some degree of relativism or at least neutrality with regard to different groups and identities. But then ironically, liberalism always sought such neutrality with respect to individuals and their conceptions of the good, and with certain qualifications might claim to be the best available 'shell' for a multi-cultural society too (Taylor et al., 1992)[15]. It is therefore perhaps not surprising that those who have pursued questions of justice from the apparently opposed standpoint of difference have arrived at conclusions that are not unlike those of liberalism (Sayer, 1995; Young, 1990a and b), although this is not acknowledged clearly by many postmodernists.

Conclusion

In the previous chapter, I argued that critical social science needs to examine its critical standpoints and the normative stances they imply. Ethical issues, concerning the nature of the good and how people should treat one another, are essential to the development of such standpoints. Currently, positive social science and normative theory are mutually estranged. The massive imbalance between the sophistication of positive social science and the poverty, at least outside political theory, of normative thinking is intolerable, but the imbalance is unlikely to be corrected given the distance of normative theory's discussions from recognizable contexts of daily life.

Normative political philosophies, such as those of communitarianism and liberalism, have long been criticized for losing contact with the empirical analysis of actual social organization. Thus, liberalism has traditionally abstracted from caring relationships, from power and dependency and from the social constitution of actions in general, presenting an image of society as an aggregate of individuals pursuing their private notions of the good, enclosed within their private property (Baier, 1994; Tronto, 1993). Though such an image might superficially appear to be objectified – for example, in the suburban environment – our actions are so tangled up with those of others, and the ways in which they affect and constrain others so complex and indirect, that it is extraordinarily difficult to decide whether individuals' actions harm others. Liberalism's positive social theory is thin and ideological – too concerned with idealized conceptions of markets and minimizing state action to want to find out what happens in existing societies. But this is not the only example of the sociological naivety of political philosophy, induced by its lack of contact with concrete social science; as Young notes, arguments about community are no less abstracted from the fabric of economic relationships present in modern, urban society (1990b).

However, no matter how frustrating we find this loose or excessive abstraction in political philosophy, we cannot simply drop it for more empirical studies of actual organizations. As Held puts it:

> ...[I]f a theory of the most desirable form of democracy [or any other form of social organization] is to be at all plausible, it must be concerned with both theoretical and practical issues, with philosophical as well as organizational and institutional questions. Without this double focus, an arbitrary choice of principles, and seemingly endless abstract debates about them, are encouraged. A consideration of principles, without an examination of the conditions for their realization, may preserve a sense of virtue, but it will leave the actual meaning of such principles barely spelt out at all. A consideration of social institutions and political arrangements without reflection upon the proper principles of their ordering might, by contrast, lead to an understanding of their functioning, but it will barely help us to come to a judgement as to their appropriateness and desirability. (Held, 1994, p. 308)

While we cannot expect theory to anticipate the specificities of particular political conjunctures, a normative theory which was more attuned to the patterning of social life, with its concrete geographies and histories could usefully inform political practice, and counter the loss of direction associated with the decline of the Left.

Notes

1 Based on an earlier essay written with Michael Storper as an introduction to papers by David Slater, David Smith and Sarah Whatmore and published in *Society and Space: Environment and Planning D*, 1997.

2 Not all theorists sympathetic to postmodernism reject or relativize moral discourse. For example, Bauman (1993) emphasizes the aporetic or dilemmatic quality of morality, not in order to abandon it but to draw attention to the inadequacy of characterizations

which suppose that moral imperatives can be followed slavishly without generating immoral side-effects.

3 This view sometimes turns up in strange places; in a recent paper, Harvey cites Engels' positivistic resistance to the alleged confusion which the inclusion of values in scientific investigation brings (Harvey, 1992).

4 In the second, Marxist half of *Social Justice and the City*, David Harvey came to reject the explicitly normative inquiry used in the first half, on similar grounds. In a more recent article relating social justice, postmodernism and the city, Harvey both repeats this argument and ventures a set of normative propositions (Harvey, 1992).

5 An additional argument is that norms are not so much directly regulative of behaviour as part of a separate discursive rationale which is only drawn upon when that behaviour is challenged. However the challenges can, of course, affect the behaviour, and actors do often worry about what is the proper course of action.

6 Many Anglo-American postmodernists invoke Foucault as the authority for this position, but this is not consistent with the recent biographical work on Foucault (Eribon, 1989).

7 The *situated* subject need not do so, for reasons given in the third point (see p. 175).

8 No better are the recent reactions to this which flip over into oversocialized conception of individuals, or worse, which reduce them to positions in discourse.

9 There is still a long way to go here, for even discussions of ecological ethics tend to neglect to specify the kinds of society in which particular normative principles could be feasibly adopted.

10 As Sarah Whatmore (1997) indicates, the appropriate domains for these concepts is contested. In *The Theory of the Moral Sentiments*, Adam Smith – often wrongly portrayed as a founding advocate of narrow self-interest – shows an extraordinary sensitivity to the moral sentiments appropriate to our relations with concrete others.

11 While we might agree that in one sense principles of justice are selective, we might also want to say they are selective in universally consistent ways.

12 For an interesting discussion of the South African case, see Smith, 1994, pp. 231–40.

13 This argument is based upon Charles Taylor's essay but modified in the light of Susan Wolf's comments on it.

14 However, like communities, not all differences and identities are good, and one has only to think of what is happening in Northern Ireland or former Yugoslavia to have some sympathy with the old liberal and Marxist wishful thinking about the decline of certain forms of difference.

15 This convergence is striking in Taylor's case since he has also been a forceful critic of liberalism's predominantly asocial conception of individuals and has given some support to communitarian arguments.

References

Abrams, P. (1982) *Historical Sociology*, Ithaca, NY: Cornell University Press.

Adam, B. (1990) *Time and Social Theory*, Cambridge: Polity.

Agnew, J.A. (1987a) *Place and Politics*, London: Allen and Unwin.

Agnew, J.A. (1987b) *The United States in the World Economy: 4 Regional Geography*, Cambridge: Cambridge University Press.

Allen, J. (1987) 'Realism as method: a review of Sayer's *Method in Social Science*' *Antipode*, 19, pp. 231–9.

Amin, A. (ed.) (1994) *Post-Fordism*, Oxford: Blackwell.

Archer, K. (1987) 'Mythology and the problem of reading in urban and regional research', *Society and Space: Environment and Planning D*, 5: pp. 384–93.

Archer, M. (1995) *Realist Social Theory: the Morphogenetic Approach*, Cambridge: Cambridge University Press.

Arthur, J. and Shapiro, A. (eds) (1995) *Campus Wars: Multiculturalism and the Politics of Difference*, Boulder, Co.: Westview.

Assiter, A. (1997) *Enlightened Women: Modernist Feminism in a Postmodern Age*, London: Routledge.

Baier, A.C. (1994) *Moral Prejudices*, Cambridge MA: Harvard University Press, 2nd edn.

Bardhan, P. and Roemer, J.E. (1992) 'Market socialism: a case for rejuvenation', *Journal of Economic Perspectives*, 6 (3), pp. 101–16.

Barnes, B. (1982) *T.S. Kuhn and Social Science*, London: Macmillan.

Barrett, M. (1987) 'The concept of difference', *Feminist Review*, 26, pp. 29–43.

Barrett, M. (1991) *The Politics of Truth: From Marx to Foucault*, Cambridge: Polity.

Barrett, M. (1992) 'Words and things: materialism and method in contemporary feminist analysis', in M. Barrett and A. Phillips (eds) *Destabilising Theory*, Cambridge: Polity.

Barrett, M. and Phillips, A. (1992) *Destabilising Theory*, Cambridge: Polity.

Bauman, Z. (1992) *Intimations of Postmodernity*, London: Routledge.

Bauman, Z. (1993) *Postmodern Ethics*, Oxford: Blackwell.

Bauman, Z. (1995) *Life in Fragments*, Oxford: Blackwell.

Baynes, K., Bohman, J. and McCarthy, T. (eds) (1987) *After Philosophy*, Cambridge, MA: MIT.

Beauregard, R.A. (1988) 'In the absence of practice: the locality research debate', *Antipode*, 20, pp. 52–9.

Bellamy, R. (1992) *Liberalism and Modern Society*, Cambridge: Cambridge University Press.

Benhabib, S. (1986) *Critique, Norm and Utopia*, New York: Columbia University Press.

Benhabib, S. (1992) *Situating the Self*, Cambridge: Polity.

Benton, T. (1993) *Natural Relations: Ecology, Animal Rights and Social Justice*, London: Verso.

Bhabha, H.K. (1994) *The Location of Culture*, London: Routledge.

Bhaskar, R. (1975) *A Realist Theory of Science*, Leeds: Leeds Books. 2nd edn 1979, Brighton: Harvester.

Bhaskar, R. (1979) *The Possibility of Naturalism*, Brighton: Harvester. 2nd edn 1989, Hemel Hempstead: Harvester Wheatsheaf.

Bhaskar, R. (1986) *Scientific Realism and Human Emancipation*, London: Verso.

Bhaskar, R. (1989) *Reclaiming Reality*, London: Verso.
Bhaskar, R. (1991) *Philosophy and the Idea of Freedom*, Oxford: Blackwell.
Bhaskar, R. (1993) *Dialectic: the Pulse of Freedom*, London: Verso.
Bhaskar, R. (1994) *Plato, Etc.*, London: Verso.
Bhaskar, R. (1995) *Plato, Etc.*, London: Verso.
Billig, M., Condor, S., Edwards, D., Cane, M., Middleton, D. and Radley, A. (1988) *Ideological Dilemmas*, Beverley Hills, CA: Sage.
Blaikie, N. (1993) *Approaches to Social Enquiry*, Cambridge: Polity.
Blaut, J. (1963) 'Space and process', in W.K. Davies (ed.) *The Conceptual Revolution in Geography*, London: University of London Press, pp. 42–51.
Bloch, M. (1989) *Ritual, History and Power: Selected Papers in Anthropology*, London: Athlone.
Blok, A. (1974) *The Mafia of a Sicilian Village 1860–1960: A Study of Violent Peasant Entrepreneurs*, Oxford: Blackwell.
Bloom, A. (1995) 'The closing of the American mind', in Arthur, J. and Shapiro, A. (eds) *Campus Wars: Multiculturalism and the Politics of Difference*, Boulder, Co.: Westview, pp. 9–18.
Bock, G. and James, S. (eds) (1992) *Beyond Equality and Difference*, London: Routledge.
Boltanski, L. and Thevenot, L. (1991) *De La Justification*, Paris: Gallimard.
Bondi, L. (1990) 'Feminism, postmodernism and geography: space for women?' *Antipode*, 22, pp. 156–67.
Bondi, L. and Domosh, M. (1992) 'Other figures in other places: on feminism, postmodernism and geography', *Society and Space: Environment and Planning D*, 10, pp. 199–213.
Bourdieu, P. (1977) *Outline of a Theory of Practice*, Cambridge: Cambridge University Press.
Bourdieu, P. (1984) *Distinction: A Social Critique of the Judgment of Taste*, London: Routledge and Kegan Paul.
Bourdieu, P. (1988) *Homo Academicus*, London: Routledge.
Bourdieu, P. (1993) *Sociology in Question*, London: Sage.
Buchanan, A.E. (1982) *Marx and Justice: The Radical Critique of Justice*, London: Rowman and Allenheld.
Buchanan, A.E. (1985) *Ethics, Efficiency and the Market*, London: Clarendon.
Butler, J. (1989) *Gender Trouble*, London: Routledge.
Butler, J. (1992) 'Contingent foundations', in J. Butler and J.W. Scott (eds) *Feminists Theorize the Political*, London: Routledge, pp. 3–21.
Butler, J. (1994) 'Gender as Performance: Interview', *Radical Philosophy*, 67, pp. 32–9.
Carling, A. (1992) *Social Division*, London: Verso.
Castells, M. (1977) *The Urban Question*, London: Arnold.
Chandler, A. (1977) *The Visible Hand*, Cambridge, MA: Harvard University Press.
Chodorow, N. (1978) *The Reproduction of Mothering*, Berkeley, CA: University of California Press.
Clifford, J. and Marcus, G.E. (eds) (1986) *Writing Culture: The Poetics and Politics of Ethnography*, Berkeley, CA: University of California Press.
Cloke, P., Philo, C. and Sadler, D. (1991) *Approaching Human Geography*, London: Paul Chapman.
Cockburn, C. (1983) *Brothers*, London: Pluto.
Cockburn, C. (1985) *Machinery of Male Dominance*, London: Pluto Press.
Cole, S. (1992) *Making Science: Between Nature and Society*, Cambridge, MA: Harvard University Press.
Collier, A. (1994a) *Critical Realism*, London: Verso.
Collier, A. (1994b) 'Values, rationality and the environment', *Radical Philosophy*, 66, pp. 3–10.
Collier, A. (1998) 'Language, practice and realism', in I. Parker (ed.), *Social Constructionism, Discourse and Realism*, London: Sage, pp. 47–58.
Connerton, P. (1989) *How Societies Remember*, Cambridge: Cambridge University Press.
Connor, S. (1993) 'The necessity of value', in J. Squires (ed.), *Principled Positions*, London: Lawrence and Wishart.

Cooke, P. (1986) 'The changing urban system and regional system in the UK' *Regional Studies*, 20, pp. 243–51.

Corbridge, S. (1993a) 'Ethics in development studies: the example of debt', in F.J. Schuurman (ed.), *Beyond the Impasse: New Directions in Development Theory*, London: Zed Books.

Corbridge, S. (1993b) 'Marxisms, modernities and moralities: development praxis and the claims of distant strangers', in D. Booth (ed.), *New Directions in Social Development Research*, Cambridge: Cambridge University Press.

Cornell, D. (1993) *Transformations: Recollective Imagination and Sexual Difference*, London: Routledge.

Cosgrove, D. (1984) *Social Formation and Symbolic Landscape*, Beckenham, Kent: Croom Helm.

Cusumano, M.A. (1985) *The Japanese Automobile Industry*, Cambridge: MA: Harvard University Press.

Daniel, G. (1962) *The Idea of Pre-History*, London: C.A. Walts and Co.

Darby, H.C. (1962) 'The problem of geographical description', *Transactions of the Institute of British Geographers*, 30, pp. 1–14.

Davidson, D. (1984) *Inquiries into Truth and Interpretation*, Boston: Clarendon Press.

Day, B. (1987) 'Rites of passage: education policy from the perspective of school leavers' *Policy and Politics*, 15, pp. 147–55.

Dear, M. (1988) 'The postmodernist challenge: reconstructing human geography', *Transactions of the Insitute of British Geographers*, New Series, 13, pp. 264–74.

Derrida, J. (1976) *Margins of Philosophy* transl. A. Bass, Chicago, IL: Chicago University Press.

Deutsche, R. (1991) 'Boy's town', '*Society and Space: Environment and Planning D*, 9, pp. 5–13.

Dews, P. (1984) 'The Letter and the line: discourse and its other in Lyotard', *Diacritics*, 14 (3), pp. 40–9.

Dickens, P.J. (1996) *Reconstructing Nature: Alienation, Emancipation and the Division of Labour*, London: Routledge.

Dittmar, H. (1992) *The Social Psychology of Material Possessions*, Hemel Hempstead Harvester.

Dobson, A. (1990) *Green Political Thought*, London: Unwin Hyman.

Dodd, N. (1994) *The Sociology of Money*, Cambridge: Polity.

Doel, M. (1992) 'In stalling deconstruction: striking out the postmodern', *Society and Space: Environment and Planning D*, 10, pp. 163–80.

Doyal, L. and Gough, I. (1991) *A Theory of Human Need*, London: Macmillan.

Dray, W. (ed.) (1966) *Philosophical Analysis and History*, New York: Harper and Row.

Dryzek, J.S. (1987) *Political Ecology*, Oxford: Blackwell.

Eagleton T. (1983) *Literary Theory: An Introduction*, Oxford, Basil Blackwell.

Edgley, R. (1985) 'Reason as dialectic: science, social science and socialist science', in R. Edgley and R. Osborne (eds), *Radical Philosophy Reader*, London: Verso.

Eribon, D. (1989) *Michel Foucault,* Paris: Flammarion.

Etzioni, A. (1988) *The Moral Dimension: Toward a New Economics*, New York: Free Press.

Fairclough, N. (1992) *Discourse and Social Change*, Cambridge: Polity.

Fay, B. (1975) *Social Theory and Political Action*, London: Allen and Unwin.

Fay, B. (1987) *Critical Social Science*, Cambridge: Polity.

Fay, B. (1996) *Contemporary Philosophy of Social Science*, Oxford: Blackwell.

Feyerabend, P. (1993) *Against Method*, London: New Left Review, 3rd edn.

Foucault, M. (1977) *Discipline and Punish* transl. A. Sheridan, London: Penguin.

Foucault, M. (1978) *The History of Sexuality* transl. R. Hurley, London: Penguin.

Foucault, M. (1980) *Power/Knowledge*, New York: Pantheon Books.

Franklin, S. (1993) 'Essentialism, which essentialism? Some implications of reproductive and genetic techno-science', *Journal of Homosexuality*, 24, 3/4, pp. 27–39.

Fraser, N. (1995) 'From redistribution to recognition? Dilemmas of a "post-socialist age"', *New Left Review*, 212, pp. 68–93.

Fraser, N. (1999) 'Social justice in the age of identity politics: redistribution, recognition and participation', in L. Ray and A. Sayer (eds), *Culture and Economy after the Cultural Turn*, London: Sage.

Fraser, N. and Nicholson, L. (1989) 'Social criticism without philosophy: an encounter between feminism and postmodernism', in L. Nicholson (ed.), *Feminism/Postmodernism*, London: Verso.

Fröbel, F. et al. (1979) *The New International Division of Labour*, Cambridge: Cambridge University Press.

Fuss, D. (1990) *Essentially Speaking: Feminism, Nature and Difference*, London: Routledge.

Geertz, C. (1973) *The Interpretation of Cultures*, New York: Basic Books.

Gellner, E. (1968) 'The new idealism – cause and meaning in the social sciences', in A. Musgrave and I. Lakatos (eds), *Problems in the Philosophy of Science*, Amsterdam: North Holland.

Gellner, E. (1970) 'Concepts and society', in B. Wilson (ed.), *Rationality*, Oxford: Blackwell, pp. 18–49.

Geras, N. (1990) *Discourses of Extremity: Radical Ethics and Post-Marxist Extravagances*, London: Verso.

Gherardi, S. (1995) *Gender, Symbolism and Organizational Cultures*, London: Sage.

Giddens, A. (1976) *New Rules of Sociological Method*, London: Hutchinson.

Giddens, A. (1979) *Central Problems of Social Theory*, London: Macmillan.

Giddens, A. (1981) *A Contemporary Critique of Historical Materialism Volume 1*, London: Macmillan.

Giddens, A. (1984) *The Constitution of Society*, Cambridge: Polity Press.

Giddens, A. (1985) 'Time, space and regionalization', in D. Gregory and J. Urry (eds), *Social Relations and Spatial Structures*, London: Macmillan, pp. 265–95.

Giddens, A. (1987) *Social Theory and Modern Society*, Oxford: Blackwell.

Gilbert, A. (1988) 'The new regional geography in English and French-speaking countries' *Progress in Human Geography*, 12, pp. 208–28.

Gilligan, C. (1982) *In a Different Voice: Psychological Theory and Women's Development*, Cambridge, MA: Harvard University Press.

Graham, J. (1988) 'Postmodernism and Marxism', *Antipode*, 20, pp. 60–6.

Graham, J. (1990) 'Theory and essentialism in Marxist geography', *Antipode*, 22, pp. 53–66.

Gray, J. (1986) *Liberalism*, Milton Keynes: Open University Press.

Gray, J. (1995) *Enlightenment's Wake*, London: Routledge.

Greenwood, D. (1994) *Realism, Identity and Emotion: Reclaiming Social Psychology*, London: Sage.

Gregory, D. (1978) *Ideology, Science and Human Geography*, London: Hutchinson.

Gregory, D. (1981) 'Human agency and human geography', *Transactions of the Institute of British Geographers News Series*, 6, pp. 1–18.

Gregory, D. (1982) *Regional Transformation and Industrial Revolution: A Geography of the Yorkshire Woollen Industry*, London: Macmillan.

Gregory, D. (1985) 'Suspended animation: the stasis of diffusion theory', in D. Gregory and J. Urry (eds), *Social Relations and Spatial Structures*, London: Macmillan, pp. 296–336.

Gregory, D. (1987) 'Postmodernism and the politics of social theory', *Society and Space: Environment and Planning D*, 5, pp. 245–8.

Gregory, D. (1988) 'The production of regions in England's Industrial Revolution', *Journal of Historical Geography*, 14 (1), pp. 50–8.

Gregory, D. (1989a) 'Areal differentiation and post-modern human geography', in D. Gregory and R. Walford (eds), *Horizons in Human Geography*, London: Macmillan, pp. 67–96.

Gregory, D. (1989b) 'The crisis of modernity? Human geography and critical social theory', in R. Peet and N.J. Thrift (eds), *New Models in Geography Vol. II*, London: Allen and Unwin, pp. 348–84.

Gregory, D. and Urry, J. (eds) (1985) *Social Relations and Spatial Structures*, London: Macmillan.

Grimshaw, J. (1986) *Feminist Philosophers: Women's Perspectives on Philosophical Traditions*, Brighton: Wheatsheaf.

Grimshaw, J. (1996) 'Philosophy, feminism and universalism', *Radical Philosophy*, 76, pp. 19–28.

Gutmann, A. (1992) 'Introduction' in C. Taylor et al., *Multiculturalism and "The Politics of Recognition"*, Princetown, NJ: Princetown University Press.

Habermas, J. (1984) *The Theory of Communicative Action Vol. 1* transl. T. McCarthy, London: Heinemann.

Habermas, J. (1990) *Moral Consciousness and Communicative Action*, Cambridge: Polity.

Hacking, I. (1983) *Representing and Intervening*, Cambridge: Cambridge University Press.

Hagerstrand, T. (1985) 'Time-geography: focus on the corporeality of man, society, and environment', *The Science and Praxis of Complexity*, London: United Nations University.

Halford, S. (1987) 'Women's initiatives in local government: tokenism or power', WP-59, Brighton, Sussex: Urban and Regional Studies, University of Sussex.

Hall, P., Breheny, M.J., McQuaid, R. and Hart, D. (1987) *Western Sunrise: The Genesis and Growth of Britain's Major High Tech Corridor*, London: Unwin Hyman.

Hansen, N.R. (1965) *Patterns of Discovery*, Cambridge: Cambridge University Press.

Haraway, D. (1985) 'A manifesto for cyborgs: science, technology and socialist feminism in the 1980s', in L. Nicholson (ed.) *Feminism/Postmodernism*, London: Routledge, pp. 190–233.

Haraway, D. (1991) *Simians, Cyborgs and Women: the reinvention of nature*, London: Free Association Books.

Haraway, D. (1997) *Modest Witness@Second Millenium*, New York: Routledge.

Harding, S. (1989) 'Feminism, science and anti-Enlightenment critiques', in L. Nicholson (ed.), *Feminism/Postmodernism*, London: Routledge, pp. 83–107.

Harding, S. (1991) *Whose Science, Whose Knowledge? Thinking from Women's Lives*, Oxford: Oxford University Press.

Harré, R. (1961) *Theories and Things*, London: Sheed and Ward.

Harré, R. (1970) *The Principles of Scientific Thinking*, London: Macmillan.

Harré, R. (1972) *The Philosophies of Science*, Oxford: Oxford University Press.

Harré, R. (1979) *Social Being*, Oxford: Blackwell.

Harré, R. (1983) *Personal Being*, Oxford: Blackwell.

Harré, R. (1986) *Varieties of Realism*, Oxford: Blackwell.

Harré, R. (1994) *Physical Being*, Oxford: Blackwell.

Harré, R. (1998) 'When the knower is also the known', in T. May and M. Williams (eds), *Knowing the Social World*, Buckingham: Open University Press, pp. 37–49.

Harré, R. and Madden, E.H. (1975) *Causal Powers*, Blackwell: Oxford.

Harris, C. (1986) *Redundancy and Recession*, Cambridge: Cambridge University Press.

Hartsock, N. (1989) 'Foucault on power: a theory for women', in L. Nicholson (ed.), *Feminism/Postmodernism*, London: Routledge, pp. 157–76.

Harvey, D. (1973) *Social Justice and the City*, London: Arnold.

Harvey, D. (1982) *The Limits to Capital*, London: Edward Arnold.

Harvey, D. (1985) 'The geopolitics of capitalism' in D. Gregory and J. Urry (eds) *Spatial Structures and Social Relations*, London: Macmillan, pp. 128–63.

Harvey, D. (1987) 'Three myths in search of reality in urban studies', *Society and Space: Environment and Planning D*, 5, pp. 367–76.

Harvey, D. (1989) *The Condition of Postmodernity*, Oxford: Blackwell.

Harvey, D. (1992) 'Social justice, postmodernism and the city', *International Journal of Urban and Regional Research*, 16, pp. 585–96.

Harvey, D. (1996) *Justice, Nature and the Geography of Difference*, Oxford: Blackwell.

Harvey, D. and Scott, A.J. (1989) 'The practice of human geography: theory and empirical specificity in the transition from Fordism to flexible accumulation', in B. Macmillan (ed.), *Remodelling Geography*, Oxford: Blackwell, pp. 217–29.

Held, D. (1994) 'What should democracy mean today?' in *The Polity Reader in Social Theory,* Cambridge: Polity.

Hempel, C. (1962) 'Explanation in science and history', reprinted 1966 in W. Dray (ed.), *Philosophical Analysis and History*, New York: Harper and Row, pp. 95–126.

Henry, N. (1992) 'The new industrial spaces: locational logic of a new production era', *International Journal of Urban and Regional Research*, 16, pp. 375–96.

Hesse, M.B. (1974) *The Structure of Scientific Inference*, London: Macmillan.

Hesse, M.B. (1980) *Revolutions and Reconstructions in the Philosophy of Science*, Brighton: Harvester.

Hindess, B. (1987) *Freedom, Equality and the Market,* London: Tavistock.

hooks, b. (1991) 'Postmodern blackness', reprinted in P. Williams and L. Chrisman (eds), *Colonial Discourse and Post-Colonial Theory: A Reader* (1993), Hemel Hempstead: Harvester Wheatsheaf, pp. 421–7.

Hoy, D.C. (1986) *Foucault: A Critical Reader,* Oxford: Blackwell.

Hull, C. (1997) 'The need in thinking: materiality in Theodor W. Adorno and Judith Butler', *Radical Philosophy*, 84, pp. 22–35.

Hutcheon, L. (1988) *A Poetics of Postmodernism*, London: Routledge.

Ignatieff, M. (1984) *The Needs of Strangers*, London: Chatto and Windus.

Jessop, B. (1990) *State Theory: Putting Capitalist States in their Place*, Cambridge: Polity.

Johnson, L. (1987) '(Un)Realist perspectives: patriarchy and feminist challenges in geography', *Antipode*, 19, pp. 210–15.

Johnston, R.J. (1993) 'Real political geography', *Political Geography,* 12 (3), 473–80.

Jonas, A. (1986) 'Rediscovering regional geography: prospectus and problems', Columbus, OH: Department of Geography, Ohio State University.

Keat, R. and Urry, J. (1982, 2nd edn) *Social Theory as Science*, London: Routledge.

Keeble, D. (1980) 'Industrial decline, regional policy and the urban-rural manufacturing shift in the United Kingdom', *Environment and Planning A*, Vol. 12, pp. 945–62.

Krige, J. (1980) *Science, Revolution and Discontinuity*, Brighton: Harvester.

Kuhn, T.S. (1970) *The Structure of Scientific Revolutions*, Chicago: University of Chicago.

Kymlicka, W. (1989) *Liberalism, Community and Culture*, Oxford: Clarendon Press.

Kymlicka, W. (1990) *Contemporary Political Philosophy*, Oxford: Oxford University Press.

Laclau, E. and Mouffe, C. (1985) *Hegemony and Socialist Strategy*, London: Verso.

Lancaster Regionalism Group (1985) *Localities, Class and Gender,* London: Pion.

Larrain, J. (1994) 'The postmodern critique of ideology', *Sociological Review,* 42, pp. 289–314.

Lash, S. and Urry, J. (1987) The End of Organized Capitalism, Cambridge: Polity.

Lawson, T. (1997) *Economics and Reality*, London: Routledge.

Le Doeuff, M. (1989) *The Philosophical Imaginary*, London: Athlone.

Lefebvre, H. (1991) *The Production of Space*, Oxford: Blackwell.

Littler, C.R. (1982) *The Development of the Labour Process in Capitalist Societies,* London: Heinemann Educational Books.

Louch, A.R. (1966) *The Explanation of Human Action*, Oxford: Basil Blackwell.

Longino, H. (1990) *Science as Social Knowledge*, Princetown, NJ: Princetown University Press.

Lukes, S. (1985) *Marxism and Morality*, Oxford: Oxford University Press.

Lyotard, J-F. (1984) *The Postmodern Condition: A Report on Knowledge* transl. J.B. Thompson, Minneapolis, MN: University of Minnesota Press.

Lyotard, J-F. and Thebaud, J-L. (1985) *Just Gaming* transl. J.B. Thompson, Manchester: Manchester University Press.

Mäki, U. (1993) 'Two philosophies of the rhetoric of economics' in W. Henderson, T. Dudley-Evans and R. Backhouse, (eds), *Economics and Language*, London: Routledge, p. 37.

Mäki, U. (1995) 'Diagnosing McCloskey', *Journal of Economic Literature,* 33, pp. 1300–18.

Malik, K. (1996) 'Universalism and difference: race and the postmodernists', *Race and Class*, 37 (3), pp. 1–18.

Mann, M. (1986) *The Sources of Social Power Vol. 1: A History of Power from the Beginning to AD 1760*, Cambridge: Cambridge University Press.

Mann, M. (1990) *The Rise and Decline of the Nation State*, Oxford: Clarendon.

Marcus, G.E. and Fischer, M.M.J. (1986) *Anthropology as Cultural Critique: An Experimental Moment in the Human Sciences*, Chicago, IL: University of Chicago Press.

Markusen, A., Hall, P. and Glasmeier, A. (1986) *High Tech America*, Winchester, MA: Allen and Unwin.

Marsh, D., Buller, J., Hay, C., Johnston, J., Kerr, P., McAnulla, S. and Watson, M. (1998) *Postwar British Politics in Perspective*, Cambridge: Polity.

Martell, L. (1994) *Ecology and Society*, Cambridge: Polity.

Martin, J.R. (1994) 'Methodological essentialism, false difference, and other dangerous traps', *Signs*, 19, 3, pp. 630–57.

Marx, K. and Engels, F. (1974) *The German Ideology*, transl. and edited by C.J. Arthur, London: Lawrence and Wishart.

Massey, D. (1984, 1996) *Spatial Divisions of Labour*, London: Macmillan.

Massey, D. (1991) 'The political place of locality studies', *Environment and Planning A*, 23, pp. 267–81.

Massey, D. (1991) 'A global sense of place', *Marxism Today*, June, pp. 24–9.

Massey, D. (1996) *Space, Place and Gender*, Cambridge: Polity.

Massey, D. and Allen, J. (1985) *Geography Matters*, Cambridge: Cambridge University Press.

Massey, D. and Meegan, R.A. (1982) *Anatomy of Job Loss*, London: Methuen.

McDowell, L. (1991) 'The baby and the bathwater: diversity, deconstruction and feminist theory in geography', *Geoforum*, 22, pp. 123–33.

McLennan, G. (1989) *Marxism, Pluralism and Beyond*, Cambridge: Polity.

McLennan, G. (1995) *Pluralism*, Open University Press.

McLennan, G. (1996) 'Post-Marxism and the "four sins" of modernist theorising', *New Left Review*, 213, pp. 53–74.

McLuhan, M. (1967) *The Media is the Message*, London: Penguin.

McNay, L. (1994) 'Bodies in transition', *Radical Philosophy*, 78, pp. 34–5.

Millstone, E. (1978) 'A framework for the sociology of knowledge', *Social Studies of Science*, 8, p. 115.

Morgan, K. and Sayer, A. (1988) *Microcircuits of Capital: 'Sunrise Industry and Uneven Development*, Cambridge: Polity.

Murphy, R. (1994) 'The sociological construction of science without nature', *Sociology*, 28 (4), pp. 957–74.

Nellhaus, T. (1998) 'Signs, social ontology, and critical realism', *Journal for the Theory of Social Behaviour*, 28 (1), pp. 1–24.

Nelson, J. (1995) *Feminism, Objectivity and Economics*, London: Routledge.

Nelson, J.S., Megill, A. and McCloskey, D.M. (eds), (1987) *The Rhetoric of the Human Sciences*, Madison, WI: University of Wisconsin Press.

New, C. (1995) 'Sociology and the case for realism', *The Sociological Review*, 43 (4), pp. 808–27.

New, C. (1996) 'Man bad, woman good: essentialisms and ecofeminisms', *New Left Review*, 216, pp. 79–93.

New, C. (1996) *Agency, Health and Social Survival: The Ecopolitics of Rival Psychologies*, London: Taylor and Francis.

Nicholson, L. (1990) *Feminism/Postmodernism*, London: Routledge.

Norris, C. (1990) *What's Wrong with Postmodernism: Critical Theory and the Ends of Philosophy*, London: Harvester Wheatsheaf.

Norris, C. (1991: revised edn.) *Deconstruction: Theory and Practice*, London: Routledge.

Norris, C. (1993) *The Truth about Postmodernism*, Oxford: Blackwell.

Norris, C. (1997) *Against Relativism*, Oxford: Blackwell.

Nove, A. (1983) *The Economics of Feasible Socialism*, London: Allen and Unwin.

Nozick, R. (1974) *Anarchy, State and Utopia*, New York: Basic Books.

Nussbaum, M.C. (1992) 'Human functioning and social justice: in defence of Aristotelian essentialism', *Political Theory*, 20 (2), pp. 202–46.

Nussbaum, M. and Glover, J. (eds) (1995) *Women, Culture and Development*, Oxford: Clarendon Press.

O'Brien, M. and Penna, S. (1998) *Theorizing Welfare*, London: Sage.

Olsson, G. (1991) *Lines of Power/Limits of Language*, Minneapolis, MN: University of Minnesota Press.

O'Neill, J. (1993) *Ecology, Policy and Politics*, London: Routledge.

O'Neill, J. (1994) 'Essentialism and the market', *The Philosophical Forum*, Vol. XXVI (2), pp. 87–100.

O'Neill, J. (1995) 'Essences and markets', mimeo, Lancaster University.

O'Neill, J. (1998) *The Market: Ethics, Knowledge and Politics*, London: Routledge.

Osborne, P. (1991) *Socialism and the Limits of Liberalism*, London: Verso.

Osborne, P. (1997) 'Friendly fire: the hoaxing of *Social Text*', *Radical Philosophy*, 81, pp. 54–6.

Outhwaite, W. (1987) *New Philosophies of Science*, London: Macmillan.

Pateman, C. (1987) 'Feminist critiques of the public/private dichotomy', in A. Phillips (ed.), *Feminism and Equality*, Oxford: Blackwell.

Pawson, R. (1989) *A Measure for Measures*, London: Sage.

Pawson, R. and Tilley, N. (1997) *Realistic Evaluation*, London: Sage.

Peacock, M. (1993) 'Hayek: realism and spontaneous order', *Journal for the Theory of Social Behaviour*, 23, pp. 249–64.

Peet, R. (1998) *Modern Geographical Thought*, Oxford: Blackwell.

Phillips, A. (1987) *Feminism and Equality,* Oxford: Blackwell.

Phillips, A. (1991) *Engendering Democracy*, Cambridge: Polity.

Phillips, A. (ed.) (1987) *Feminism and Equality*, Oxford: Blackwell.

Phillips, A. (1991) 'So what's wrong with the individual? Socialist and feminist debates on equality' in P. Osborne (ed.), *Socialism and the Limits of Liberalism*, London: Verso, pp. 139–60.

Pickles, J. (1986) *Geography and Phenomenology*, Cambridge: Cambridge University Press.

Pile, S. (1994) 'Maculinism, the use of dualistic epistemologies and third spaces', *Antipode*, 26 (3), pp. 255–77.

Pile, S. and Rose, G. (1992) 'All or nothing? Politics and critique in the modernism-postmodernism debate', *Society and Space: Environment and Planning D*, 10, pp. 123–36.

Plant, R. (1991) *Modern Political Thought*, Oxford: Blackwell.

Poole, R. (1991) *Morality and Modernity*, London: Routledge.

Potter, J. (1997) *Representing Reality*, London: Sage.

Potter, J. (1998) 'Fragments in the realisation of relativism', in I. Parker (ed.), *Social Constructionism, Discourse and Realism*, London: Sage, pp. 27–46.

Pred, A. (1986) *Place, Practice and Structure*, Cambridge: Polity.

Pred, A. (1989) 'The locally spoken word and local struggles', *Society and Space: Environment and Planning D*, 7 (2), pp. 211–34.

Pudup, M.B. (1988) 'Arguments within regional geography', *Progress in Human Geography*, 12, pp. 369–90.

Putterman, L. (1990) *Division of Labor and Welfare*, Oxford: Oxford University Press.

Quine W.V.O. (1961) *From a Logical Point of View*, Cambridge, MA: Harvard University Press.

Rattansi, A. (1994) '"Western" racisms, ethnicities and identities', in A. Rattansi and S. Westwood (eds), *Racism, Modernity and Identity: on the western front*, Cambridge: Polity.

Rawls, J. (1971) *A Theory of Justice*, Oxford: Oxford University Press.

Rawls, J. (1993) *Political Liberalism*, New York: Columbia University Press.

Ricoeur, P. (1982) *Hermeneutics and the Human Sciences* transl. J.B. Thompson, Cambridge: Cambridge University Press.

Roemer, J.E. (1994) *A Future for Socialism*, London: Verso.

Robbins, B. (1998) 'Science-envy: Sokal, science and the police', *Radical Philosophy*, 88, pp. 2–5.

Rorty, R. (1980) *Philosophy and the Mirror of Nature*, Oxford: Oxford University Press.

Rosaldo, R. (1987) 'Where objectivity lies: the rhetoric of anthropology', in J.S. Nelson, A. Megill and D.M. McCloskey (eds), *The Rhetoric of the Human Sciences*, Madison, WI: University of Wisconsin Press, pp. 87–110.

Sack, R.D. (1980) *Conceptions of Space in Social Thought*, London: Macmillan.

Sack, R.D. (1987) *Human Territoriality: Its Theory and History*, Cambridge: Cambridge University Press.

Saunders, P. (1986) (2nd edn) *Social Theory and the Urban Question*, London: Hutchinson.

Savage, M., Barlow, J., Duncan, S. and Saunders, P. (1987) 'Locality research: the Sussex programme on economic restructuring and change', *Quarterly Journal of Social Affairs*, 3, pp. 27–51.

Sayer, R.A. (1976) 'A Critique of Urban Modelling', *Progress in Planning*, 6 (3), pp. 187–254.

Sayer, A. (1981a) 'Abstraction: a realist interpretation', *Radical Philosophy*, 28, pp. 6–15.

Sayer, A. (1981b) 'Defensible values in geography: Can values be science-free?' in R.J. Johnston and D.T. Herbert (eds), *Geography and the Urban Environment*, Vol. 4. Chichester: Wiley, pp. 29–56.

Sayer, A. (1982) 'Explanation in economic geography', *Progress in Human Geography*, 6, pp. 68–88.

Sayer, A. (1983) 'Defining the urban', *Geojournal*, 9 (3) pp. 279–85.

Sayer, A. (1985) 'The difference that space makes', in D. Gregory, J. Urry (eds), *Social Relations and Spatial Structures*, London: Macmillan, pp. 49–66.

Sayer, A. (1986) 'New developments in manufacturing: the just-in-time system', *Capital and Class*, 30, pp. 43–71.

Sayer, A. (1991) 'Behind the locality debate: deconstructing geography's dualisms', *Society and Space: Environment and Planning D*, 23, pp. 283–308.

Sayer, A. (1992) *Method in Social Science: A Realist Approach*, London: Routledge, 2nd edn.

Sayer, A. (1994) 'Realism and space: a reply to Ron Johnston', *Political Geography*, 13 (2), pp. 107–9.

Sayer, A. (1995) *Radical Political Economy: A Critique*, Oxford: Blackwell.

Sayer, A. and Morgan, K. (1986) 'A modern industry in a declining region: links between method, theory and policy', in D. Massey and R.A. Meegan (eds), *The Politics of Method*, London: Methuen.

Sayer, A. and Storper, M. (1997) 'Ethics unbound: for a normative turn in social theory', in *Society and Space: Environment and Planning D*, 15 (1) pp. 1–18.

Sayer, A. and Walker, R.A. (1992) *The New Social Economy: Reworking the Division of Labor*. Cambridge, MA: Blackwell.

Schor, N. and Weed, E. (1994) (eds) *The Essential Difference*, Bloomington and Indianapolis, IN: Indiana University Press.

Scott, A.J. and Angel, D.P. (1987) 'The US semiconductor industry: a locational analysis', *Environment and Planning A*, 19, pp. 875–912.

Seers, D. (1972) 'What are we trying to measure?', *Journal of Development Studies*, 8 (3), pp. 21–36.

Sen, A.K. (1984) *Resources, Values and Development*, Oxford: Blackwell.

Sen, A. (1992) *Objectivity and Position*, The Liddley Lecture, University of Kansas.

Sheppard, E. (1996) 'Site, situation, and social theory', *Environment and Planning A*, 28, pp. 1339–44.

Sheppard, E. and Barnes, T. (1990) *The Capitalist Space Economy*, London: Pion.

Sim, S. (1988) '"Svelte discourse" and the philosophy of caution', *Radical Philosophy*, 49, p. 31.

Simmel, G. (1965) *Essays on Sociology, Philosophy and Aesthetics*, K.H. Wolff (ed.), London: Harper and Row.

Simonsen, K. (1991) 'Towards an understanding of the contextuality of mode of life' *Society and Space: Environment and Planning D*, Vol. 9 (4) pp. 417–32.

Sismondo, S. (1993) 'Some social constructions', *Social Studies of Science*, 23, pp. 515–53.

Slater, D. (1989) 'Peripheral capitalism', in D. Peet and N. Thrift (eds), *New Models in Geography*, Oxford: Blackwell, pp. 267–94.

Slater, D. (1992) 'On the borders of social theory: learning from other regions', *Society and Space: Environment and Planning D*, 10, pp. 307–28.

Slater, D. (1997) 'Spatialities of power and postmodern ethics – rethinking geopolitical encounters', *Society and Space: Environment and Planning D*, 15, pp. 55–72.

Smith, A. (1759) Revised edn 1982, *The Theory of Moral Sentiments*, Indianapolis, IN: Liberty Fund.

Smith, D.M. (1994) *Geography and Social Justice*, Oxford: Blackwell.

Smith D.M. (1997) 'Back to the good life: towards an enlarged conception of social justice', *Society and Space: Environment and Planning D*, 15, pp. 19–36.

Smith, N. (1987) 'Dangers of the empirical turn: some comments on the CURS initiative', *Antipode*, 19, pp. 59–68.

Smith, N. (1990) 'Uneven development and location theory', in R. Peet and N. Thrift (eds), *New Models in Geography, Vol. 1*, London: Unwin Hyman, pp. 142–63.

Smith, N. (1992) 'History and the philosophy of geography: real wars, theory wars', *Progress in Human Geography*, 16, pp. 257–71.

Soja, E.W. (1985) 'The spatiality of social life: towards a transformative retheorisation' in D. Gregory and J. Urry (eds), *Spatial Structures and Social Relations*, London: Macmillan, pp. 90–127.

Soja, E.W. (1986) 'Taking Los Angeles apart: some fragments of a critical human geography', *Society and Space: Environment and Planning D*, 4, pp. 255–72.

Soja, E. (1989) *Postmodern Geographies*, London: Verso.

Sokal, A. and Bricmont, J. (1998) *Intellectual Impostures*, London: Routledge.

Soper, K. (1986) *Humanism and Anti-Humanism*, London: Hutchinson.

Soper, K. (1990) Feminism, humanism and postmodernism, *Radical Philosophy*, 55, pp. 11–17.

Soper, K. (1991) Postmodernism, critical theory and critical realism, in R. Bhaskar (ed.), *A Meeting of Minds*, London: The Socialist Society.

Soper, K. (1995a) *What is Nature?* Oxford: Blackwell.

Soper, K. (1995b) 'Forget Foucault?' *New Formations*, 25, Summer, pp. 21–7.

Spivak, G.C. (1987) *In Other Worlds: Essays in Cultural Politics*, London: Methuen.

Squires, J. (1993) *Principled Positions*, London: Lawrence and Wishart.

Steele, D.R. (1992) *From Marx to Mises*, La Salle, IL: Open Court.

Stones, R. (1996) *Sociological Reasoning: Towards a Post-Modern Sociology*, London: Macmillan.

Storper, M. (1987) 'The post-Enlightenment challenge to Marxist urban studies', *Society and Space: Environment and Planning D*, 5, pp. 418–26.

Storper, M. and Salais, R. (1996) *Worlds of Production: the Action Frameworks of the Economy*, Cambridge, MA: Harvard University Press.

Strohmayer, U. and Hannah, M. (1992) 'Domesticating postmodernism', *Antipode*, 24, pp. 29–55.

Tallis, R. (1988) *Not Saussure*, London: Macmillan.

Taylor, C. (1967) 'Neutrality and political science', in A. Ryan (ed.) (1973) *The Philosophy of Social Explanation*, Oxford: Oxford University Press, pp. 139–70.

Taylor, C. (1987) 'Overcoming epistemology', in K. Baynes, et al. (eds), *After Philosophy*, Cambridge, MA: MIT, pp. 464–88.

Taylor, C. (1989) *Sources of the Self: the Making of the Modern Identity*, Cambridge, MA: Harvard University Press.

Taylor, C. (1992) *Multiculturalism and the Politics of Recognition*, with commentaries by A. Gutmann (ed.), S.C. Rockefeller, M. Walzer, S. Wolf, Princetown, NJ: Princetown University Press.

Thompson, E.P. (1967) 'Time, work-discipline and industrial capitalism', *Past and Present*, 38.

Thompson, E.P. (1979) *The Poverty of Theory*, London: Merlin.

Thrift, N.J. (1983) 'On the determination of action in space and time', *Society and Space: Environment and Planning D*, 1, pp. 23–57.

Thrift, N. (1990) 'The making of a capitalist time consciousness', in J. Hassard (ed.) *The Sociology of Time*, London: Macmillan.

Thrift, N. (1997) *Spatial Formations*, London: Sage.

Tomlinson, J. (1990) *Hayek and the Market*, London: Pluto Press.

Toye, J. (1987) *Dilemmas of Development*, Oxford: Blackwell.

Tronto, J.C. (1987) 'Beyond gender differences in a theory of care', *Signs*, 12, pp. 644–63.

Tronto, J.C. (1993) *Moral Boundaries*, London: Routledge.

Ullmann, S. (1962) *Semantics*, Oxford: Blackwell.

Urry, J. (1986) 'Capitalist production, scientific management and the service class', in A.J. Scott, and M. Storper (eds), *Production, Work, Territory*, Hemel Hempstead, Herts: Allen and Unwin, pp. 41–66.

Urry, J. (1987) 'Society, space and locality', *Society and Space: Environment and Planning D*, 5, 4, pp. 435–44.

Urry, J. (1996) 'Sociology of time and space', in B. Turner (ed.) *Companion to Social Theory*, Oxford: Blackwell.

Valentine, G. (1989) 'The geography of women's fear', *Area*, 21, pp. 385–90.

Veatch, H.E. (1962) *Rational Man*, Bloomington, IN: Indiana University Press.

Wade Hands, D. (1994) 'Conjectures and reputations: the sociology of scientific knowledge and the history of economic thought', *History of Political Economy*, 29 (4), pp. 695–740.

Walby, S. (1986) *Patriarchy at Work*, Cambridge: Polity.

Waldron, J. (1992) 'Superceding historic injustice', *Ethics*, 103, pp. 4–28.

Walzer, M. (1983) *Spheres of Justice*, Oxford: Blackwell.

Warde, A. (1988) 'Industrial restructuring, local politics and the reproduction of labour power: some theoretical considerations', *Society and Space: Environment and Planning D*, 6, pp. 75–95.

Wellmer, A. (1972) *Critical Theory of Society*, New York: Seabury Press.

Whatmore, S. (1997) 'Dissecting the autonomous self: hybrid cartographies for a relational ethics', *Society and Space: Environment and Planning D*, 15, pp. 37–54.

White, H.I. (1987) *The Content of the Form*, Baltimore, MD: Johns Hopkins University Press.

Williams, R. (1962) *Communications*, Harmondsworth: Penguin.

Williams, P. and Chrisman, L. (eds) (1993) *Colonial Discourse and Post-Colonial Theory: A Reader*, Brighton: Harvester Wheatsheaf.

Willis, P. (1977) *Learning to Labour*, Aldershot, Hants: Gower.

Wolfe, A. (1989) *Whose Keeper? Social Science and Moral Obligation*, Berkeley and Los Angeles, CA: University of California Press.

Wolf, S. (1992) 'Comment' in Taylor, C. (1992) *Multiculturalism and the Politics of Recognition*, with commentaries by A. Gutmann (ed.), S.C. Rockefeller, M. Walzer, S. Wolf, Princetown, NJ: Princetown University Press, pp. 75–86.

Wright, E.O. (1994) *Interrogating Inequality: Essays on Class Analysis, Socialism and Marxism*, London: Verso.

Yanagisako, S. and Delaney, C. (eds) (1995) *Naturalizing Power*, London: Routledge.

Young, I.M. (1990a) *Justice and the Politics of Difference*, Princetown, NJ: Princetown University Press.

Young, I.M. (1990b) 'The ideal of community and the politics of difference', in L. Nicholson (ed), *Feminism/Postmodernism*, London: Routledge, pp. 300–23.

Index